Multiple Intelligences

Best Ideas from Research and Practice

Mindy L. Kornhaber
The Pennsylvania State University

Edward Garcia Fierros
Villanova University

Shirley A. Veenema
Project Zero, Harvard University
Phillips Academy, Andover, Massachusetts

PEARSON

Boston   New York   San Francisco
Mexico City   Montreal   Toronto   London   Madrid   Munich   Paris
Hong Kong   Singapore   Tokyo   Cape Town   Sydney

Senior editor: Arnis E. Burvikovs
Series editorial assistant: Christine Lyons
Manufacturing buyer: Andrew Turso
Marketing manager: Tara Whorf
Production coordinator: Pat Torelli Publishing Services
Cover designer: Suzanne Harbison
Editorial-production service: Chestnut Hill Enterprises, Inc.
Electronic composition: Stratford Publishing Services, Inc.

For related titles and support materials, visit our online catalog at
www.ablongman.com.

Library of Congress Cataloging-in-Publication Data

Kornhaber, Mindy L.
    Multiple intelligences : best ideas from research and practice / Mindy L. Kornhaber, Edward Garcia Fierros, Shirley A. Veenema.
        p. cm.
    Includes bibliographical references and index.
    ISBN 0-205-34259-0
    1. Learning, Psychology of—Case studies.   2. Multiple intelligences—United States—Case studies.   3. Cognitive styles in children—United States—Case studies.
4. Education, Elementary—Curricula—United States—Case studies.   I. Fierros, Edward Garcia.   II. Veenema, Shirley, A.   III. Title.
    LB1060.K67 2004
    370.15'23—dc22   2003017818

Printed in the United States of America

10 9 8 7 6 5 4 3 2 1   07 06 05 04 03

Contents

Foreword

A PRACTICAL THEORY

Individuals, organizations, and societies differ in their location on the theory–practice continuum. In general, individuals and institutions of the United States and Britain are impatient with theory: we want to know what works and, perhaps as an afterthought, why it does. Those who live on the European Continent are far more desirous of theory. Such persons almost always begin with a theoretical framework, and they may relegate practical matters to a later day.

Theory and practice are often contrasted with one another, as I have just illustrated. But I happen to agree with the influential social psychologist Kurt Lewin, who moved from Germany to the United States in the 1930s. Lewin famously quipped, "There is nothing so practical as a good theory." It is for others to say whether the theory of multiple intelligences (hereafter MI theory), which I developed in the late 1970s and the early 1980s, is a good theory. But that MI has proved a spur to practice cannot be doubted. In the two decades since the theory was first published, an impressive number of practices all over the world have been attributed to MI. Without question this theory has demonstrated its practicality.

As it happens, MI theory was not created as a spur to educational practice. At the time of its formulation, I was a cognitive–developmental psychologist, with some training in brain study, and I addressed my theoretical formulations to my fellow scholars. MI theory did not create much of a stir among my fellow psychologists, however; most were—and remain—content with the standard IQ account of intellect. However, almost as soon as they heard about it, many educators immediately sensed that MI theory spoke to them. Interest arose initially among those who work with young children, those who address special needs, those who cultivate particular talents, especially in the arts, and those who lived in the continental United States. But now, twenty years later, MI theory has become a well-traveled "meme" (Richard Dawkins's term for a unit of meaning that may last); there are few areas of education where it remains unknown.

I can claim very little credit for the practical applications and implications of MI theory. Ideas about how to bring about "MI classrooms," "MI curricula," "MI assessments," and the like sprung in most cases from dedicated practitioners. Initially, I was delighted by the interest in these ideas. Gradually, I came to see that some of the practices were better founded and more likely to prove successful than were others. I was horrified by the misunderstanding displayed by some educators and the mischief wrought by a few others. While never viewing myself as a traffic cop or a censor, I have on occasion noted those applications that seem to me to be meritorious, and those that seem ill-considered or counterproductive (Gardner, 1999).

Much—perhaps too much—has been written about MI theory from the perspective of educational practice. Nearly all of what has been written has come from individual practitioners. Much of this writing suffers from one of two flaws: (1) the author has only a superficial understanding of the theory—indeed, sometimes I have wondered whether the author has even read the original publications; (2) the author is promoting a particular set of practices, often to the exclusion of other, equally tenable ones.

The book whose foreword you are now reading is unique. Mindy Kornhaber and her colleagues, Ed Fierros and Shirley Veenema (whom I'll dub the Kornhaber trio), display a deep understanding of the theory of multiple intelligences. I have worked alongside Mindy for well over a decade; she understands the theory extremely well, and she has made valuable contributions to its current version. Equally important, the Kornhaber trio began their study with no particular ax to grind. Instead, they elected to study forty-one diverse schools, each of which had at least three years of experience working with MI ideas. The trio surveyed these schools carefully, interviewing key personnel and collecting qualitative data and information on student outcomes. They identified the features that characterize effective MI schools. And in this book, they present their findings through the prism of rich case studies of five schools and six classrooms that embody the best of MI practices.

When Mindy Kornhaber first became interested in the practical implications of MI theory, she quipped, "MI theory is popular because it doesn't come with directions. Educators can say they've adopted it without doing anything differently." Alas, there was something to Mindy's quip. It is possible to wave the MI flag without having to think, change, or grow. However, as this book convincingly illustrates, those educators who take MI ideas seriously embark on a challenging course, one that is likely to alter their practice in fundamental ways.

As they introduce us to committed practitioners, the three authors invoke a useful term, one reminiscent of both the American philosopher John Dewey and the Russian psychologist Lev S. Vygotsky. The term used by Kornhaber and colleagues is *tool*. And indeed, MI ideas and practices are best thought of as a toolkit: a versatile set of cognitive and tangible tools that can serve the ingenious and diligent practitioner.

In this book, you will be introduced to a myriad of educational practices that are inspired by MI theory. Some concern the meat and potatoes of school: the basic literacies, the foundational subjects. Others cast a net more widely, involving the arts, the community, the terrain of interdisciplinary work. Students in the classes portrayed here may be learning how to run a business, probe rivers from a natural and a cultural perspective, explore their own heritage and that of other immigrant groups, or go on an archaeological dig. They do so in schools that span the country, from Maine to Washington State, from New York to New Mexico.

It makes little sense to grasp a physical tool properly unless you have a goal in mind, whether it is hammering a nail, building a ship, or fixing a leaking faucet. By the same token, it makes little sense to wield an educational tool unless you have put forth an educational goal. The educators described in this book do not "do MI" for its own sake. Instead, they use MI so that youngsters can become literate, master the ways of thinking of important disciplines, express themselves in various artistic symbol systems, understand the community and the broader world in which they live, and achieve a better understanding of themselves and an enhanced capacity to deal with others in civil and productive ways.

As researchers grounded in theory as well as practice, Kornhaber and colleagues develop an informal theoretical framework with which to think about educational innovation. They explain the cognitive operations involved in the several intelligences; they introduce various entry points to lessons and topics; and they formulate the set of compass points by which educators can orient their practice and chart their progress. These tools are introduced as a means of thinking about one's educational goals and how best to achieve them. They are brought to bear in each of the rich case studies that form the heart of this stimulating book. And, like the components of any good toolkit, they are available to be drawn on for new goals in new settings.

Without question, MI ideas and practices have taken on a life of their own in our time. Were I and the dozens of MI books to disappear suddenly from the face of the earth, experimentation of the sort described in these pages would continue. Yet it is important—crucial—to step back from the hundreds of experiments, and the thousands of claims and counterclaims, to organize the most effective educational examples, and to set forth the most powerful concepts and theories. The Kornhaber trio has succeeded in this endeavor.

Writing in the United States in the year 2003, I feel compelled to add a remark about context. The United States is going through one of its periodic pendulum swings in education. Following relatively progressive periods like the 1920s, the 1960s, and perhaps the late 1980s, a strong reaction has set in. Tests and standards are "in," and when students don't do well, the solution is to add more tests and more standards. Educational experimentation, attention to individual differences, concern with the arts and interdisciplinary work, interest in provocative questions rather than "right" answers, are "out." One closes one's eyes to these trends at one's peril. Yet, if educators are professionals, and if education is a discipline rather than a set of fads, then educators must insist on working in ways that they know engage students' minds and lead to deeper understanding, no matter how countercyclical these approaches may seem. Otherwise, we risk an educational landscape—and especially a public educational landscape—where youngsters are perennially bored and from which gifted practitioners and families with means flee.

Much as I would like to, I cannot simply assert that MI theory is right, or that MI practices are destined to succeed. We do not have enough data to make such claims, though this book moves us in a positive direction. I feel confident in declaring that the trends governing educational policy in American society at present are not healthy and that their limitations will become apparent, sooner or later. As we await the next pendulum swing in education, it is important that we maintain an open mind about both theory and practice and continue to experiment, in ways that are prudent and that allow for some measure of accountability. At the heart of MI theory is the belief that each individual has a rich and differentiated mind; that no two persons have exactly the same cognitive configuration; and that education is most likely to be successful if it pays attention to these individual differences in the course of fashioning curriculum, pedagogy, and assessment. Theories and practices that reflect these beliefs are likely to have a long and successful life in education. The ideas and practices described in this book will provide rich sustenance for many readers over the long haul.

—Howard Gardner, Cambridge, MA

REFERENCES

Gardner, H. (1999). *Intelligence reframed.* New York: Basic Books.

Preface

Howard Gardner launched the theory of multiple intelligences, "MI," with his 1983 book, *Frames of Mind*. Gardner's aim was to counter psychology's most widely accepted concept: the idea that general intelligence, or *g*, governs human problem solving. Instead of a single, general intelligence, often measured by IQ tests, Gardner argued that there were at least seven "intelligences" that individuals deploy in varying ways to carry out real-world problem solving.

In a decade's time, something unexpected happened: MI—a theory about human intelligence—became contemporary education's most popular idea. In a grassroots fashion, teachers and principals throughout the United States and across the world put MI into practice.

Because Gardner's original intention was to change psychology's view of intelligence, he did not provide guidelines in *Frames of Mind* for applying MI in schools. This situation encouraged many teachers, staff developers, consultants, and policymakers to generate their own approaches to implementing MI. As a result, dozens of books are now available to help educators draw on the theory. Ours shares some features of these books: it is readable, it offers concrete and practical information, and it's meant to be a resource for engaging and developing a wide variety of learners. Yet, this book has several important differences.

First, this is the only book about implementing MI based on a national investigation of diverse schools that associate MI with improvements for students. Most other books about MI are based on the experiences of a single teacher, school, or staff developer. In contrast, this book identifies approaches that are successful across particular classrooms, schools, and student populations. Thus, it presents a powerful, research-driven description of effective practices involving MI.

Second, this book highlights, and richly illustrates, organizational practices that allow MI to be applied throughout a school. Most books about MI have emphasized how to apply the theory in the classroom, even though classroom innovation is hard to sustain without schoolwide support.

Third, this book recognizes that powerful learning environments require the integration of ideas, not just one idea. Therefore, this book shows how administrators have used MI alongside other ideas about teaching, learning, and school change to engage students and advance students' learning. It also reveals the classroom strategies that master teachers use to enable a wide range of students to produce excellent work.

Finally, this book was developed by investigators who have worked for many years at Project Zero, the research group at Harvard's Graduate School of Education that has been Howard Gardner's organizational base since 1967. This book therefore draws deeply on the best ideas about multiple intelligences, learning, and school development as well as on the work of very talented practitioners who have shared their ideas with us.

WHO WILL FIND THIS BOOK USEFUL?

This book is meant primarily to serve kindergarten through grade 8 educators, broadly defined, who want to integrate multiple intelligences into their practice in ways that are associated with benefits for students. Among those who will find this book useful are:

- *Teacher educators:* Gardner's theory of multiple intelligences is often introduced in teacher education courses. This book provides approaches for incorporating MI that are grounded in research alongside richly illustrated and practical materials that support thoughtful and effective implementation.
- *Classroom teachers:* The classroom examples described in this book highlight teacher practices that engage students' multiple intelligences in ways that foster their knowledge and skills. The examples include tips on how to get started and materials to use. The examples also emphasize the underlying thinking strategies that these teachers use. These strategies provide insights into the ways teachers select classroom materials and activities so that they enhance the skills and understanding of a broad range of learners.
- *School administrators:* This book is a strong resource for principals and other school administrators who seek to build schoolwide practices that support all students. It includes a history and description of five schools that associate MI with positive outcomes for students. It explains how the schools came to adopt MI, the professional development that was used to bring the theory into practice, and the particular challenges each principal faced.
- *Educators of special needs children:* One of the key findings from our investigation is that educators strongly associate MI with benefits for students with learning disabilities. MI enables educators to think more broadly about human capabilities and the ways that these can be developed. It also fosters a school culture that is respectful of all kinds of learners. In the schools we profile, all students have ways to contribute constructively from their areas of strength. At the same time, these schools recognize that most students—from learning disabled to gifted—have areas in which they need to stretch and grow.
- *Professional development personnel:* This volume offers professional development personnel new approaches for enhancing schoolwide practices. It provides new ways to help educators reflect systematically about their work and develop practices that serve learners

throughout the school. This book's detailed school and classroom examples should provide useful supplements to the examples staff developers already employ.

- *System changers:* This book is designed for people who may already be using MI but who want to take the theory to a broader and deeper level. It is a useful resource for implementing MI not just in a few isolated classrooms but rather on a schoolwide basis. It does so by highlighting Compass Point Practices. These are the practices SUMIT's researchers have found to be widely in use among schools that associate MI with improvements in student outcomes.
- *School board members and other policymakers:* This book highlights both the educational improvements associated with MI and the practices in place where such improvements have occurred. These Compass Point Practices and outcomes associated with them provide a valuable knowledge base to gauge existing MI-influenced efforts or to implement systemic efforts to advance learning across a wide diversity of students.

In short, this book should be the primary resource for anyone seeking to implement MI systemically and effectively at the K-8 level. The ideas from practice and research contained here are meant to help educators build schoolwide environments in which all students can flourish.

THE DESIGN OF THIS BOOK

Given the many demands educators face, we designed this book in two parts, so that individual readers can efficiently gather the information that is most useful to them.

In Part I, called Implementing Multiple Intelligences: Theory and Research, you'll find:

1. Overviews of the theory of multiple intelligences and two other frameworks that have originated at Project Zero, a research group at Harvard University's Graduate School of Education. You can think of these frameworks as tools for building learning environments that allow MI to be used in powerful ways for a broad range of learners. These tools address three central components of the school:

- MI is a tool for focusing on learners' cognitive abilities
- The Entry Points Framework is a tool for developing curriculum,
- Compass Point Practices act as a tool for developing organizational practices across classrooms and the school.

Readers familiar with MI and Entry Points might choose to focus on the Compass Point Practices, which are extensively described for the first time in this volume.

2. Findings about the relationship between MI and student outcomes. This information will be especially useful to those who seek evidence about MI and school and student improvement.

Part II presents views of schools and classrooms. Its eleven chapters contain:

1. Overviews of five diverse public elementary schools, each of which has been strongly influenced by the theory of multiple intelligences. The overviews include the history of MI's implementation, the school demographics, and outcomes that the school associates with MI.

2. Richly illustrated examples of curriculum drawn from each of the five schools. Each of the curriculum examples are organized into five sections:

- *At a Glance* presents a very brief overview of the unit and how it intersects with MI, Entry Points, and the Compass Point Practices.
- *What Is. . . ?* This section provides a more detailed description of the unit.
- *Strategies* describes the strategies that individual teachers used to make the unit work in the classroom.
- *What Happens?* This section details the teaching and learning activities that take place during the unit.
- *Revisiting the Frameworks* interprets the unit in light of MI, Entry Points, and Compass Point Practices.

The five sections for each curriculum example are like the transparent pages of an old anatomy textbook: separate pages that highlight the skeletal system, the circulatory system, the organs, nervous system, and muscles. You can learn something important by reading any one section. Together, the five sections provide the whole picture of how teachers have been able to draw on MI in ways that are linked to students' learning.

We invite you to read on, to learn about effective school and classroom practices that incorporate MI, and to explore these ideas in your own classroom and school.

Acknowledgments

A great many institutions and individuals have enabled us to produce this volume. We are exceedingly grateful to the educators at the schools who participated in this research. A complete list of the forty-one schools appears in the Appendix. We especially thank the principals who led the schools we have profiled in detail: Marilyn Davenport, Sheryl Harmer, Douglas Lockwood, Mary Ellen ("Mel") McBride, and Natalie McKenna. We are most grateful to the teachers whose classroom work we have highlighted: Renée Blodgett, Chimene Brandt, Carolyn Chadwell, Charlene Farris, Nan Hamner, Donna Schneider, and Marge Staszak. These educators generously shared their time to help us understand how they go about the complex task of enabling diverse young thinkers to produce wonderful work.

We thank the Geraldine R. Dodge Foundation and the Schwab Foundation for Learning for their financial support of the Project on Schools Using Multiple Intelligences Theory (SUMIT). We wish to express our appreciation to officers and consultants at the Schwab Foundation, including Alexa Culwell, Scott Flemming, Lisa Garrison, and Scott Saliman, and to Robert Perry at the Geraldine R. Dodge Foundation for their insights and encouragement.

We thank Linda Campbell for introducing our work to Allyn & Bacon. We are especially grateful to editors Paul A. Smith and Arnis E. Burvikovs for their advice and patience.

Our appreciation goes to the following reviewers for their helpful comments on the manuscript: Barbara M. Britsch, Lourdes College; Ken Dobush, Eastern Connecticut State; Micki Hartwig, Upper Iowa University; Emilie Johnson, Lindenwood University; and Leslie Owen Wilson, University of WI Stevens Point. Thanks also to Myrna Breskin for her diligent editing as well as to Officer Mark Rhodes for recovering the original copyedited manuscript after its mysterious disappearance.

Our project benefitted enormously from the dedication and energy of three interns: Michael Broom, Natalie Corrigan, and Rita Rodriguez Sattler. We are deeply grateful to many colleagues at Project Zero, our research home at Harvard University, who provided intellectual sustenance and friendship over many years. We are also grateful to our new colleagues at The Pennsylvania State University and Villanova University for their support. Our heartfelt thanks go to Howard Gardner, whose ideas and mentoring made this work possible.

PART ONE

Implementing Multiple Intelligences
Theory and Research

1

Tools for Putting MI into Practice

Tools are instruments for doing work, and virtually every sort of work uses them. In the work of schooling children, we employ tools such as blackboards and computers, maps and chalk. However, many of the most important educational tools are not three-dimensional things. Instead, they are ideas about how to work with students, curriculum, materials, and colleagues.

The theory of multiple intelligences, "MI," is one of the ideas, or tools, that many educators use in their work. Yet, in most complex work—from building a house to managing a business—many tools are necessary. In this chapter we describe three tools that are needed to engage students' multiple intelligences in ways that advance their learning. Each tool is meant to enhance knowledge and skills across a broad range of students. The tools we present are not the only tools that can be used. However, they are a good basic set, because they deal with three fundamental aspects of schooling: the learner, the curriculum, and the school as an organization.

Here are the tools we'll focus on:

- MI, a tool for focusing on learners' cognitive abilities;
- Entry Points, a tool for developing curriculum;
- Compass Point Practices, a tool for developing organizational practices across classrooms and the school.

In this chapter, we present the background to these tools and describe them in detail.

If you are new to these ideas, keep in mind that it takes time and practice to feel comfortable using any tool. Remember your early attempts at using a sewing machine or a new piece of software? Like those tools, the ones we describe here will become familiar and helpful as you work with them.

If you are already working in schools, you might want to think about how your current practice includes ideas that are similar to and different from the tools presented here. Educators sometimes find that many of their ideas align with the tools we'll describe, but that they did not necessarily have a language for expressing or naming these ideas. Having ways to describe what you do, or having names for the ideas, helps you to reflect systematically on your practice. This, in turn, allows you to see more clearly the strengths in your practice and also to see possibilities for further development. In addition, when educators have a shared vocabulary, it can help them to communicate about their practice and to build a stronger learning environment for their students (Kornhaber 1999; Kornhaber and Krechevsky, 1995; Schön, 1983).

THE THEORY OF MULTIPLE INTELLIGENCES: A TOOL FOR FOCUSING LEARNERS' COGNITIVE ABILITIES

Background

The theory of multiple intelligences (MI) was developed by Harvard psychologist Howard Gardner and first presented in *Frames of Mind: The Theory of Multiple Intelligences* (Gardner, 1983/1993). In *Frames of Mind*, Gardner took issue with the way that most psychologists had characterized intelligence since the beginning of the twentieth century. That traditional psychological view was based largely on studies of mental tests. According to that view, all human problem solving is governed by one underlying mental ability. This ability is known as general intelligence, or g. However, Gardner's years of research in the arts, developmental psychology, and neuropsychology led him to cast doubt on the centrality of g.

- If general intelligence governed all problem solving, then young children should show roughly the same rate of intellectual development in mastering language skills, drawing, math, dance, or other areas. Yet, development across these areas occurs at different rates. For example, children typically develop sophisticated language skills far faster than they develop sophisticated skills in math.
- If g prevailed, then child prodigies should excel across the board, in music, as well as in painting, chess, and math. However, prodigies rarely, if ever, fit such a pattern. They typically excel in only one or two areas.
- If g were the rule, then autistic savants or stroke victims should have weak capacities across the board. Yet, there are brain-damaged people who can play music beautifully but who are severely impaired in their use of language; there are others who can communicate well, but who cannot solve basic math problems.

Rather than attempting to explain all of human intelligence in terms of g and the mental testing that supports it, Gardner began with a very different question: What are the mental abilities that support the wide range of adult roles found over time and across cultures? So, for example, what abilities enable people to become teachers, carpenters, musicians, engineers, storekeepers, hunters, architects, doctors, religious leaders, farmers, or stockbrokers? What enables human beings to repair a car's faulty wiring, navigate the ocean, or negotiate a peace treaty? Rather than defining intelligence in terms of mental test results, or IQ scores, Gardner defined an intelligence as a psychobiological potential to solve problems or fashion products that are valued in one or more cultures (Gardner, 1999). In other words, an intelligence is a capacity inherent in the human brain that is developed and expressed in social and cultural contexts.

Evidence and Criteria

To uncover the abilities or "intelligences" that support these diverse roles, Gardner considered research from his own fields of developmental psychology and neuropsychology as well as more far-ranging disciplines such as cross-cultural anthropology and evolutionary biology. To determine whether a capacity should be called an intelligence, Gardner argued that each possible intelligence should meet most, if not all of the following criteria:

- It should be seen in relative isolation in prodigies, autistic savants, stroke victims, or other exceptional populations.
- It should have a distinct developmental trajectory. That is, different intelligences should develop at different rates from their beginning manifestations in infancy to full adult usage.
- It should have some basis in evolutionary biology. In other words, an intelligence ought to have helped our human ancestors to survive and ought to be evident in other mammals.
- It should be captured in symbol systems. Given its importance, humans would likely have found a way to transmit information that draws on the intelligence, as they do, for example, in notations for math, language, music, spatial relations, and various forms of movement.
- It should be supported by evidence from psychometric tests of intelligence. Gardner drew on this kind of evidence, which commonly uncovers verbal, spatial, and numerical abilities. However, unlike traditional psychologists, he did not rely on evidence from psychometric tests to the exclusion of other information.
- It should be distinguishable through experimental psychological tasks. For example, experimental psychologists have found that different neural structures help to support different kinds of mental processing.
- It should demonstrate a core, information-processing operation. That is, there should be nearly automatic mental processes that handle information related to each intelligence. For example, barring neurological impairment, human beings automatically break up streams of sound into the words of their own language; discriminate greater or lesser numbers in small groupings of objects; attempt to make sense of facial expressions in interpersonal encounters; and make distinctions between pitches when they hear music.

The Eight Intelligences

Using this definition and these criteria, Gardner has now identified eight intelligences:

Linguistic intelligence allows individuals to communicate and make sense of the world through language. Those who have a keen sensitivity to language in its spoken and/or written forms demonstrate this strength as poets, writers, lawyers, and public speakers. Linguistic intelligence is highly valued and rewarded in school.

Logical-mathematical intelligence enables individuals to use, appreciate, and analyze abstract relationships. In Western culture, this capacity is often harnessed in mathematical reasoning and scientific investigations. Mathematicians, scientists, and engineers deploy this intelligence at high levels. Like linguistic intelligence, logical-mathematical intelligence is emphasized in school.

Spatial intelligence enables people to perceive visual or spatial information, to transform this information, and to recreate visual images from memory. Blind people skillfully employ this intelligence, using it to create mental maps of their environments. It is commonly seen operating at high levels in architects, artists, surgeons, and pilots.

Musical intelligence allows people to create, communicate, and understand meanings made out of sound. It is manifested to high degrees among composers, musicians, and acoustic engineers.

Bodily-kinesthetic intelligence entails using all or part of the body to solve problems or create products. This intelligence seems to stand in stark contrast to the reasoning prized in traditional tests of intelligence. Yet, advanced forms of problem solving and creativity are evident in the activities of choreographers, rock climbers, and skilled artisans.

Interpersonal intelligence is the capacity to recognize and make distinctions among others' feelings and intentions and to draw on these in solving problems. Successful teachers, actors, therapists, political leaders, and salespeople rely on strong interpersonal intelligence.

Intrapersonal intelligence enables individuals to recognize and distinguish among their own feelings, to build accurate mental models of themselves, and to draw on these models to make decisions about their lives. Intrapersonal intelligence is sometimes seen in skillful autobiographies and, more generally, among those individuals who make sound choices about their life and work.

Naturalist intelligence allows people to solve problems by distinguishing among, classifying, and using features of the natural world. This intelligence is commonly seen in people's ability to categorize different kinds of plants and animals and has been harnessed to the task of distinguishing among human-made objects. It is essential to the work of landscape architects, hunters, archeologists, and farmers.

Some Important Points

There are several points about MI that are especially important for educators to keep in mind:

First, Gardner notes that the exact number of intelligences is less important than the notion that intelligence is multiple rather than primarily dependent on *g*. Over time, Gardner may find other abilities that qualify as intelligences when judged against his criteria. In fact, the naturalist intelligence was established several years after the others, once evidence to support it had been uncovered.

Second, barring brain damage, all individuals possess all the intelligences. Though we have often heard educators or parents describe a youngster as "bodily-kinesthetic" or "linguistic," this convenient shorthand runs counter to the theory. What differs across people is not the intelligences they possess, but their *profiles of intelligence*. That is, individuals differ with regard to the relative strengths and weakness among their intelligences. For instance, some people will be stronger in spatial intelligence than they are in musical or in bodily-kinesthetic intelligence. Other individuals may be stronger in logical-mathematical and spatial intelligence than they are in linguistic or interpersonal intelligence. Still others may be strong in intrapersonal, linguistic, and musical intelligence than they are in logical-mathematical or naturalist intelligence. While school has traditionally prized a profile strong in linguistic and logical-mathematical intelligences, individuals with markedly different "profiles of intelligence" are successful in the real world.

A third nuance stems from the theory's focus on real-world roles. Even a brief consideration of real-world roles—journalist, mathematician, dancer—reveals that *each real-world role draws on a combination of intelligences*. For instance, a journalist certainly requires strong linguistic ability. However, to be successful, a journalist likely also needs keen interpersonal skills to conduct good interviews, and reasonable logical-mathematical skills to weigh evidence and make judgments about conflicting sources of information. A mathematician certainly requires strong logical-mathematical skills. However, a mathematician may also rely on spatial skills for visualizing relationships and likely also draws on interpersonal intelligence to make mathematical ideas understood and interesting to others. A dancer needs bodily-kinesthetic strengths, but she must also use musical intelligence to align her movements with the mood and meter of the music, spatial skills to organize these movements on stage, and intrapersonal and interpersonal intelligences to access her own feelings and convey these to an audience. In short, each of the intelligences contributes to real-world success. We believe that if schools thoughtfully engage a wider range of students' strengths, they will help more students to succeed in school and beyond.

Interpreting MI for School Use: Some Issues to Consider

The multiplicity of intelligences and their utility in the real world is a two-edged sword for schooling. Many educators have rightly seen that schools' traditional focus on linguistic and logical-mathematical intelligences has left many students on the sidelines.

On the other hand, in an effort to use MI and enable more students to succeed, educators have oftentimes divided the curriculum up into seven or eight discrete "intelligence activities." For instance, educators may divide a unit on reptiles into centers that ask students to move like a reptile, create a reptile song, read reptile books, and draw or sculpt reptiles, do reptile math problems, etc. Staff developers, consultants, and numerous writers have widely advocated this approach, and it is commonly used when educators first try adapting the theory to practice. There is no doubt that this approach offers a clear line from theory to curriculum. However, some awkward things happen when MI—a tool for understanding cognitive abilities—is used as a tool for curriculum development. Superficial activities may become more frequent and some of the substance of the curriculum may be sacrificed. Because of such problems, MI has sometimes been criticized for watering down standards, rather than enabling richer learning across the student population. To use MI well, one needs tools aimed more specifically at developing curriculum that engages learners who have different profiles of intelligence. The following section, "Entry Points," provides a tool for curriculum development devised by Howard Gardner.

ENTRY POINTS: A TOOL FOR DEVELOPING CURRICULUM

Background

Several years after MI was put into practice, Howard Gardner devised a framework that was more appropriate for constructing curriculum to support success among learners with very different profiles of intelligence. In developing this framework, Gardner was considering this question: What are some of the characteristics or features of the disciplines that also reflect the different ways that people can learn? By asking this question, Gardner sought to devise a map that respected the complexity of individuals' profiles of intelligence and the richness of math, literature, science, history, art, and other disciplines.

Gardner provided an initial description of such a framework, which he called entry points, in his 1991 book, *The Unschooled Mind* (revised in Gardner's 1999 book, *The Disciplined Mind*). Gardner regards the entry points as different doors, each of which leads into the same room—the subject or topic being studied. He asserts that each curriculum unit can be divided into entry points, with each entry point allowing learners to encounter the substantive knowledge, concepts, and skills of the disciplines.

While individual learners' profiles of intelligence may lead some students to prefer some entry points over others, Gardner argues that it is important for students and teachers to approach a topic through multiple entry points. The use of multiple entry points allows students to gain different perspectives on the same topic. By having a range of perspectives, students' understanding is deepened: they become more able to go beyond rote recall and to find new ways to represent and apply what they have learned. Rather than being left with one static idea of a topic, they are more likely to transfer information about the topic from one context to another.

The Entry Points Framework

The Entry Points Framework we are using in this book is described below. To illustrate the entry points, we draw on Gardner's example, which shows how each entry point can be applied to the topic of evolution (Gardner, 1991a, 1999). However, as you read the following example, you may also want to develop your own illustration, using a topic that you have taught or plan to teach.

> *Narrative:* The narrative entry point deals with the story or stories that are central to a topic. Typically a rich, or "generative," topic will offer several possible narrative entry points, some of which may be recounted or performed as dramatic narratives. For instance, for the topic of evolution, there is the narrative involving Darwin's own life, his voyage to the Galapagos Islands, or even various traditional folk stories about how different animals and plants came to have their unique form.
>
> *Logical-Quantitative:* This entry point focuses on numerical aspects of a topic and/or on deductive, logical reasoning, of the sort that can often be captured by *if-then* syllogisms. A more quantitative entry point for the topic of evolution might entail looking at Darwin's effort to map the

distribution of different species across different islands. A logic-focused entry point might pose syllogisms for the students to explore: if there were no variation within a species, then what might happen when its environment changed?

Aesthetic: The aesthetic entry point engages artistic aspects of, or representations of, a topic. It may also focus on sensory features associated with the topic. An aesthetic entry point for evolution might be to examine different drawings Darwin made of finches or other species he studied on the Galapagos and to describe how their shapes/morphologies differ.

Experiential ("Hands-on"): This entry point provides students opportunities to do work involving the physical "stuff" of the topic. For example, for the topic of evolution, students might breed fruitflies, or do virtual simulations of evolutionary processes, and document what they observe.

Interpersonal: The interpersonal entry point involves working together with others to learn about a topic. One way to incorporate the interpersonal entry point in the topic of evolution is to form research teams to carry out real or simulated experiments in breeding fruit flies.

Existential/Foundational: This entry point deals with fundamental, philosophical questions about the nature of the topic, why it exists, and/or what is its meaning or purpose. For the topic of evolution, this entry point might explore questions such as "Why are new species created and others die out?" or "What is the purpose of variation within species?"

The Entry Points Framework (a tool for curriculum development) clearly complements MI (a tool for understanding learners' cognitive abilities). Because different students have different profiles of intelligence, some students will be more engaged by pursuing a logical-quantitative entry point while others may find an aesthetic entry point more intriguing. But again, Gardner believes that it is important to use a variety of entry points to enhance students' perspectives and understanding of a topic.

Applying Entry Points in the Classroom: Some Issues to Consider

We have heard from teachers that the Entry Points Framework may be somewhat easier to implement than MI. Implementing MI seems to demand that the teacher have a reasonable grasp of each student's different profile of eight intelligences. This is a tall order, especially at the beginning of the year and especially for new teachers! In contrast, the Entry Points Framework allows the teacher to engage diverse learners by focusing on a more manageable number of points: one topic and a handful of entry points. (It's often best to start with fewer entry points and build up your repertoire, especially if you are relatively new to teaching or to these ideas.) Because the entry points largely map onto different intelligences, nearly all students should find ways to get at the substance of the topic using their strengths. At the same time, teachers can orchestrate entry point activities so that their students can also have opportunities to develop skills in their weaker areas.

Let's get concrete: Imagine a state curriculum framework that requires fourth graders to understand area and perimeter. Oftentimes, these concepts are taught didactically, through teacher presentations and math workbooks that rely heavily on the logical-quantitative entry point. Many students come to some understanding of area and perimeter in this fashion. However, many of these same students could come to an even stronger understanding if they could explore and represent these concepts through the entry points. This would give them somewhat different perspectives on these concepts and help them to apply what they have learned. In addition, some students do not grasp these concepts well, if at all, through the usual didactic methods. These students need different approaches to exploring area and perimeter in order to develop an understanding of these concepts and to see why they are important.

There are many ways to support students' understanding of these concepts through the Entry Points Framework. For example, the teacher could develop an experiential/hands-on approach: "Design a new playground that would fit within the current playground space, and be able to contain a new playhouse big enough to fit six students.") Interpersonal and aesthetic entry points could be included: "You are an architect, hired by the school to develop a new playground. As part of your planning process, it's important to interview people around the school to understand what they like about the existing playground and what they would like to change. Write up what you've learned from others about how to improve the playground. Then, draw a plan for the new playground that incorporates students' and teachers' suggestions. Calculate the perimeter and area of your design. Can your new design be incorporated into the existing playground space?" As students grapple with questions of the design's dimensions or making the new playground fit within the space of the existing one, there are many opportunities for teachers and students to engage the existential/foundational entry point: "What's the purpose of considering area and perimeter? What roles do these mathematical concepts play in the world we live in?"

Strive for Substantive Engagement

Depending on the topic, the Entry Points Framework may not allow every student's strongest intelligence to be used. For instance, in the unit on area and perimeter a student who has keen musical intelligence may not have an opportunity to draw on this strength in a substantive way. (It's true that in this and in many other units, such a student could invent a song. While this exercise allows the student to use his or her musical strengths, it is not clear that it will build their understanding of the topic.) Instead, this unit engages a variety of the student's other intelligences, some relatively strong, others less so, in order to provide a variety of opportunities to develop an understanding of the concepts of area and perimeter.

It's important to strike a balance between always engaging a student through his or her strongest intelligences and tackling what's to be learned in a substantive way. We argue that the balance should be tilted to allow students' strengths to be engaged substantively, rather than superficially, in the learning at hand. If there is not an opportunity for substantive engagement of an intelligence in a particular unit, this can be offset with opportunities in other units. Social studies or language arts oftentimes allow greater opportunities for music to be incorporated and used within the aesthetic entry point. By balancing entry points across different units and different subject areas, students can have opportunities to use their strengths and to do so in substantive ways, that is, in ways that really build their understanding.

Using the Entry Points Framework opens up the curriculum to students with different profiles of intelligence. By engaging different learners and having them grapple with several entry points, students' understanding is more likely to expand. Yet, the process of advancing all students' achievement extends beyond work with individual students' profiles of intelligence and the curriculum. This process also encompasses organizational practice. A sound set of organizational practices can help teachers to sustain and develop the good work that they do in their own classrooms. Such practices can also enable teachers throughout a school to build knowledge and skills across a wide range of learners. Therefore, in addition to a tool for understanding individual learners' strengths and a tool for building curriculum, we need a tool for organizational practice. The next section introduces a new tool developed through our research into schools that use MI.

COMPASS POINT PRACTICES: A TOOL FOR DEVELOPING ORGANIZATIONAL PRACTICES ACROSS CLASSROOMS AND THE SCHOOL

Background

Another tool, one that complements the two we've just discussed, is Compass Point Practices. These are practices found in schools that use MI and that associate the theory with benefits for students. They can guide you toward developing schools and classrooms that support students who learn in many different ways. The Compass Point Practices provide a tool for thinking systematically about classrooms and schools, for identifying areas of practice that are strong and those that can be made stronger.

The Compass Point Practices stem from the work of a three-and-a-half-year research investigation based at Project Zero, called the Project on Schools Using MI Theory or SUMIT. SUMIT was funded by the Schwab Foundation for Learning and the Geraldine R. Dodge Foundation. Its aim was to identify, document, and disseminate practices that are employed in schools that link MI with benefits for students.

To identify and document these practices, SUMIT researchers carried out two investigations. The first was aimed at understanding the big picture, and focused on this question: What are the practices in place across schools that use MI and associate the theory with positive outcomes for students? To answer this question, we conducted telephone interviews with educators at forty-one such schools, nearly all of which had been employing MI for three or more years. (The Appendix provides a brief description of each school.)

While a conceptual tool like the Compass Point Practices is useful by itself, it becomes much more powerful when complemented by vivid, concrete illustrations. To provide such illustrations, SUMIT's second investigation focused on documenting rich examples that incorporated the practices identified through our earlier telephone interviews. To develop these examples, we visited eight schools. There we had in-depth conversations with teachers and administrators. We observed classrooms in action and gathered examples of teachers' and students' work. We also spoke with students about their work, classrooms, and schools. In Part II of this book, we document exceptional practices at five schools and include detailed examples of six curriculum units. Together, the Compass Point Practices described below and the examples from Part II provide powerful ways for you to think about and develop your own work.

WHAT'S GOING ON IN SCHOOLS THAT USE MI AND THAT ASSOCIATE POSITIVE OUTCOMES FOR STUDENTS WITH THE THEORY?

To get a broad picture of the practices in place in schools that use MI and that associate the theory with improvements for students, we conducted forty-one interviews with educators from many different kinds of schools. The schools were from eighteen different states and one Canadian province. All but seven were elementary schools, reflecting the fact that the theory

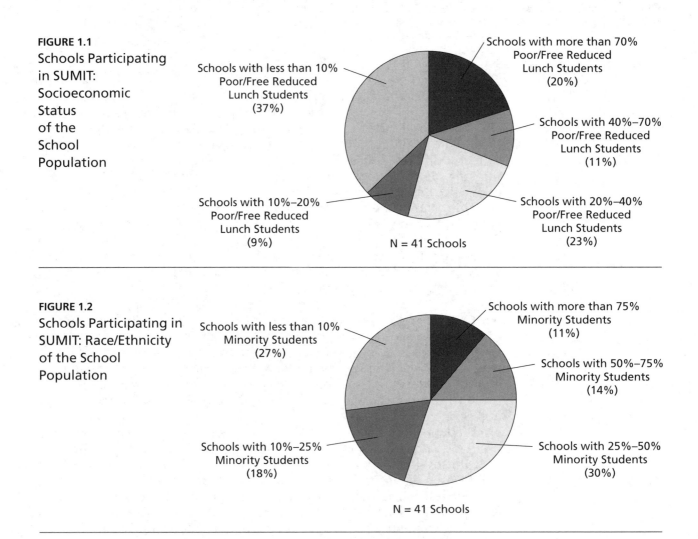

FIGURE 1.1
Schools Participating in SUMIT: Socioeconomic Status of the School Population

Schools with less than 10% Poor/Free Reduced Lunch Students (37%)

Schools with more than 70% Poor/Free Reduced Lunch Students (20%)

Schools with 40%–70% Poor/Free Reduced Lunch Students (11%)

Schools with 20%–40% Poor/Free Reduced Lunch Students (23%)

Schools with 10%–20% Poor/Free Reduced Lunch Students (9%)

N = 41 Schools

FIGURE 1.2
Schools Participating in SUMIT: Race/Ethnicity of the School Population

Schools with less than 10% Minority Students (27%)

Schools with more than 75% Minority Students (11%)

Schools with 50%–75% Minority Students (14%)

Schools with 25%–50% Minority Students (30%)

Schools with 10%–25% Minority Students (18%)

N = 41 Schools

was first and most frequently adopted by educators of younger students. Thirty-nine were public schools. None was a charter school. Across the schools, there were many different kinds of student populations, ranging from all affluent to all poor, all students of color to all white. By looking at schools with many different kinds of student populations in many different parts of the country, we hoped to identify practices that could be useful to educators in a great range of schools and classrooms.

In these interviews, we asked educators about their school's history, their student population, and their community. We asked about how MI was implemented in their schools, and about the schools' organizational, curriculum, and assessment practices. We also asked educators about outcomes or improvements that had taken place in the school and whether the educators associated these with MI or other interventions.

In analyzing transcribed interviews, we first looked at what educators told us about outcomes. This revealed that across the schools we studied, educators reported that MI contributes to improvements in test scores, student discipline, parent participation, and the schooling of students with learning disabilities.

OUTCOMES ASSOCIATED WITH USING MULTIPLE INTELLIGENCES

Standardized Test Outcomes

Nearly four-fifths of the schools in our survey reported improvements in standardized test scores. At nearly half of the schools, educators associated these improvements with MI. For example, Shirley Atkinson, the principal at the Moore Alternative School, an elementary school in Winston-Salem, North Carolina, reported, "a significant increase in achievement as measured by the California Achievement Test. . . for Grade 2 to Grade 3 to Grade 4." Continued gains in scores as children moved up the grades was an important indicator to this principal that the school was engaging students over the long term and increasing their capacities. "You know, to me that's

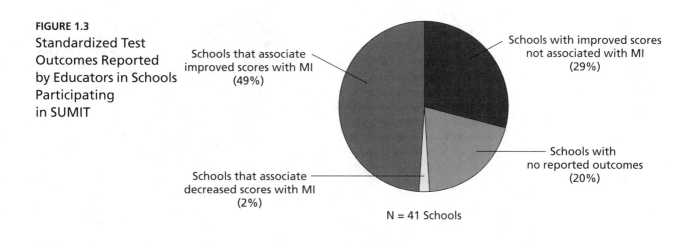

FIGURE 1.3

Standardized Test Outcomes Reported by Educators in Schools Participating in SUMIT

Schools that associate improved scores with MI (49%)

Schools with improved scores not associated with MI (29%)

Schools with no reported outcomes (20%)

Schools that associate decreased scores with MI (2%)

N = 41 Schools

powerful," she said. A teacher at the West Boylston Middle School in West Boylston, Massachusetts, made clear the connection between MI and achievement gains in her school: "Our achievement has been increased on a positive note. I think children have more opportunities to achieve better, to reach higher grades, to reach higher performances, because they have different modalities and different ways to express themselves." It is reasonable to think that when MI influences instruction, teachers present material in ways that engage more students and enable them to grasp it.

Student Discipline

Educators in more than four-fifths of the schools in our survey reported improvements in student discipline. In more than half of the schools, educators associated this improvement with the implementation of multiple intelligences. Educators spoke enthusiastically about these improvements. For example, Mr. Les Anderson, the principal at the Russell School in Lexington, Kentucky, stated that, "this year, our in-school suspension referrals are down 50 percent when we weren't doing anything else except incorporating MI." Carmen Hadrias, the principal of the Madrona Non-Graded School in Edmonds, Washington, noted that, with MI "there is a humongous difference at this school. Kids are able to resolve their conflicts on their own, and teachers can deal with the students' conflicts much better than they ever have before. So the teachers and the students have the skills to resolve the conflict. In theory, rarely does anybody come in the office and I have to do anything to them. Mostly, I just sit there while they solve their problems."

Our analysis of interviews and our school site visits indicate that improvements in discipline occur partly because schools that use MI find ways to engage a very broad range of learners. Students with strengths in areas that schools traditionally prize (logical-mathematical and linguistic intelligences) as well as students whose strengths reside in other areas are constructively involved in learning. Because students can be constructively engaged, fewer students act out. As we'll discuss in more detail a bit later,

FIGURE 1.4
Improvements in Student Discipline Reported by Schools Participating in SUMIT

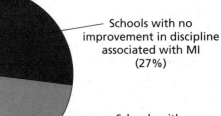

Schools that associated improvement in discipline with MI (54%)

Schools with no improvement in discipline associated with MI (27%)

Schools with no reported improvement (19%)

N = 41 Schools

discipline problems are also reduced because MI helps to foster respect for a variety of strengths and to build an appreciation for the fact that everyone has areas in which to improve. In an engaging and respectful environment, students have fewer reasons to misbehave.

Parent Participation

Parental involvement in education is important because it has long been associated with increased student achievement. In 80 percent of the schools SUMIT studied, educators reported improvements in parent participation. Sixty percent of the schools associated improved parent participation with MI theory.

One reason that MI seems to foster greater parent participation is that the theory validates the thinking and skills found across a wide range of real-world roles and occupations. In the schools we studied, skill in community work, the arts, trades, as well as academics and the professions were valued. As a result, parents with a wide range of abilities and occupations—and not only parents who had time or who had experienced success in school—felt comfortable in their children's schools and wanted to participate in school activities. The diversity of real-world roles was often incorporated into the curriculum (in Part II, see Schneider's Ink and the Archaeology Dig, two curriculum units that build on real-world roles).

Douglas Lockwood, the principal at the Searsport Elementary School in rural, Searsport, Maine, reported that the influence of MI on parent participation "has been unbelievable. We have twenty-two regular people who come in every single day. I mean, that's amazing. MI has given us real reasons to have parent volunteers." This was true in part because parent volunteers at Searsport were encouraged to share their knowledge of local history and culture.

Dr. Chris Mann, the principal at the Jesse Wowk School, in British Columbia, Canada, indicated yet another reason why MI might be linked to improved parent participation. As part of the process of implementing new

FIGURE 1.5

Improvements in Parent Participation Reported by Schools Participating in SUMIT

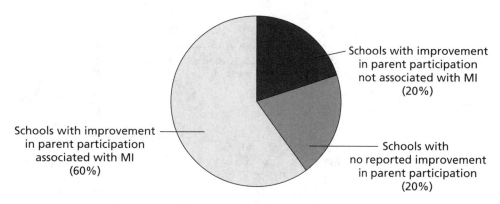

Schools with improvement in parent participation not associated with MI (20%)

Schools with improvement in parent participation associated with MI (60%)

Schools with no reported improvement in parent participation (20%)

N = 41 Schools

ideas in the school, the schools often reached out to parents. As this principal remarked, "We brought the parents on gently with us and, right from the beginning, we told them what we were doing, and we were doing it because we felt that it was good for kids and good for their children. The nice thing about MI theory is that it makes sense. . . . Each child has strengths in certain areas, and we want to expose them to a variety of ways to do things. They [parents] say, 'Oh that makes sense.'"

Students with Learning Differences or Disabilities

Educators in nearly four-fifths of the schools associated MI with improvements for students with learning differences. Valerie Gardner, the principal of Champlain Valley High School in Hinesburg, Vermont, asserted, "I would say that without a doubt it [MI] makes a huge difference. . . . They [students with learning differences] feel good about being able to choose and play on strengths, while they're also working on weaknesses in other areas so that they can become effective." In our visits to schools, we observed—and teachers reported—that youngsters with learning disabilities worked constructively within regular classrooms and generally could not be distinguished from other students who had not been diagnosed (see Part II, Schneider's Ink, for a detailed example of such a classroom).

When we realized just what a powerful tool MI seemed to be for students with learning differences, we sought to understand how educators were using the theory with these students. But time and again, the principals and teachers we spoke with said that they were not devising MI-influenced practices specifically for these youngsters. Instead, they told us their efforts to incorporate MI supported a wide-range of learners, including those with learning disabilities.

Once we uncovered this outcome and those concerning parent participation, student behavior, and test scores, we set out to identify in our interview data the kinds of practices that tapped multiple intelligences and that were widely shared across these schools. These are the Compass Point Practices that we highlight next.

FIGURE 1.6
Improvements for Students with Learning Disabilities

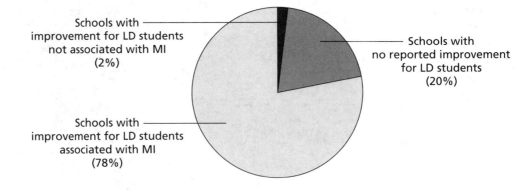

Schools with improvement for LD students not associated with MI (2%)

Schools with no reported improvement for LD students (20%)

Schools with improvement for LD students associated with MI (78%)

N = 41 Schools

THE COMPASS POINT PRACTICES

Rather than putting forth strict rules or guidelines for using MI, our project uses the metaphor of "Compass Points." These are practices worth steering toward to engage students' multiple intelligences in ways associated with student learning. Our interviews and later site visits underscore the importance of six Compass Points Practices.

1. Culture

The cultures of the schools we studied—their prevailing values, beliefs, and attitudes—share several themes. Among these are deeply held views that all children have strengths and can learn; that care and respect among people in the school is essential; that learning should be exciting; and that hard work, especially by adults in the school, is necessary to sustain such an environment.

A belief in children's strengths and potential   Educators in the schools using MI express beliefs that all children can learn, all children can succeed, and all children have strengths. Children bring their particular array of strengths to school, and it is the educators' job to enable these strengths to be fully realized. For example, Chris Mann, the head of the Jessie Wowk School, commented that, with MI, "the underlying attitude and underlying frame of reference that we all have is actually quite remarkably different" than those found in other settings. We are "not thinking of any child as a loser, but rather thinking of them all as successful and [our task is] finding ways for each of them to represent their learning. . . ." Patrick Cawley, principal of the Freeman School in Phillipsburg, New Jersey, said, "I consider all of them gifted. We just have to find out what the gift is." He went on to explain that, prior to implementing MI in his school, "there weren't experiences in the content of the classrooms that would allow anyone but the language- and the math-oriented child to shine. . . . By providing an array of experiences, a number of other kids have now come forward." Marilyn Davenport, principal of the Governor Bent School, in Albuquerque, New Mexico, emphasized, "We want every child who comes to our school to be successful. That's why we go about meeting their needs, and the framework of MI allows us to do that."

Advocacy of care and respect   Most of the schools advocate values of care and respect among all members of the school community. Marilyn Davenport noted that, "I can't go anywhere without [getting] fifty hugs. They just love me, and I love them. They know that. They know they're valued. They know they're respected." Sheryl Harmer, principal of Glenridge Elementary in Renton, Washington, highlighted the connection between seeing children's potential and a culture of respect and care: "I think kids really have a respect for each other and an empathy for each other, because they realize that they have strengths and weaknesses." Chris Mann expressed the same idea: "MI theory has only helped to augment something good that was begun and make it that much stronger: The kids are respectful toward one another." In part because of such values across the great majority of schools in the study, discipline problems were either minimal or had been greatly reduced.

A reading buddy at the McCleary School highlights the importance of caring and contributing in the culture of the schools in the SUMIT study

Educators noted that a culture of care and respect entails not only efforts to meet students' needs but also providing them with opportunities to contribute to the school and the wider community. Marilyn Davenport commented that, "Children need to feel that they belong and that they are competent." She noted that many of her students can survive the harsh circumstances they face "as long as there is kindness and there are opportunities for them to give." Opportunities to contribute come in many forms across these schools. In some schools, students participate in projects that serve the elderly, disabled, and homeless. Schools also ask older students to work with younger students in reading, writing, and other curricular areas. For example, there is a program for "reading buddies" at the McCleary School in Pittsburgh, Pennsylvania. As Sheryl Harmer of Glenridge Elementary, put it, "We've tried very strongly to make sure that students have lots of different ways to feel like they are contributing members of this group."

A belief that learning is exciting. Adults and youngsters in many of the schools maintained that learning in their schools is "exciting," "an adventure," and something undertaken with "enthusiasm." A parent at the Governor Bent School noted that her son's teacher, Carolyn Chadwell (whose "Math Labs" is highlighted in Chapter 5), "has an ability to bring out the joy in learning for every child. She does this by actively engaging them, by delighting all of their senses, by building a community of respect for diverse learners with special needs and talents, and by challenging them to be their best. . ." Her son, on his first afternoon at the school, offered this comparison: "In my other school I'd be on my eighteenth ditto by now." Kathy Carr, the principal of the Dover School, near Dover, Florida, reported that "we are a very, very enthusiastic school." At the county's Science Olympics, where Dover students win many gold medals, Carr noted with delight that participants from other schools "always know we're there. I guess you could say we're loud, but we just say we're enthusiastic!" McCleary School students' enthusiasm is obvious to visitors. "Visitors come into the rooms and they can't believe that children will go right up to them and start talking about their work." We experienced this for ourselves in our site visit. A youngster spontaneously came up to us with her topographical map of the Arctic, and exclaimed: "Did you know that there are seven countries in the Arctic!?" Similarly, after a child at the Governor Bent School showed us his poster of hurricanes and tornadoes, he volunteered to "get back to us" with more information about the differences between these two kinds of storms.

Educators work hard. The persistence and dedication manifested by youngsters at many of the schools is modeled for them by their teachers. Teachers and administrators in the schools we investigated work hard to enable a broad range of students to learn. However, the work for most of them appears to be worth it. Sheryl Harmer of Glenridge Elementary said, "I think the acknowledgment needs to be there that it [using MI] does take extra effort. It takes time in preparation and extra dedication, and unless you really believe fundamentally that this is worthwhile and that children are going to benefit from that effort, you won't go that extra mile." Tom Hoerr, the director of the New City School, in St. Louis, Missouri, expressed the same view: "Using MI requires a great deal of work and energy. There is no doubt that our teachers are working longer hours and harder than they were before this. From my perspective, there's got to be a return for the investment. There clearly is or we wouldn't be doing it." Hoerr's "return" is "that our kids use more different routes to learn and to demonstrate their understanding. I'd argue that that increases quality." In addition, "they know more about themselves as people." The return for teachers and administrators at McCleary Elementary comes from seeing students, most of whom are severely at-risk, view themselves as learners and to perform better in the middle school than students from the other five feeder schools.

Educators' emphasis on the hard work entailed in implementing MI makes it clear that the theory does not provide quick and easy solutions. Instead, for many educators, the theory of multiple intelligences opens up new possibilities, which yield successes with energy, time, and dedication. This effort, alongside the belief in students' potential, a sense of joy in learning, and values of care and respect yield a culture that supports the development of skills and knowledge for a wide range of students.

2. Readiness: Preparing people to work with multiple intelligence and other new ideas

Success in applying the theory of multiple intelligences, and other new ideas, appears to be related to when and how the teaching staff is introduced to it. "Timing is everything," said Natalie McKenna, the principal of the John F. Kennedy School in Brewster, New York. Principals emphasized the importance of building teachers' awareness of the different kinds of learners as a precursor to implementation. They employed many different approaches to building this awareness.

In some schools, there was a history of educational philosophies and practices in place that complemented MI. For instance, at the Briarcliff School in Shoreham, New York, teachers had many years' experience with "constructivist learning." This entailed building youngsters' understanding through diverse kinds of explorations and materials. In addition, for a number of years before learning of MI, the staff had devised activities that built on youngsters' different cognitive levels. Alongside this history of appreciating each learner's starting place, the school and surrounding district had a strong arts curriculum. Therefore, the staff was comfortable with incorporating musical and artistic activities. Given all this, the teachers felt a natural readiness for MI, and their task became figuring out how to draw on the theory wisely.

However, in the vast majority of schools, readiness for using MI wasn't quite so effortless. The process typically took a year or more. For example, the McCleary School was started by a team of teachers who developed its design. The design incorporated multiple intelligences and museum learning, the arts, and community involvement. The team won a grant that allowed its members a year to study various school reforms, visit other schools, and refine their design. Only after this extended process did the school open and begin its work with students.

In most other schools, the implementation of MI occurred while the school was up and running. For example, at Edgemont Montessori, a public elementary school in Montclair, New Jersey, the teachers were addressing the whole child with the materials and child-centered philosophy that are common to Montessori schools. However, the new principal, Adunni Anderson, wanted the teachers to extend the frameworks they use to examine their practice. "Of course, I took it easy. I was the new person on the block. . . [But] I said to them, 'we have to be about educating all children and responding to all the learning needs of kids.'" To help address the learning needs and development of all children, the principal gave "gifts" of articles about MI to the teachers. She also occasionally used the time before everyone was assembled for staff meetings for a "sponge activity." For example, she asked teachers to think back on their day to see how they'd drawn on a particular intelligence in their classroom. The teachers would then share their experiences, jot down ideas in their journal, and then move on to the formal part of the meeting.

In other schools, such as the Wheeler School in Louisville, Kentucky, building awareness entailed more formal learning opportunities. Several educators from this school attended a conference at which Howard Gardner spoke. They then shared the information with the staff: Wheeler's Judy Hummel described how readiness for MI grew in her school: "As staff became more and more aware of MI and understood, and read more and more research on it, we developed our own interest in it." At this school, and many others, teachers had opportunities to visit schools in which the theory was being applied and to ask questions of their colleagues at other schools. Many schools also hired consultants or staff developers who specialize in MI to do workshops to explore how the theory might be put into practice.

Alongside building awareness of the theory among the school staff, principals fostered readiness by encouraging teachers to apply the theory at a rate that felt sensible to them—perhaps in one or two units or projects—rather than plunging in all at once. Most principals noted that teachers were applying the theory at varying paces, and that their teachers were at varying points along a continuum of experience with the theory.

In short, while teachers at Briarcliff felt that appying MI was "just like breathing," educators elsewhere needed support, preparation, and time to adopt and use the theory. MI, like most other tools, only began to feel comfortable as teachers gained familiarity and experience with it.

Just as teachers were supported to take on MI, in the schools we visited students were helped to develop readiness for new work. Curriculum examples in Part II of this book, such as Schneider's Ink (Chapter 8) and the Heritage/Traditions Unit (Chapter 10), show that students and their parents were given materials in advance of these projects in order to help them get ready for undertaking new work. To build readiness for new undertakings, teachers in these classrooms and schools engaged in a substantial process of preparing students.

In essence, in these schools new ideas aren't just "delivered" to teachers or students with the expectation that they will be done. Instead, students and teachers are helped to get ready for new ideas and new work. This period of preparation supports teachers and students to successfully tackle complex new assignments.

3. Tool: MI is used as a means to foster high-quality work

Our interviews reveal a common pattern in the implementation of MI. When educators begin using MI, they often try to adapt their work to the theory. For example, curriculum, school periods, classroom learning centers, and even students might be labeled with the different intelligences. Within a couple of years of applying the theory, most educators rethink this approach. Ultimately, schools that use the theory effectively "keep the cart before the horse." They clearly use MI as a means to help students acquire knowledge and skills in the disciplines. MI does not replace those things. Sandra Kase, the principal of the Claremont School in the Bronx, New York, expressed this idea clearly, "[We use] MI to support what we need to do for kids; [rather than] manipulating what we do with kids to support MI."

The use of MI as a tool takes a variety of forms. In Briarcliff Elementary, the teachers used the terminology of the intelligences as a tool in their own thinking and in their communication with each other. MI was not explicitly mentioned to the students. At Briarcliff, even students who struggled in their learning, and who were helped to find areas of competence, were not taught the theory. Rather they, and their parents, were helped to see that they were, for example, capable artists or good at interacting with other children. Instead of using the vocabulary of MI with students, the teachers used everyday language to help children appreciate and develop their abilities.

At other schools, for example the Russell School and the New City School, children were introduced to the theory. In both schools, there was an emphasis on intrapersonal intelligence. This emphasis was aimed at helping children to know their own strengths, to appreciate their strengths, and to deploy them in their learning.

The Archaeology Dig at Searsport Elementary School substantively engages almost all the intelligences. At this and other schools studied by SUMIT, educators avoided superficially incorporating every intelligence in every unit

Another way that MI serves as a means of learning is by helping teachers to open up the curriculum. While many teachers reported that they initially started using MI by teaching everything in seven ways, most schools were, as Searsport's Doug Lockwood described it, "way over that kind of thinking." That initial practice was transformed into efforts to draw on several, rather than all, intelligences in substantive ways during a curriculum unit. For instance, at Searsport Elementary, in Maine, children learned about the local town history in part through an archaeological project (highlighted in Part II). This included opportunities to draw on many, but not all of the intelligences. In this project, children, with the help of amateur archaeologists and a local museum curator, carried out an excavation of one of the town's abandoned outdoor shipyards. They researched the finds from each of their dig sites, organized their finds into collections, and prepared them to be exhibited in the local museum. In this effort, all but musical intelligence were exploited to a significant degree. Music was not added simply to tap all seven. There were other opportunities in the school day and week to draw on that intelligence in a more authentic fashion.

In sum, across these schools—whether the theory was explicitly taught or not—educators used MI to develop knowledge and skills that are broadly recognized and to help students carry out work of high quality. MI was used much more as a means than as an end in and of itself. While it is possible to teach all topics in seven or eight ways, there is a wide consensus across these schools that it is better to draw on the intelligences in ways that substantively contribute to, rather than distract from, the learning at hand.

4. Collaboration: Informal and Formal Exchanges

Educators, like all other people, have their own profiles of strengths. Yet, they are responsible for creating learning environments that serve a wide range of students. To develop classrooms and schools that foster knowledge and skills among many different kinds of learners, teachers in the schools we studied sought to complement their own areas of strength by drawing on the knowledge and strengths of their colleagues. Through informal and formal collaborations, teachers were better able to develop the strengths and skills of their students.

An example of informal collaboration comes from the McCleary School in Pittsburgh, Pennsylvania, in which nearly every student is considered at-risk. During a study of the city's rivers (see Chapter 3), one classroom teacher, Chimene Brandt, realized then that it would be helpful if her second and third graders were equipped with some new skills to document what they observed on their river field trip. Through a brief conversation, she and Nancy Fralic, the school's part-time art teacher, brainstormed lessons for the class. One lesson entailed conveying the techniques for sketching. As the art teacher explained it, students tend to record the details of their observations, but in sketching, they need to draw broader outlines and fill in the details later. When the students returned from their field trip, Fralic provided a second lesson on blending colored chalk to create backgrounds and using wet chalk to create a more detailed foreground. The result of this informal collaboration was that students gained new drawing skills with which they could represent what they had seen.

The success of this informal collaboration was shared at a larger group meeting in the school's "Elegant Room" (the teachers' wicker-furnished

An informal collaboration between the classroom and art teacher at the McCleary Elementary School enabled students to skillfully represent their observations of Pittsburgh's rivers.

lounge that had been largely ceded to the youngsters). The collaboration was also documented on paper in order to share it with other teachers in the school. Both the classroom teacher and the art teacher emphasized how powerful such informal collaborations can be in engaging students and equipping them with skills to carry out a particular piece of work.

One example of formal collaboration comes from the Dover School in Dover, Florida. This elementary school serves a population with a large Spanish-speaking minority, and many of the students are children of migrant workers. The school has two full-time music teachers and two full-time art teachers. Throughout the curriculum, teachers encourage children to use spatial and musical strengths, and abilities in other arts areas, to learn and to express their understanding. To enable teachers to draw on the youngsters' different strengths, teachers receive one full day a month to work in teams to develop rich curriculum units.

Another example of formal collaboration comes from the John F. Kennedy School (highlighted in Chapter 7), where several classrooms are paired, so that two teachers work with a large group of students throughout the day. In addition, special services are "pushed in" to support full inclusion of all students. At any point in time, any teacher in the room—ranging from the regular classroom teacher, to the speech therapist, to the reading teacher—can be leading instruction.

In sum, collaborations among teachers can bring the range of expertise and strengths available across the school staff. Such collaborations in turn help engage diverse students' strengths and improve their opportunities to learn.

5. Choice: Meaningful curriculum and assessment options

The educators we spoke with find that applying MI requires providing students with meaningful choices for learning and for demonstrating their knowledge. Meaningful choices are ones that are of interest both to the student and to the wider society (not just to one or the other). It is important to note that these choices are guided or controlled. Alan McCloud, principal of the McWayne Elementary School in Batavia, Illinois, described it this way: "We honor children's choices. But we also control that. We tell students, the last four times you did a project, you have done a visual representation. Let's see if we can't have you do something in another format. So that we try to build confidence in other areas. . ."

The project-based curriculum used by the Briarcliff School highlights one route to achieving both choice and high-quality student work. In each of the school's classrooms, a long-term investigation of a topic was underway. Children explore the topic in various substantive ways. For example, in one classroom in which spiders were the topic, children could make large models of spiders, create computer drawings of spiders, develop a spider game based on spider facts, and survey classmates about their attitudes toward spiders and graph the results.

These choices allowed children to draw on a range of intelligences to build their understanding. Youngsters, even those identified as having learning disabilities, were extremely engaged in their learning. Many spontaneously came to us to explain what they had done and why their arachnids looked and behaved as they did.

In the Rivers Study at the McCleary School, students visited, observed, and sketched rivers. Their classrooms included collections of artwork involving rivers. The teachers encouraged students to generate hypotheses about how rivers flow and to test these using sand and water in a stream table. In addition, the students could build river and bridge structures, and they could read about rivers. Although about 20 percent of the school's youngsters are considered learning disabled, the choices teachers offered allowed nearly every child to become involved and to learn. The youngsters were also able to use these different choices to help demonstrate their understanding of how rivers formed and the role of rivers in the water cycle. For example, a drawing of a rainy day scene was used to prompt one youngster to give a detailed explanation of the water cycle. The stream table activity was used by the teacher to elicit information from students about how rivers form and change.

The use of choices applies not only to project–like curricula, but also to fundamental curricular areas. For example, at the West Boylston Middle School, some teachers used to assign the same reading to all students. Sharron Bouvier, a teacher at the school, explained, "Seven years ago, I would have passed out the same novel to every single child and said, 'By Friday, you have to have pages 1 through 20 read. Next Wednesday, you have to have up to page 40 read.'" But once she began drawing on MI, she thought differently about how to organize reading assignments. "Now I try to get novels that all focus around the same theme, but there are books that would appeal to different intelligences. . . . The kids have a choice. They would all be reading a biography, but they have a choice. They might want to read a biography about a sports character, or a musician, or someone in government, or a ballerina. . . . I can plug in things that they are more interested in and by giving them a choice, they respond better."

Providing controlled choices enables a wide range of learners to become constructively involved. Through controlled choice—choices that make sense not only to the student but to adults—students can draw on a wider range of intelligences to gain new knowledge and skills.

6. Arts: A significant role in the school

The arts play a vital role in nearly all the schools we have studied. A significant role for the arts makes sense in these schools, because MI theory specifies that musical intelligence and spatial intelligence (which is used extensively in the visual arts) are fundamental ways of solving problems.

Many of the schools in our study reported that they had an extensive arts curriculum. For example, the Russell Elementary School offered classes in Suzuki violin, band, art, and dance. The school also produced an original opera, using a script that the children wrote, sets that they designed and painted, and music that they developed and were helped to record. Similarly, art, general music, instrumental music, and elective Suzuki classes were offered at the Briarcliff Elementary School.

While many schools emphasized the arts as "ends in and of themselves," most schools also employed the arts as a means for expanding children's knowledge and understanding in other curricular areas. For example, in one art class for second and third graders at Russell, the children were asked to paint a watercolor to illustrate the song, "America, the Beautiful." However, the children—city youngsters, most of whom came from poverty—had difficulty representing the song's lyrics. Therefore, the art teacher used most of the art lesson to help the students grasp the meaning of "amber," and metaphors such as "waves of grain." Through debate, and discussion of the concepts of "foreground" and "background," she also enabled students to envision "purple mountains." The class's exploration of lyrics left only eight

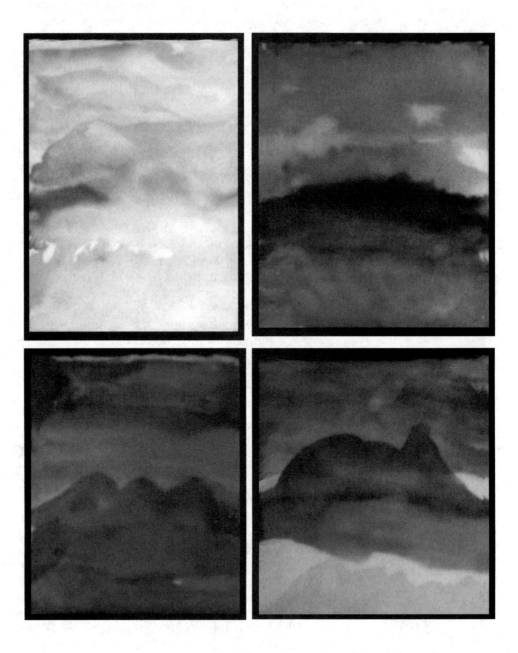

Watercolors produced by second- and third-grade students at the Russell Elementary School reflect an understanding of "America, the Beautiful."

At the McCleary School, a student used his group's rainy day mural to explain the water cycle.

minutes for the actual watercolor paintings. Yet, as the children's paintings demonstrate, the youngsters now understood the vocabulary and imagery of the song.

In the River Study at the McCleary School, the murals that children drew in one second- and third-grade classroom reflected not only what they had seen at the river, but advanced their conceptual understanding of the water cycle. When three boys were asked about the large chalk mural they had drawn, they began by talking about the concrete objects depicted: the tall houses, streets, and the gray sky full of rain. But when asked about how their mural fit with the river murals generated by their classmates, one of the boys (pictured at the far left) provided an extended explanation. He noted that rain forms from evaporation of water on the earth's surface, that condensation of water vapor yields clouds, that smaller raindrops collide and become larger ones, and that that made the rain that was falling on the houses and streets in his picture.

In some years, the Governor Bent School had no art teacher. Nevertheless, the arts pervaded the classrooms. For instance, in a number of classrooms (including one highlighted in Chapter 6), teachers used spiral-bound "squiggle books" to inspire an interplay of creative writing and imaginative drawing. In the example on the next page, a second grader has created both an elaborate Halloween illustration and a story rich with detail.

In our interviews as well as our site visits, learning experiences involving the arts powerfully engage students. The students, even those with learning disabilities, participate eagerly and enthusiastically. As the brief examples from the Governor Bent, McCleary, and Russell schools illustrate, the arts in these schools supported the development of children's knowledge and skills across many curricular areas.

One dark, gloomy halloween night, the mouse kids were trick-or-treating. Many of them were dressed as "Supermouse." But wile the supermice were trying to fly, they landed all over Mouse Village. Three of them landed in the grasses out of town! They landed with a big

THUMP! "Could you stop landing with capital letters?" exclaimed Eddy. "It messes up the page." "How are we going to get back to town?" questioned Freddy. Meanwhile, back in Mouse Village, the rocket expedition to the moon for cheese was taking off. . . .

Squiggle books are used extensively at the Governor Bent School. They combine detailed artwork and detailed stories.

NAVIGATING FARTHER

Together, these six Compass Point Practices engage students' multiple intelligences and help teachers to foster knowledge and skills across a range of students. You can think of the Compass Point Practices as directions that schools and classrooms ought to steer toward to effectively engage the many ways that students learn. We invite you to begin this journey by exploring Part II. There we provide extended examples from a diverse set of public elementary schools in which these practices are prominent.

BOX 1.1 THE COMPASS POINT PRACTICES

Culture: a supportive environment for educating diverse learners.

The school environment is notable for a belief in students' strengths and potential, care and respect, joy in learning, and educators' hard work.

Readiness: awareness-building before implementation

There are efforts to introduce and explore MI and other new ideas prior to calls for implementing them in classrooms.

Tool: MI is a means to foster high-quality student work

MI is used as a route to promote students' skills and understanding of curriculum, rather than as an end in itself or as an additional piece of the curriculum.

Collaboration: informal and formal exchanges

In informal and formal exchanges, educators readily share ideas, provide constructive suggestions, and complement their own areas of strength by drawing on the knowledge and strengths of others.

Controlled Choice: meaningful curriculum and assessment options

Educators provide students wtih options for learning and for demonstrating their knowledge that are meaningful both to the student and in the wider society.

Arts: a significant role in the life of the school

The arts are used to develop students' skills and understanding within and across disciplines.

PART TWO

Views of Schools and Classrooms

The following chapters highlight the work of teachers and principals in five schools during the period between 1997 and 2000. Each of these chapters offers dynamic illustrations of MI, the Entry Points Framework, and the Compass Point Practices. In this section, you'll find two kinds of chapters: school overviews and examples of curricula.

1. Overviews of five diverse public elementary schools, each of which has been strongly influenced by the theory of multiple intelligences. These overviews include the school demographics, the history of MI's implementation, and outcomes that the school associates with MI.

2. Richly illustrated examples of curriculum drawn from each of the five schools. Each of the curriculum examples is organized into five sections:

- *At a Glance* presents a very brief overview of the unit and how it intersects with MI, Entry Points, and the Compass Point Practices.
- *What Is. . . ?* This section provides a more detailed description of the unit.
- *Teacher Strategies* describes the strategies that individual teachers used to make the unit work in the classroom.
- *What Happens?* This section details the teaching and learning activities that take place during the unit.
- *Revisiting the Frameworks* interprets the unit in light of MI, Entry Points, and Compass Point Practices.

The five sections for each curriculum example are like the transparent pages of an old anatomy textbook: pages that highlight the skeletal system, the circulatory system, the organs, nervous system, and muscles. You can learn something important by reading any one section. Together, the five sections provide the whole picture of how teachers have been able to draw on multiple intelligences in ways that advance students' learning.

2 The McCleary School

The curriculum example we have selected from the McCleary School is entitled the Rivers Study. It is an interdisciplinary curriculum that engages multiple intelligences with the aim of building students' understanding of the water cycle and the importance of rivers to the city of Pittsburgh. We highlight this unit as it was taught by one of its key developers, Ms. Chimene Brandt, to the second and third graders in her classroom. The strategies she uses, and many of the activities, are ones that teachers throughout the McCleary School have applied to a wide variety of topics, including the Arctic, libraries, Egypt, theater, the savannah, and mammals. Before presenting the Rivers Study, this chapter puts that unit in context by providing an overview of the McCleary School. The chapter also highlights the Compass Point Practices that enable McCleary's teachers to engage students' multiple intelligences and advance their learning.

OVERVIEW OF THE McCLEARY SCHOOL

The McCleary School, Pittsburgh, Pennsylvania.

The McCleary School is a small K-5 elementary school located in the Lawrenceville section of Pittsburgh. The school occupies a corner location in a largely residential neighborhood of older, worn-looking attached houses. The school's parking lot and playground share a blacktopped space separated from the street by a high chain-link fence. The school building itself is compact, mostly pale brick, two stories, and a hundred years old. The main door is metal and windowless. Tall, double-arched windows gracefully counteract the school's somewhat industrial appearance.

The inside of the McCleary school belies its stern exterior qualities. A renovation in the early 1990s left intact beautiful, old architectural details. Just up the stairs from the street-level entry is a large circular space called the atrium. The atrium serves as a central gathering and performing place. The school's small main office—a front counter, a secretary's space, and a cramped principal's office—is on the first floor opposite the atrium. Two sets of stairs, decorated with elaborate wrought-iron railings, follow around a large curved stairwell to the second floor. There, the round stairwell is surrounded by large, portable display boards. These provide an exhibition area for student work or artwork. The first and second floors hold the school's ten large classrooms, replete with arches, high ceilings, and hooked coat closets, sinks, and enormous windows. A small gym and cafeteria are in the basement level, a music room on the first floor, and a well-equipped library on the second floor. There are a full-time librarian, part-time music and physical education teachers, an art teacher, who works part-time in some years, and two full-time resource teachers who work closely with classroom teachers to support this school's full-inclusion teaching.

McCleary's student population has varied widely in size. When the school opened it was overcrowded with almost 300 students. After elementary schools were redistricted, McCleary's population was reduced in 1998–1999 to approximately 180 students in eight classrooms. Thirty percent of the students are African American, 67 percent are white. Poverty is widespread: 77 percent of the students receive free or reduced meals. Twenty percent of the students have been diagnosed with disabilities. Few students entering kindergarten know the alphabet or can distinguish letters from numbers.

Yet, at the McCleary School, these at-risk students become powerfully engaged learners. They learn to evaluate and critique their own and others' work, to revise using information from these evaluations, to work with others, and to carry out long-term projects that yield high-quality products. These crucial skills and behaviors are associated with different short-term versus long-term test results. In the short term, scores of students within the school have been mixed. Some districtwide tests have shown very favorable comparisons in math and reading against nineteen other Pittsburgh elementary schools with similar populations. Some assessments, like the Metropolitan Achievement Tests, showed powerful gains over four years, while the Iowa Test scores were persistently low. However, over time, the importance of this school's approach is powerfully and clearly manifested. A study by Pittsburgh's central administration found that, in middle school, students from McCleary markedly outperformed students from the seven other feeder elementary schools every year for four years in a row, even though McCleary's students were typically more at-risk. In every academic subject they had the largest proportion of A's and the lowest proportion of failing grades. They also had the most students on high honor roll, the best attendance, and the fewest behavior problems. From these sorts of results it is possible to say that McCleary is working well toward achieving its mission: "to initiate every child on a journey of lifelong learning." Alongside these achievements, the school has been recognized with a Title I Parent Involvement Award and chosen by Title I as a model of best practices.

THE COMPASS POINT PRACTICES

How does the McCleary School enable at-risk youngsters to become capable learners? The framework of the Compass Point Practices is helpful in understanding the successes achieved by the students and teachers at this school. (In this, and all the school overview chapters, we review the Compass Point Practices in an order that allows the story of each school to be clearly told.)

Readiness

The McCleary School began operating in 1992. It was based on a synthesis of ideas crafted by a group of educators who worked together in another inner-city school in Pittsburgh. These teachers submitted a concept paper to the Pittsburgh-based Heinz Foundation, which was then looking to foster grassroots school reform. The concept paper sought to engage inner-city students in learning by drawing on the wide range of their strengths and by incorporating museums and museum–like experiences in education. This original concept paper yielded a one-year grant of $325,000 to develop a school design. To develop their initial ideas, teachers visited schools both in this country and abroad, and they spoke with teachers and scholars of education. "It was like a postgraduate education of the first order," said Mary Ellen ("Mel") McBride, who later became McCleary's principal.

Central to the teachers' design for the new school was Gardner's theory of multiple intelligence. The teachers' design also called for depth of engagement rather than broad coverage of curriculum. Along with these emphases, the teachers gave a prominent role to community involvement, museum experiences, and an arts-integrated curriculum.

Unlike the other schools highlighted in this book, the McCleary School incorporated the theory of multiple intelligences from its very beginning. Despite that, preparatory and ongoing efforts were still needed to help teachers to apply the theory in the classroom. One of the ways that teachers did this was through their professional development. Much of this professional development was school-based. Mel McBride noted, "We don't believe in workshops. We don't believe in bringing in experts for a day. . . . [That is] "time that we could be talking and learning from our own experiences." One of the ways that the educators learned from each other at McCleary was by sharing readings and holding discussion groups to reflect on what they'd read. "We began reading Gardner's books and having discussions," said Mrs. McBride.

In the first year of the school's operation, the teachers were enthusiastic and eager, but the actual curriculum was not articulated in detail. The staff did not necessarily have the experience or education to carry out long-term, in-depth projects. Building on her own experiences, Mrs. McBride decided to model a project. The project arose out of the fact that the school's cafeteria was a bleak, undecorated basement space. The students didn't like being there, and they often acted out. Mrs. McBride, in consultation with them, decided to make the cafeteria much more like a restaurant. Students learned about the different jobs that make a restaurant work, and about food preparation, recipe math, and nutrition. They also learned about social skills that are needed to make a restaurant a pleasant place to be (including good manners and talking in an inside voice). During lunchtime for the rest of the year, students assumed some of the different "front" jobs, including greeting "guests," designing menu boards, and decorating the space, complete with tablecloths. The restaurant project provided some opportunities to learn about nutrition and about how restaurants worked, and it markedly reduced behavior problems at lunchtime. In addition, the teachers gathered insights and ideas about how to develop and run a long-term project. Among the lessons for the teachers was that the project should matter to the students and that it was helpful if the project allowed them to take on real-world roles.

Alongside modeling a project, teachers got help in developing curriculum from a grant that provided sustained support from outside experts. This grant, called Vision 21, brought together five Pittsburgh schools with mentors from Bank Street College. Over a three-year period, Bank Street educators coached teachers in developing long-term projects, which they called "studies," of a given topic. The Bank Street coaches, according to Mrs. McBride, "believe that children should be given a variety of ways to show what they know." To do this, they mentor teachers in efforts to incorporate many different disciplines and media. As the Rivers Study will make clear, this mentoring provided McCleary's teachers with a clear structure for engaging students' intelligences and developing their knowledge and skills.

Culture

The culture of the McCleary weaves together four important strands: a belief in children's strength and potential, respect and caring among all members of the school, joy and enthusiasm in learning, and hard work.

A belief in children's strengths and potential. The McCleary School's statement of values and beliefs highlights that: "Every child can learn, has a drive to learn, and has a right to learn and to develop all of his intelligences." Clearly, these sorts of values are far easier to state than they are to enact. This is especially true with students who are at-risk. At the McCleary School, teachers recognize the difficulties in their students' lives. During our visit, they and their students told us about youngsters who had witnessed crimes, who had lost family members to violence and mental illness, or who had been separated from parents by court order. However, it was the students' efforts to surmount these difficulties, and their successes in overcoming them, that provided the central theme to such stories.

We learned, for instance, that a third grader we saw calmly offering more than a dozen different ways to categorize mammals (nocturnal, diurnal, predator, prey, omnivore, carnivore, vegetarian, land or water dwellers . . .) had been in several foster homes. When she first came to the school, she could not sit still or listen. But this year, she knows how well she's doing. When a new child came in and acted wild, she commented, "I used to be like that." This child's situation was one of many that illustrate the belief that McCleary's teachers maintained in their students' potential to learn. Students in the school were seen as very capable of beating the odds against them.

Care and respect.   Mrs. McBride asserted that "the social and psychological needs of the students" have to be addressed for learning to take place in her school. One of the ways these needs are met is by providing continuity for the students through looped classrooms. Children in kindergarten move together with their teacher into first grade. Second and third graders, and fourth and fifth graders, have combined classrooms. This allows them to have the same teacher and most of the same classmates for two years in a row. As a result, students and teachers get to know each other well and to work better together.

Care and respect are also inculcated by teaching students how to interact in ways that promote learning. For example, in Stephanie Hornick's kindergarten classroom, we watched as students, who sat in a circle, shared their journals. One by one, students took turns walking slowly around the inside perimeter of the circle so that his or her classmates could see the journal work. Classmates were taught that if they wanted not only to look at the journal but also to touch it, they first had to ask the author, "May I touch it?" This kind of careful sharing sets the stage for the well-behaved, but not uncritical, discussions of students' work that takes place in the upper grades of the school. In these discussions, students talk about the qualities that they like in the work as well as make suggestions for how to improve the work even more.

Students at McCleary School are taught how to be respectful and caring toward each other's work.

Instruction on how to get along with each other takes place regularly. In Ms. Brandt's room, we saw a brief fight between a boy whose mother had just been hospitalized and a boy with autism who had been annoying him. Ms. Brandt took one boy in each hand and walked them out into the corridor as the other students continued working. She calmly but intensely asked the first boy, "What else could you have done besides hit him? Let's think." They decided that he could go to the teacher, he could ask to be placed in a separate group, or he could move himself away from the other child. He could not hit another child. The school also hired a community member to work as the "trouble-shooting aide." This aide visits most classrooms daily to give students ideas for getting along and to praise their good deeds. She also mediates conflicts among them. Such ongoing efforts to create a caring and respectful environment have paid off. Over four years, the number of disciplinary referrals has been reduced by more than 75 percent.

Excitement, enthusiasm, and joy.   These qualities are far more common than discord at the McCleary School. Mrs. McBride reported that "People come from all over the country to see us, and they come into the rooms and they can't believe that children will go right up to them and start talking about their work, what they are doing." When we visited the school several months later, exactly the same thing happened. For example, a student working on a study of the Arctic excitedly showed us her topographical map of the region: "Did you know that there are seven countries in the Arctic Circle!?" she exclaimed. On several occasions students leaped to make connections between their current in-depth studies and studies undertaken in previous years. For instance, during the Arctic unit, students began recalling and comparing the life traditions of the Netsilik and the traditions of the Masai, which they had studied the year before. They also spontaneously compared behaviors of the savannah animals with the behaviors of animals they were now studying in the mammal unit. This kind of spontaneous transfer of knowledge from one year to the next is extremely unusual among young students, and it reflects the depth of the curriculum as well as students' enthusiasm and investment in their learning.

Hard work.   The enthusiasm and work ethic that students demonstrated at McCleary was modeled by their teachers. These educators chose to work in an urban school, and they were clearly devoted to fostering these students' learning. Their commitment was evident in long hours that most of the staff put in. The teachers also enrolled in extra courses to help them gain expertise, including a seven-week summer course in teaching students the writing process.

Just as teachers worked hard to do their best, they instilled ideas about hard work in their students. They did this in part by rarely accepting a student's initial product. Instead, they taught students how to critique their work and make it even better. "Everything we do, we assess," said Mel McBride. One of the assessment tools teachers relied on was rubrics (Goodrich, 1997; Goodrich Andrade, 2000; Wiggins, 1998), which they developed together with their students. In developing rubrics, the teachers and students articulated the characteristics that a strong piece of work should possess. They rated the degree to which students have incorporated the characteristic on a four-point scale, with a four reflecting the highest degree possible.

Rubrics provided standards against which students could assess their work, and also helped to guide their effort. For example, in Michele Gnora's class, we observed fourth and fifth graders using a rubric to assess their own montage boxes. Each box was both supposed to illustrate a key life cycle event, such as birth, death, or marriage, and to incorporate good collage techniques. After all the students had presented and reviewed their own box to the class, Ms. Gnora asked, "Who gives their box the highest rating?" Our expectation was that all students would rate themselves highly. In fact, not a single hand was raised. All the students knew that, with more work, they could do even better.

Collaboration

Collaboration at McCleary was fostered by the staff's shared commitment to at-risk students and to a set of shared classroom practices intended to serve them. Across the school, teachers employed the theory of multiple intelligences, rubrics, long-term studies introduced by Bank Street College, and arts in the curriculum. Collaboration was an explicit part of the design for the school. "Our school depends on a staff committed to cooperation and consensus building," stated the original concept paper. "We envision a school . . . where the entire staff works energetically and collegially with each other. . . ."

Much of the collaboration at McCleary was informal: every classroom door was left open, and everyone talked with each other about his or her work. "When it comes to questions," said teacher Stephanie Hornick, "I feel really comfortable going to anybody." Todd Shaffer, a teacher new to the school, remarked, "People were just offering me help all the time. . . . I never thought for a minute that I couldn't walk into anybody's room and ask them for anything, whether it was as simple as borrowing some materials or asking them how to teach oral reading more effectively."

A somewhat more structured route toward collaboration was the use of a common topic for an in-depth study across two or more classrooms. For example, the Rivers Study underway in Ms. Brandt's room was also being used in another classroom. Common topics, some of which were recycled in later years, enabled the teachers to share ideas and experiences and to build on each other's insights as they worked on a particular unit. Oftentimes, collaborative efforts, such as the Rivers Study, were shared more formally at staff meetings. Mel McBride encouraged and supported collaborations, partly by holding meetings devoted to such efforts.

Collaboration also grew out of the school's effort to provide full-inclusion classrooms for students with special needs. To do this, classroom teachers and the special education teacher often worked together in the classroom. For example, during small-group activities, the special educator, Tammy Smith, supported several students in reading or another area, while the classroom teacher worked with, and monitored, other groups. (Schneider's Ink, a curriculum example described in Chapter 8, highlights a collaboration between a classroom teacher and special educator.)

Classroom teachers and specialists collaborated to bring together their separate strengths to benefit the whole class of students. As Chimene Brandt put it, typically "specialists are used for preps. . . . I don't believe in that." Instead, she and the other classroom teachers consulted with the specialists to make the curriculum as rich as possible. For example, the librarian regularly worked with classroom teachers to orchestrate books and other media to support instruction for many topics and learners. In the Rivers Study, described in the next chapter, both the librarian and the art teacher brought resources and ideas that engaged many different kinds of learners. Ms. Brandt believes that collaboration among teachers models important behaviors for students: "They see teachers working together, helping each other, and learning from each other. That is very powerful."

Arts

The McCleary School placed a strong emphasis on the arts. The concept paper envisioned a staff that "attempts to integrate arts throughout the school." Extensive collaborations between classroom teachers, art special-ists, and the librarian was one means of achieving this aim. In every class-room, there were posters with art reproductions in different styles. There was also artwork related to particular units of study. For example, during the River Study, there was a large cluster of various artists' depictions of rivers in Ms. Brandt's room. Along with reproductions of work by adult artists, artwork produced by students spilled forth from all the classrooms into the corridors. (For readings on the arts and education, see Eisner, 2002; Gardner, 1990).

One of the aims of the school was to be the "53rd Street Museum" (because the school is on the corner of McCleary and 53rd Street). Local artists and galleries sometimes lent their work to be displayed around the atrium. In addition, the atrium served as a performance space. For example, during an Arctic Study the students decided to do a play. They wrote it themselves, drawing on "all the research they had done" about Arctic life and how people provided food, shelter, and clothing for themselves in the far north. Then they rehearsed it and performed it for the rest of the school.

The McCleary School also benefited from collaborations with some of Pittsburgh's art institutions. For instance, instructors from the Art Institute of Pittsburgh came every week to work with students who were especially interested in the visual arts. The school also got a grant that gave students and teachers extensive access to the Carnegie Museum. Museum docents and other staff also visited the school regularly over the course of a year and helped teachers draw on the museum's resources to enrich the curriculum.

Mrs. McBride reported that "all this gorgeous artwork" occasionally led a visitor to "think that all we do is play." But Mrs. McBride, and the rest of the staff, argued that the arts contributed to students' understanding: If you "interviewed the child about what he's attempting to show in that mural, that collage, that model, that map, you will hear tons of information." The arts in the McCleary School provided a way for students to draw on the range of their abilities to represent and reflect on what they learned.

Controlled Choice

The McCleary School teachers employed a rich system of controlled choice. In this system, teachers worked with students to develop and select choices that could foster new skills and new knowledge.

In all the extended studies that take place at the McCleary School, a whole classroom of students first brainstormed many possibilities about what they wanted to learn and the ways they might pursue this learning. Teachers then guided the selection of questions and methods to help students focus on choices that were likely to illuminate the central concepts they wanted students to master during the study. For example, in the Rivers Study, Ms. Brandt guided students to choices that would help them understand "How do rivers begin?" and "Where does the water come from?"

Through brainstorming and careful selection, teachers supported students' interest and commitment to do work. "If I sat down and told students exactly what to do the whole time and never asked them what they thought, they wouldn't have any ownership," said Todd Shaffer.

Choice at McCleary was evident in the range of activities that were available during the in-depth studies and sometimes during other units of curriculum. For example, across study topics, students commonly chose to take field trips, read about a topic, write about it, and build models related to it. Within these choices, students were still guided: If a teacher found a student sticking just to the block modeling area or to journal writing, the teacher encouraged, and sometimes assigned, work on other activities. Sometimes, teachers began the in-depth study time by assigning students to their preferred activity and then rotating them into activities outside their comfort zone. In this way, students got to do work that they enjoyed and to develop skills in new areas.

Another way that teachers helped students focus on meaningful choices was by telling them that work presented to the class must incorporate central concepts, ideas, or information from the study topic. Mel McBride explained, "We don't want a pretty picture with a car in it," unless that work is connected to the curriculum. For many topics, students are told that they can "write a play about it, write a song about it, you can do a mural about it, you can do a map about it. But you must be able to show what you know through the choices you make."

Because in-depth studies are pursued for about an hour each day, the preferences students exercised during that time were balanced by other forms of instruction. For example, a block of time was set aside for math instruction each day. There was also a writing period during which students used a process involving brainstorming ideas, drafting, editing and revising, and publishing. This balance of choice within the in-depth studies combined with more prescribed curriculum enabled students both to invest in learning and to acquire fundamental skills.

MI Is Used as a Tool

Even though MI was a cornerstone for the school, the theory never dominated the curriculum. Mrs. McBride stated, "we never said that today we are going to do art because we want to do multiple intelligences. That is ridiculous. We said, 'today we are going to study the Masai and their war dances. . . .'" In other words, the teachers focused on developing a rich substantive curriculum. They did not focus on including every intelligence in every curriculum unit.

The school's classrooms and display spaces reflected an instrumental use of MI. There were few, if any, posters about MI on view, and teachers didn't talk to students about the theory. Yet, with the theory in mind, teachers provided students with many different ways to explore or investigate a topic, and students produced work that drew on a variety of intelligences: maps, writing, drawings, three-dimensional models in all kinds of media, and performances of student-written plays.

Finally, the theory was never seen as a justification for students' weak performances. Teachers at the McCleary School encouraged students to use their strengths to learn, but also required them to develop skills in areas that were weak. Ms. Hornick spoke of one young first grader who still "can't write any words except maybe his name," but who is "a genius when it comes to building with blocks. So . . . if someone is having a hard time making the road go the way they want it to, he can explain it and help the other kids. This is so important because . . . if he wasn't given the opportunity to be creative like he is, I could see him as a kid totally hating school." While she appreciated this ability and used it to keep him engaged in schooling, she did not substitute his skill in block modeling for a skill in writing. This struggling child was nevertheless expected to work hard on his writing. In fact, Ms. Hornick said, he was expected to work on it as much as the best writers in the class.

In sum, teachers at the McCleary School kept a substantive curriculum and necessary skills in the forefront of their classrooms. They harnessed MI, not for the sake of "doing the theory," but to enable students to produce their best work.

The Compass Points Practices that infuse the entire McCleary School make it possible for students to draw on all their intelligences in ways that advance their learning. The Rivers Study, presented in the following chapter, incorporates many of these same practices. As you read about this study, you might consider ways that the arts, collaboration, or other Compass Points Practices can be harnessed within your classroom to bring similar kinds of curriculum and learning experiences to your own students.

CHAPTER 3

The Rivers Study

THE RIVERS STUDY AT A GLANCE

The Rivers Study is a second- and third-grade interdisciplinary curriculum unit taught by Chimene Brandt and other teachers at the McCleary School in Pittsburgh, Pennsylvania. The Rivers Study gives students the opportunity to learn about rivers using a "KWL" question-based approach. That is, the study of rivers begins with three broad questions:

- What do you already **know** about rivers?
- What do you **want** to know?
- How we will **learn** about the rivers?

With Ms. Brandt's facilitation, the students arrive at two central questions to explore for a period of three to four months:

- How do rivers begin?
- Where does the water come from?

A third grader's chalk drawing of the Allegheny River

The students explore these two questions and arrive at answers to them through a variety of activities that include visits to the rivers that are a prominent part of Pittsburgh's landscape. During these visits, students record their observations in words and drawings. Back in the classroom, they develop models of the landscape, read about rivers, and write about rivers.

MI in This Unit

- The activities included in the Rivers Study allow students to draw on many different intelligences to acquire and demonstrate their knowledge of rivers.
- Different activities draw on different combinations of intelligences. For example, field trips to the rivers tap students' naturalist, spatial, and linguistic intelligences; group work on murals and three-dimensional models engages students' interpersonal, naturalist, spatial, and bodily-kinesthetic intelligences.

Entry Points in This Unit

- The activities in the Rivers Study tap all of the entry points.
- The existential entry point is central to the questions the students and teacher decided to pursue: How do rivers begin? Where does the water come from?
- The aesthetic, logical-quantitative, and interpersonal entry points are prominent in many of the activities.

Compass Point Practices in This Unit

- The Rivers Study is a good example of a unit in which the theory of multiple intelligences serves as a tool in the teaching of substantive areas: the theory is there, but not taught directly to the students.
- The arts are prominent throughout this classroom and in the McCleary Elementary School as a whole.
- Students have controlled but meaningful choices in the range of ways they can learn and represent their understanding.

WHAT IS THE RIVERS STUDY?

I love to teach this way, and I love for kids to learn this way,
because we're not dumbing down anything.

—Chimene Brandt
Second- and third-grade teacher
The McCleary School
Pittsburgh, Pennsylvania

The Rivers Study is an interdisciplinary unit focused on two questions: How do rivers begin? Where does the water come from? Students pursue these questions through a range of interdisciplinary activities that draw together science, social studies, language arts, visual arts, and mathematics.

In the Rivers Study, students take a field trip to observe the Point, the place where Pittsburgh's three rivers converge.

Through their activities over a period of three to four months, students develop an understanding of the entire water cycle, the stages of the river from its source, river ecology, and the mutual influences that exist between rivers and cities.

Developing an understanding of how rivers begin and where water comes from is a tall order for young students. Ms. Chimene Brandt, the teacher who developed this unit, explained the central role that MI plays in fostering this understanding: "I thought about all the different areas I could pull in so that kids would have so many different ways to work through something that was really difficult." Providing many different, yet substantive, approaches to the topic enables learners with different profiles of intelligence to grasp the material and demonstrate what they have learned.

As part of this unit, Ms. Brandt takes her class on a field trip to Washington's Landing, from which they can see the Point, the place where the Monongahela, Allegheny, and Ohio Rivers converge in the city of Pittsburgh, Pennsylvania.

During their visit, the students observe the rivers and the environment surrounding them, including the plant life, buildings, bridges, and boats. They record what they observe using pencils or pastels on sketch paper affixed to clipboards. They also write fieldnotes in spiral notebooks. While at Washington's Landing, the teacher, Chimene Brandt, reminds students of the questions they developed together in class before the field trip.

Back in the classroom, Ms. Brandt has students engage in a variety of activities, each one intended to build their understanding of rivers. For example, the students write about what they have observed. They build models of rivers in various media. They generate and test hypotheses about how rivers form using a stream table, a working model of a river. They sketch and paint murals of river scenes, and they read about rivers in fiction and nonfiction.

In the Rivers Study, students create many different representations of their observations.

These various activities make it possible for students with different profiles of intelligence and interests to participate and to learn. For example, some students may develop an understanding of how rivers begin by reading about rivers. Other students' understanding of this may grow from discussions that occur as they test hypotheses at the stream table. Through a range of ongoing substantive activities, Ms. Brandt's students become engaged in their learning about rivers and develop a good deal of knowledge about the topic.

The Rivers Study is structured around a questions-based approach that can be useful in advancing students' understanding across a broad range of disciplines and grades. The questions that are central to the study can be explored in ways that draw on many different intelligences. As you read more about this particular study, you may want to keep in mind a topic or unit that can be developed using this approach.

STRATEGIES: A QUESTIONS-BASED APPROACH COMBINED WITH RUBRICS

> *You always have to have in mind what direction you want to go in. . . .*
> *One of the major goals was to examine the question 'How do rivers begin'*
> *and then to follow the river through all of its stages.*
> —Chimene Brandt

The Rivers Study is an interdisciplinary unit designed to build students' understanding of the rivers, which are a prominent part of the environment for those who attend Pittsburgh's McCleary School. In this unit, and throughout the McCleary School, two strategies help to develop this understanding and to enable students to produce high-quality work: a questions-based approach and the use of rubrics.

The Questions-Based Approach

According to the school's principal, Mary Ellen "Mel" McBride, the questions-based approach helped the McCleary School to take MI from theory into classroom practice. The entire school was introduced to this question-based approach about eighteen months after it opened through work with Bank Street College in New York. In this question-based approach students are treated as investigators. Their questions can be answered through various types of activities. The questions-based approach enabled teachers to address topics both substantively and through many different activities that engage learners with different profiles of intelligence. As Chimene Brandt put it, the questions-based approach "seemed to be MI, but not called MI."

BOX 3.1 RIVERS STUDY QUESTIONS

The Rivers Study, like all other studies at the McCleary School, begins with three questions:

- What do we know about rivers?
- What do we want to know about rivers?
- How are we going to learn about rivers?

At the very beginning of the study, the teacher facilitates a whole-class brainstorming session. In this session, students generate many responses for each one of the three central questions. Each of the three questions serves a variety of purposes:

What do we know about rivers?   In this brainstorming activity, the teacher encourages students to tell what they already know about rivers. The question serves as a preassessment or diagnostic aide. That is, it helps the teacher to size up students' initial information and understanding. A second purpose is to help the teacher to build a "word bank" of vocabulary pertaining to rivers. Third, it helps to prime, or activate, students' thinking about rivers. Finally, it helps the teacher to dispel erroneous beliefs or ideas that students may voice about rivers.

What do we want to know about rivers?   Through this question, the teacher learns what the students are interested in and can begin to bring together students' interests with the goals and standards held by the teacher and district. In the beginning of brainstorming for this question, the teacher accepts any reasonable question that the students offer. After the initial brainstorming, she and the class choose a few questions from among those that were offered. The questions that are selected help to focus the class's study, and build on students' interests.

How are we going to find out about rivers?   During this brainstorming session, the teacher encourages students to devise approaches to answering the questions they have posed about rivers. The teacher, together with the students, then choose from this session a range of activities that allow students to learn about the topic. The chosen activities enable them to draw on many different intelligences and helps them develop knowledge and skills important to the topic and to the school district.

As the brainstorming for each question takes place, a student or the teacher records all the students' responses. After the brainstorming, the teacher often asks children "to think about how their responses are related. How could we group them? What categories come out at you?" Ms. Brandt plays an important role here: she listens to hear the students' interests and ideas while she is also thinking about how to incorporate these in the service of understanding the study's central questions ("How do rivers start?" "Where do rivers come from?").

When categories have been suggested, one or more students use large markers to neatly write the categorized lists of questions on sheets of butcher paper, which may run several feet long. These sheets are posted in the room for the duration of the study and they act like connective strands: The teacher and students refer back to the categorized list when information or ideas gleaned from their activities shed light on questions they have posed.

Rubrics and Modeling

The second strategy that is widely employed in the Rivers Study and throughout the McCleary School is the use of rubrics. Rubrics are an approach to making assessment criteria publicly known and available to students while the students can still use them to shape their work. (This practice stands in contrast to end-of-unit assessments, which may not artic-ulate criteria at all and which typically occur too late to shape students' thinking or work in the unit.) In this unit, rubrics specify the qualities that are important for a given work to incorporate. To make the criteria for good

FIGURE 3.1 A rubric for students' chalk drawings was developed during a class discussion about what the chalk drawings should incorporate.

Natural landscape: The mural depicts several natural elements of the landscape that students observed on the class trip.

Manmade elements: The mural depicts features of the landscape that have been created by people and that students observed on the class trip.

Recognizability: Viewers should be able to recognize what the artist says is in the drawing.

Fine details: Details are depicted in the mural using wet chalk.

Blending: Bigger objects and sections of the drawing use sides of different chalk to blend colors

Foreground/Background: The mural incorporates a foreground and background.

Ms. Brandt's rubrics for her second and third graders are very simple. They consist of characteristics or criteria that she and the students have determined are important for a work to be of high quality. She does not use a numerical scale to show the degree to which students have attained the particular criterion, although teachers of older students at the McCleary School do incorporate a scale. With younger students, Ms. Brandt's aim is not so much to score student products but rather to "immerse" students in thinking about the qualities that go into good work and whether their own work includes those qualities.

work known, teachers and students throughout McCleary spend time *at the beginning* of an activity to discuss the kind of qualities that good work should demonstrate. For example, before students begin drawing, the teacher might ask, "What do you think should be included in your chalk drawings? What else?" Ms. Brandt asserts that eliciting characteristics of high-quality work in conversation with students helps them "to think critically about their work" from the outset and, ultimately, to generate stronger work.

Along with discussing the criteria for good work and developing rubrics from such discussions, Ms. Brandt helps students to look at their work in relationship to the rubric qualities. To foster this kind of critical looking and thinking, Ms. Brandt will sometimes ask, "What do you see?" "What else might you want to include?" She reminds students of the rubric by asking, "What kinds of qualities are important to have in your sketch?" In a piece of writing that students do after their field trips, she'll guide them, to "look over your trip writing. What qualities are included? Do you think you can add more?"

To make the rubric qualities as concrete as possible, Ms. Brandt often uses exemplary students' work as a model. (The strategy of highlighting strong qualities within student work is one that is used as well by Mrs. Hamner in Language Artists, Chapter 6, and Ms. Staszak in the Heritage/ Traditions Unit, Chapter 10). She asks students to examine the work and compare it to the rubric's qualities. As she holds up the work, Ms. Brandt asks the rest of the class questions, "What do you like about this work? Why is it good?" She stretches them to leap further by asking, "Do you have any suggestions to make it even better?"

WHAT HAPPENS DURING THE RIVERS STUDY?

Students have multiple ways of showing what they know. . . .
It's not just, 'look at this textbook and answer questions. Read it and answer questions.'
The kids have many ways of learning something.
—Chimene Brandt

The Rivers Study incorporates many different kinds of activities. Some of these involve the whole class. Others take place in small groups or are carried out individually. Some activities are required of all students, while

---

BOX 3.2 MATERIALS NEEDED

Most of the materials for the Rivers Study are common classroom supplies for writing and drawing, like notebooks and pencils. Others, like chalk, sketchbooks, butcher paper, clay, and other kinds of modeling materials are easy to obtain. Murals require poster board or chart paper and tempera paint. Papier mâché and homosote boards are often used in some of the big models at the McCleary School. (See Box 3.6) It is helpful to have one or more large tables which students can use for painting murals or producing other large pieces of work. The stream table will require the most elaborate set-up. To build a stream table, fill a square plastic container with dirt, rocks, sand, and organic material. At one end, add a hole beneath which there is a bucket to catch water. Use a small pump at the other end to pump water into the table. If it's not possible to build a stream table, a trip to a local stream may be a good substitute.

others are more "open-ended." This variety of activities enables students to use a range of their intelligences to investigate the two central questions of the study: "How do rivers begin?" and "Where does the water come from?" It also enables them to represent what they are learning in different ways and to come to a more multifaceted understanding of the topic.

The Rivers Study takes place over three to four months. On most days, the Rivers Study activities occupy about one hour of class time. During this hour, everyone in the class participates in one or more activities. Although students can choose among the activities, choice is controlled. Ms. Brandt monitors and guides students' choices to ensure that over the course of the study students participate in a range of activities. She noted that, if left to their own, "Some kids would build all the time . . . but [with guidance] they soon discover that painting's not bad either, and they really enjoy it."

At the McCleary School, studies typically conclude with a culminating activity. The culminating activity is often a presentation of a large work that all students have contributed to. For some studies at the McCleary School, this work has been a dramatic presentation or an exhibit of student work. As we'll see below, the culminating activity is the presentation of the City and Country Models.

The following section illustrates the range of activities that are pursued during the Rivers Study. As you read through the section, you might think up a number of other activities to include in a study of rivers, or another topic, in your own classroom or school.

Whole-Class and Small-Group Activities

The first three activities described below (brainstorming, site visits, post-trip meetings) involve the whole class. The remaining activities involve small groups of students. Ms. Brandt tends to have everyone do post-trip writings at the same time, either individually or in small groups. The other small-group activities take place simultaneously. For example, the chalk drawings, river murals, reading, block construction, and stream table operate at the same time in different areas of the room. To divide the children among these areas, Ms. Brandt calls for students to raise their hands if they want to participate in a given activity. She then assigns them on the basis of her understanding of where a child needs to spend time in order to learn, where the child has already spent time, and how she feels a particular small group of students will work together. (You might want to compare this informal approach to creating groups with the method Mrs. Chadwell uses in Math Labs, Chapter 5).

Brainstorming Meetings
At the beginning of each new study, Chimene Brandt holds several brainstorming meetings in which the whole class participates. These meetings are structured around the KWL approach. So, for example, in the first meeting, the teacher encourages students to answer the question "What do you already know about river?" As described previously, this discussion helps the teacher to understand what students already know, enables her to correct mistaken ideas about the topic, primes students for the learning ahead, and starts the class on learning topic-related vocabulary.

The second meeting is devoted to the question, "What do you want to know about rivers?" The initial brainstormed responses are categorized

BOX 3.3 ARRANGING A CLASSROOM FOR THE RIVERS STUDY

A classroom with a well-thought-out organization makes it easier to conduct in-depth studies and to maintain a rich environment for inquiry. Ms. Brandt divides her room so that children can work in small groups or individually in each section of the room. The room arrangement also makes it easy for students to rotate through the sections of the classroom. Bookshelves section the room into small areas. Some, like the block area, have one primary use; others, like the area with a large work table, have several functions. The meeting area serves as both a meeting area for the whole class and small groups.

Designated areas will change with each study. For example, the stream table will be replaced with a bookmaking area and the bookshelves moved to form check out and reading areas for a study of libraries later in the year.

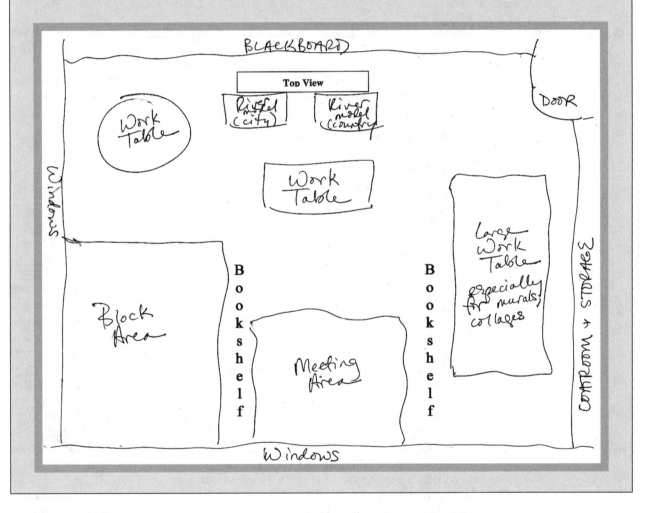

into groups. Ms. Brandt asks them whether any of the brainstormed items are alike or can be grouped. This is followed by what Ms. Brandt calls a "negotiation." "I brought some ideas [about what to learn] and they have ideas, and let's sort of mesh them together." In this process, Ms. Brandt makes sure that central questions (How do rivers begin? Where does the water come from?) for the study are clearly spelled out.

Once she and the students decide what they want to learn about rivers, a third brainstorming discussion addresses the question, "How will we learn about rivers?" In this process students generate many different ways to investigate what they want to learn. Because the KWL strategy is prominent throughout the McCleary School, students at the second and third grade already have a repertoire of approaches to learning about a topic. This includes reading about the topic, interviewing people, building models, visiting the site, and viewing documentaries. (Documentaries and museum visits are especially useful when the study focuses on faraway places and times.)

In each of these brainstorming meetings, all responses are initially written down, then reviewed, categorized, and edited. After this, a polished version of the list is written up in large print on long sheets of butcher paper. These lists are posted to serve as a guide and reference for the entire period of study.

Site Visits

During the Rivers Study, students take several trips to observe the rivers from different vantage points and to gather a range of information. These trips, which typically last about a half-day, help to shed light on the two main questions (How do rivers begin? Where does the water come from?) and on a number of subsidiary topics the students and teachers thought were important to learn about, including:

- the stages of the rivers from beginning to end;
- the animal and plant life of the river;
- water cleanliness;
- the work and people associated with the river;
- the river-related history of Pittsburgh;
- the recreational aspects of the river.

Many of these issues are addressed in the visit to Washington's Landing, highlighted at the beginning of this chapter. For example, the visit enables students to explore the stages of the river: Viewing the Point, they see the confluence of the Allegheny and Monangahela at a stage between their source and endpoint and the formation out of this of a third river, the Ohio. Because the Point includes one of Pittsburgh's earliest settlements, this visit also helps students to begin thinking about the interplay between the rivers and the growth of the city of Pittsburgh. The roads, bridges, and boats that the students observe also help to fuel this exploration. Later trips to a mill site, a dock, a park on the riverfront, and locks and dams allow students to continue to learn to investigate the questions they have raised.

Site visits require students to be active observers. Students are supported to do this by class discussions in advance of the visit, by bringing a clipboard of their questions to the site, by supplies of paper and materials for documenting their observations, and by an art lesson that prepares them to record what they see (see Box 3.4 on collaboration). During these trips all the students sketch what they observe using pastels or other media. They are also required to take written fieldnotes, which may also incorporate observational drawings. Preparation for the site visits, and the assignments at the site, help students to build observational, writing, and drawing skills. It also enables students to collect and represent information that they need to answer their questions.

Post-Trip Meetings

After each trip, Ms. Brandt convenes a post-trip meeting. The entire class spends about fifteen minutes together in the meeting area of the classroom to "talk about everything we saw on our trip." Post-trip meetings provide time for children to reflect on what they observed, to share their observations, and to hear about what their classmates noticed. The students use their fieldnotes and sketches from the river to support this discussion. In the course of these meetings, Ms. Brandt asks students what they learned about rivers from their trip. She guides them to think about their two central questions: "How do rivers begin?" "Where does the water come from?" She writes their responses on large flip charts and tapes the sheets on the walls of her room. These sheets provide a reference for them and also serve as a public document of their visit. For example, from their trip they now have at least one answer to the question, "How do rivers begin?" The Ohio begins from two other rivers flowing together.

Another aim of these meetings is to build vocabulary pertaining to their observations. During the course of the meeting, if a child reports seeing a bridge, Ms. Brandt will try to elicit a detailed description of the structure, and uses this as opportunity to introduce words such as *span, roadway, arch,* and *cables.* She records new vocabulary on the butcher paper that documents each trip.

Trip Writings

Following the trip meetings, Ms. Brandt asks students to find a space in which "to do some quiet writing" for about fifteen minutes. Depending on the preceding discussion, Ms. Brandt might ask all the children to write on a common topic. For example, she might ask them to write about the bridges that they noticed and encourage them to use some of the new vocabulary words. Or, she might ask them to write on a more global topic, such as "What did I see at the river?" This allows them to represent and draw on the class discussion in an individual piece of writing. At other times, the students choose the topic for their trip writing. Students may incorporate pictures into their writing to help capture and convey their ideas.

Alongside consolidating vocabulary and providing writing practice, Ms. Brandt uses trip writings to build shared standards for good writing. During writing time, Ms. Brandt circulates around the room, checking in with students and supporting their efforts. Through this, she can also see good work as it is being produced. After individual writing time is over, she will often share examples of strong written work with the class. Ms. Brandt notes that children in her class "really feel motivated to share their work" and that students "are motivated by their peers' success." The class discusses what they liked about the piece of writing. The teacher sometimes asks the class to make suggestions about how to make the writing even stronger. Following these kinds of conversations, Ms. Brandt gives the students more time to review their own writing and to revise it.

Chalk Drawings

To enable students to do a good job representing what they saw at the river, Ms. Brandt collaborated with Nancy Fralic, the school's art teacher, who devised two art lessons to support the unit. In one lesson prior to the site visit, the art teacher helped students to understand the principles of sketching. Younger students typically draw the details of a picture, but through Ms. Fralic, they learned that to sketch something, they first have to draw broad outlines and only then fill in the details. Once students returned from their site visit, Ms. Fralic provided a second lesson. In this lesson, students

This chalk drawing of a river scene highlights techniques that students learned for blending colors and creating details. These techniques equipped them to represent their observations.

used their river sketches as a reference to create colorful chalk drawings of river scenes. Students learned that bigger, broader areas of their drawings could be filled using the sides of colored chalk and that different colors could be blended together. To portray finer details, students learned that they could dampen the point of the chalk and get sharper lines.

You can see these techniques in the chalk drawing above, in which the water and river bank combine broad strokes of lighter and darker shades, while the bridge, and the figure, his hat, and fishing pole are portrayed with sharp, dark and fine lines.

Students critique their own and their classmates' chalk drawings, using a number of criteria developed in the process of constructing rubrics. (See

---

BOX 3.4 COLLABORATING ON THE CHALK DRAWINGS

Interdisciplinary units of study provide an opportunity to collaborate with colleagues. These units can bring together teachers whose strengths in different areas enable students to produce rich and complex work. In the Rivers Study, the collaboration was prompted by Ms. Brandt, who sought to enable her students to record their fieldtrip observations both in writing and pictures. She approached the art teacher, Nancy Fralic, who then developed lessons in sketching and chalk techniques.

This collaboration clearly supported the production of strong student work, but it also provided an opportunity for the whole teaching staff to learn from each other. Near the end of the Rivers Study, Ms. Fralic and Ms. Brandt joined their colleagues in the teachers' "Elegant Room," a wicker-filled lounge largely ceded to the school's students. There they displayed some of the students' work, discussed the lessons that supported it, and provided handouts to help other teachers in the school follow the sequence of lessons and visits.

Rubric Figure 3.1 on p. 48.) For example, the students and teachers felt that it was important for the drawings to portray things that were observed on the field trip. Another jointly developed criterion was that viewers should be able to recognize what the artist says is represented in the drawing. The students also said the drawings should incorporate the different chalk techniques that they had learned from the art teacher. Articulating these qualities and reviewing work in light of them enabled students to produce strong work.

The Stream Table

A stream table is a small-scale model of a river system that makes observation of the natural processes of river formation easier to see. According to Ms. Brandt, "The stream table helps kids to really see how streams and rivers are created and how they behave. . . ."

The stream table consists of a square or rectangular plastic container, about six inches deep and about three feet long, filled with dirt, rocks, sand, and organic material. A small water pump (or hose attached to a sink) is used to pump water into one end of the table to create a stream. The water flows out on the other side of the table into a bucket.

Students work at the stream table in small groups with the classroom teacher (or another adult). The teacher asks the students to generate hypotheses about what will happen when the water is turned on. One student from the group records all the hypotheses. Chimene Brandt's students provided hypotheses like: "The water will flow out the other end into the bucket." "The sand and dirt and twigs will move downriver faster than the rocks." "The water will change the shape of the river." "Some of the water will sink into the dirt."

Once students develop several hypotheses, the water is turned on. They observe what happens as the water flows and then discuss whether their observations help to support or disconfirm their hypotheses. The teacher then asks them to develop new hypotheses based on their last observations, the hypotheses are recorded, and then the water is turned on again so students can again test what actually happens.

River Murals

River murals are another small-group activity involving three students. Each group of students works over a period of several days to design and paint their murals. The murals are made using tempera paint and poster board or butcher paper, which is spread out on a long rectangular table. To help the students generate ideas for what to paint in the murals, the teacher asks them to reflect on their trips. The students also review their sketches, chalk drawings, and the text from their field notes.

When students complete their mural, they present it at a class meeting. In these presentations, each group of students is expected to provide a description of their mural and to establish a clear link between what they have depicted and what they have learned about rivers. This helps them continue to explore the two central questions of the Rivers Study and to consolidate their understanding of the role the river plays in the city of Pittsburgh. For example, one group of three boys depicted a rainy day city scene in their mural, a subject that initially seemed unrelated to the topic at hand. During their presentation, though, they were asked to explain how their mural, which they titled "The Rain Process," might fit together with the

"How do rivers begin?" "Where does the water come from?" Here a student demonstrates his understanding of these questions by using his group's mural of a rainy, city scene to explain the entire water cycle.

river scenes that their classmates had painted. One of the boys (shown on the far left in the photo above) gave a full and rich description. He explained that rain forms from evaporation of water on the earth's surface. Condensation of evaporated water forms clouds. The smaller raindrops in clouds collide to become larger ones that, in turn, fall on the houses and streets shown in his city scene. In essence, the student could connect the group's city scene to the entire water cycle and to one of the central questions of the study: Where does the water come from?

In the presentations, students also describe their understanding of the importance of the rivers to the city and its people. For example, one group of students talked about how the rivers provide many people with jobs, and they noted that the city's early industries relied on the rivers for transportation and to power mills. They described the need for bridges across rivers so that people could get to work. They also talked about the tourist and recreational aspects of the river: That the river made it possible for Pittsburgh to have boating, beautiful views, and parks for people to enjoy. The mural activity therefore helps students to reflect on their river visit, to consider the study's central questions, to gain presentation skills, and to consolidate skills in the visual arts.

River Readings

Ms. Brandt's classroom, and all the other classrooms in the McCleary School, have well-stocked classroom libraries, which have been purchased with the school's Title I funds. The library in Ms. Brandt's room occupies bookshelves on either side of the meeting area. When meeting time is over, individual students or small groups of youngsters use the meeting area for silent reading or reading in small groups. They can draw on a variety of

Within the block activity area, students can work alone or in small groups to construct representations of Pittsburgh's buildings, bridges, and rivers.

books from their classroom library, including poetry, fiction, and nonfiction. In addition, because the school librarian works closely with the classroom teachers to support the studies that the teachers undertake, students can read books that they have selected from the school library. Through these resources, students can gain information about the water cycle, plant and animal life along rivers, the use of rivers in transportation and industry, the role of rivers in the history of Pittsburgh, and they also build reading skills and vocabulary.

Block Activity

As a result of McCleary School's coaching from Bank Street College, teachers throughout the school incorporated into their classrooms a large area for building blocks. As the photograph above shows, in the Rivers Study, students working alone or in small groups construct elaborate bridges, the rivers beneath them (using tape), and buildings along the waterfront. The block area is also used to help students develop math knowledge and concepts, including shapes, perimeters and area, proportion, scale, and ratio. The block area also provides opportunities for lessons in organization, sharing, and cooperation.

The Culminating Activity: River Models

For the culminating activity of the Rivers Study, all students participate in constructing one of two large river models over the course of about two weeks. Working in two groups, the students, in conversation with the teacher, first decide what to include in their group's model. Following this

BOX 3.5 MATERIALS NEEDED FOR RIVER MODELS

The complexity of the models will dictate the materials needed for the culminating activity. Models will need a sturdy base—heavy cardboard, wood, or homosote. Other supplies should include assorted papers, cardboard, glue, and paint. Also think of ways to add texture, like applying sand or shavings from sharpened pencils to wet glue or paint.

discussion, the students work around a large table to make a draft sketch of the model. Some may draw background features first, leaving details in the foreground for others to tackle. They critique it and redraw it. They may then make an initial three-dimensional model out of clay. Following this, they develop a large-scale model using papier mâché and other materials.

One model depicts the river in a rural, or country, setting. Drawing on knowledge gleaned from the stream table activity, from readings, and from river visits, this model highlights how rivers begin. The country model includes snow-capped mountains made of papier mâché, painted rivers flowing down the mountains, and rivers surrounded by a rural landscape. The second model shows the river in an urban setting. It focuses on the influence of the river on the city and its people. The city model includes city buildings, dams, locks, bridges, and boats used in leisure and commerce (see Box 3.6).

The process draws on students' language, spatial, kinesthetic skills and naturalist intelligences (for example, the naturalist intelligence is engaged in solving problems like this: "If we're showing the river near the source, we need to show where the water is coming from . . ."). Clearly, it also draws on interpersonal and personal intelligences, as students organize themselves and each other to tackle particular tasks and get the whole model completed.

As part of this culminating activity, Ms. Brandt asks students, "What do our models show us about what we know about rivers?" Eager students fill the room with responses: "The water is cleaner at the source." "The river is youngest at the source." "The rivers at the Point are middle-aged." "Rivers are oldest near the ocean." "The plant life along the river banks holds the soil in place." "The country model has more green and plant life." "The river . . . picks up dirt along the way." "Cities form near rivers." "The river is wider on the city model." "The city model shows the Monangahela and the Allegheny meet to form the Ohio." These answers, as well as their work and comments in the Rivers Study's other activities, help to reveal that these young students have learned many things through this extended unit, including where the water for rivers comes from, how rivers begin, and the interrelationship of Pittsburgh's city and rivers.

BOX 3.6 MAKING MODELS

The city model (above) shows the kind of detailed scenery that can be added with papier mâché, paint, and clay models. The country model (below) shows how to build a base for the model on two layers. The bottom layer is a ³⁄₈″ sheet of particle board, and the top layer is a ³⁄₈″ sheet of homosote. The homosote provides a durable and pliable construction surface. It is soft enough to bend into realistic grades and install and remove pins or tacks easily. The added support of particle board gives the model additional support.

REVISITING THE FRAMEWORKS

In the Rivers Study, students are able to show their learning in multiple ways.

—Chimene Brandt

Multiple Intelligences in This Unit

Figure 3.2 highlights that the activities used during the Rivers Study enable students to learn and to demonstrate their understanding in multiple ways. It is important to emphasize that not every intelligence is used in each activity, or even across all the activities. It is better to have rich activities that allow learners to develop an understanding of rivers than it is to introduce more activities primarily because they allow all intelligences to be used.

Entry Points in This Unit

The Entry Points Framework provides a tool for examining the curriculum and opening it up to diverse learners. Accessing a topic through a variety of entry points helps students to engage and to develop a multifaceted understanding of the topic. For example, because Ms. Brandt's study of rivers incorporates many different entry points, her students can tell you about rivers, build models of different stages of the river, and document what they know in writing, chalk, and other media. The Rivers Study allows students to learn about rivers using a full range of entry points:

Narrative: Students read stories about the river, they write about their class visits to the river, and they consider how the river influences their own and their families' life events.

Aesthetic: Students create sketches and murals of the river. They study artworks in which rivers are depicted. They may also read and write poetry about rivers.

Logical-Quantitative: In the stream table activity, students generate and test hypotheses about what happens to rivers under various conditions. A more strictly quantitative entry point is involved when students work with the concepts of ratios, scale, proportion, area, and perimeter in constructing block models.

Experiential: Students visit rivers to observe them firsthand and record their observations.

Existential: Students consider how rivers form, where water for them comes from, and how rivers shape people's lives.

Interpersonal: Students work together in various group activities, such as creating the river and country models, block constructions, and murals.

Compass Point Practices in This Unit

Compass Point Practices provide a tool for building the classroom and school into organizations that engage multiple intelligences in ways that are associated with positive outcomes for students. The six Compass Point Practices are solidly in place across the McCleary Elementary School. The Compass Point Practices are also evident in Ms. Brandt's classroom.

Linguistic	Spatial	Interpersonal	Intrapersonal	Logical-Mathematical	Musical	Bodily-Kinesthetic	Naturalist	ACTIVITIES
X	X					X		River Field Trips: Students visit river sites, observe natural and manmade features of the environment, and record observations in field notes and drawings.
X		X	X			X	X	Trip Writings: Students write about their field trip, critique and revise writing, and incorporate new vocabulary.
	X					X	X	Chalk Drawings: Students learn and use techniques for rendering river scenes in chalk drawing.
X	X	X		X		X		Stream Table: Small groups of students and the teacher use a working model of a river to generate and test hypotheses.
X	X	X				X	X	River Murals: Working in small groups, students paint tempera murals of rivers and present these during whole class meetings.
X								River Readiness: Students read fiction and non-fiction books about rivers either alone or in small groups.
	X	X		X		X	X	Block Activity: Students work alone or in small groups to build block models of river scenes.
X	X	X		X		X	X	Country and City Models: Large groups of students have an extended time to build models of the river close to its source and a model of the river in the city. They use these different models to show what they know about rivers.

FIGURE 3.2   Multiple Intelligences in the Rivers Study

Culture: There is an expectation in McCleary's classrooms, including Chimene Brandt's, that everyone is respected and can learn, that learning is exciting, and that it requires work. In this culture, students are accustomed to articulating high standards, thinking critically about their efforts, and revising what they do to produce high-quality work.

Readiness: Students are prepared in advance to undertake the work of the Rivers Study. The KWL approach entails initial sessions that draw out students' existing knowledge, primes them to think about the topic, and gets them to generate ideas about how to explore the topic.

Choice: In the Rivers Study, students brainstorm ideas in response to the question "What do you want to learn?" and then Ms. Brandt guides them to a set of questions that include important learning goals. Students also have choices among the activities that they want to pursue during Rivers Study time. Students' choices are "negotiated" with the teacher, so that students' interests as well as key areas of knowledge and skill are incorporated into the study.

Collaboration: The Rivers Study was greatly influenced by the collaboration of the classroom teacher and the art teacher on the chalk murals. The librarian also supports this and other studies at the McCleary School by finding resources related to the topic. Collaboration is also evident in efforts by teachers to share their successes, as Ms. Brandt and Ms. Fralic did with the Rivers Study.

Arts: There are a variety of art activities (e.g., murals, sketches, chalk drawings) in the Rivers Study that engage students and enhance their understanding. A much more limited role is given to music in this study.

Tool: In this unit, the teacher focuses primarily on helping students to understand rivers. Ms. Brandt draws on MI as a tool to help students engage curricular content and represent their understanding, but does not teach the theory.

4 The Governor Bent School

We have selected two examples of curriculum and teaching strategies from the Governor Bent School. The first is an ongoing approach to literacy, entitled Language Artists, as taught by Nan Hamner in her first- and second-grade classroom. The second is called Math Labs, and it was developed and taught by Carolyn Chadwell, a third-grade teacher. Each of these examples provides detailed descriptions of classroom practice that engage students' multiple intelligences and yield high-quality student work. To see these examples within the context of the school, this chapter first provides an overview of the Governor Bent School. Then, through the framework of the Compass Point Practices, it illustrates how the Governor Bent School as an organization fosters exceptional work on the part of teachers and students.

OVERVIEW OF THE GOVERNOR BENT SCHOOL

The Governor Bent School, Albuquerque, New Mexico

The Governor Bent School is located in the northeast section of Albuquerque, New Mexico, on a slightly out-of-the way street, opposite a church, a parking lot, and a large, red-brick apartment building. In front of the school is a semicircular driveway, along which are low cactuses, and a signboard that sports a changing array of inspirational messages ("CURL UP WITH A GOOD BOOK" "HAPPY NEW YEAR, SET GOALS") from the school's principal, Marilyn Davenport. From the street, the school appears to be a small, one-story brick building, built in the 1960s, but just to the right of the building is a gate in a chain-link fence through which one enters a sizable campus. A covered walkway begins just past the gate. Along the left side of the walkway is the school's office, a large dome-shaped cafeteria, and finally a gym. On the right side of the walkway are three short rows of permanent classrooms and then several longer rows of portable classrooms. At the end of the classrooms is an expanse of bare-dirt playground, recently renovated with swings, slides, and climbing structures in bright red, yellow, and blue.

The school has a large and diverse student population. In 1998–1999, it served approximately 730 students in kindergarten through grade 5. About 48 percent of the students are white, 37 percent are Latino, and African Americans, Native Americans, and Asians together comprise about 15 percent of the student body. About a third of the students receive free or reduced-price meals, although the school itself does not receive Title I funds. There are many Spanish-speaking children, and the school receives federal bilingual funds that it devotes to providing all children with Spanish and English language skills.

In recent years, the district has helped to support smaller class sizes. At Governor Bent, classes are not larger than twenty-four students, and they typically include about three students with special needs. Per pupil expenditure was modest, less than $4,500 per year.

Governor Bent's physical plant, student population, and funding seem ordinary. Yet, parents throughout the district seek to enroll their children in the school. The school regularly had the highest test scores among Albuquerque's seventy-nine elementary schools, it has been designated a National School of Excellence, and over the course of eight years, five of its teachers won New Mexico's teacher-of-the-year awards. All of these things signal that wonderful teaching and learning occur there. How has this seemingly ordinary place become so extraordinary?

COMPASS POINT PRACTICES

The development of the Governor Bent School and the ways in which extraordinary teaching and learning have been supported there can be understood through the framework of the Compass Point Practices. We describe the Compass Point Practices in an order that allows the Governor Bent School's story to be clearly told.

Readiness

I had to work with their belief systems.

—Marilyn Davenport
Principal
The Governor Bent School
Albuquerque, New Mexico

When Marilyn Davenport first arrived at the school she found "a great deal of frustration." There had been a shift in student population. In the 1960s, the surrounding area was made up primarily of single-family homes, and the students were predominantly white and middle class. Gradually, the neighborhood's open spaces were built up with apartment complexes and, over time, many of these became rundown and overcrowded. The children who lived in these circumstances behaved differently—some quite defiantly, according to Mrs. Davenport—and they had weaker academic skills than the students the teachers were used to. When Mrs. Davenport took over the principalship, "There was an awful lot of talk about 'those children,' the ones we used to have, and that these are no longer the kind of children we want to deal with." There was a lot of yelling. No one was happy to be there.

Fortunately, Marilyn Davenport had a great deal of experience. She had been a principal in two other schools and had served as the head of curriculum for the district. She understood, both from her professional experience and from extensive reading of educational research, that there was no "one way that things have to be taught." She also understood that teachers have "a great deal of autonomy when they close the classroom door. And they will do what *they* think is best, not what you think they should be doing." Therefore, Mrs. Davenport didn't tell teachers what to do, other than calling for an end to yelling. (Instead, she had teachers send their difficult youngsters to her.) Rather than issuing a lot of directions, she set her sights on helping teachers to think differently about what to do. Toward that end, she said, "I had to work with their belief systems."

For a year and a half, Mrs. Davenport worked with teachers' beliefs about the bases of learning: "I knew that they really wanted the children to learn. That's what they were so frustrated about: The students weren't learning." Two main points emerged and became a common language. The first was, "The child has to feel like he belongs here." Students cannot be "separated into those who do and those who don't belong." The second point was that "everybody must feel like they are competent learners. Therefore, you've got to design activities to help them feel competent."

These two common points provided a lens through which teachers came to view their classroom practices. They began to ask themselves, "Is this activity enabling all students to belong? Is this activity helping students to feel competent?" As Marilyn Davenport explained, the teachers "definitely wanted the children to feel more competent. So, what could they do with them? Well, then they were ready to know that there was this theory of multiple intelligences that makes sense. The theory is wonderful. The implementation is far more difficult."

To support the implementation, the staff organized study groups. First, the teachers in these study groups listed what they were already doing that engaged a range of children's strengths. This helped to validate their practice and to learn more about each others' practice. They also spent time talking about particular intelligences and seeking ideas about how to engage students who demonstrated strength in a particular intelligence. With a small grant, some of the teachers had opportunities to visit schools where MI was already being implemented. From these discussions and visits, the staff came to an important realization: While it was vital to respect each of the intelligences, it was equally important not to isolate the intelligences and simply "cover" each one every day. Instead, the intelligences needed to be incorporated into a well-designed curricula that fostered children's competence and enabled diverse learners to feel that they belong in the classroom.

MI Is Used as a Tool

Because the teachers realized that the intelligences needed to be integrated in learning activities, MI has always functioned as a tool at Governor Bent. This was evident throughout our visit: While the names of the intelligences were posted on some bulletin boards, there were no MI lessons or MI activities. Instead, there was a great deal of rich curriculum in math, language arts, social studies, science, physical education, and the arts. All this was aimed at enabling diverse learners to participate and to become competent.

The many ways that teachers engage students are evident in the two classroom examples we highlight from the Governor Bent School. For example in Language Artists (Chapter 6), Nan Hamner helped children to develop language skills through art and visual representation, fine motor work, group work, reading, writing, and listening. Though the students could tap many different intelligences, Mrs. Hamner was not teaching them MI theory. Instead, she taught the structure and components of writing and an appreciation for figurative language.

At Governor Bent, and at all the schools we visited, the theory of multiple intelligences was an important tool, but not an exclusive one. This, of course, makes sense. Building rich school and classroom environments is like building a house: more than one tool is necessary. Thus, Mrs. Davenport has also helped to educate the staff about several other conceptions of intelligence. Mrs. Davenport and the staff have considered Robert Sternberg's ideas about creative, analytical, practical, and successful intelligence. They also were influenced by the work of Arthur Costa, who has emphasized a dozen "intelligent behaviors" found among adults who are high achievers in many different occupations. The Governor Bent staff has added many additional behaviors needed to be a successful student, including persistence, organization, goal-setting, humor, thoughtfulness, cooperation, a positive attitude, kindness, mastering impulsivity, and respect for others (see Costa, 1991; Sternberg, 1996).

In essence, according to Marilyn Davenport, the more ways educators have to consider intelligence, the more likely they are to harness and deploy it. She urges teachers to use MI, alongside other tools, to enable students to participate, feel competent, and gain knowledge and skills.

Culture

The culture of the Governor Bent School is notable on several accounts. It is certainly a place where care and respect are fundamental values. At the same time, it is a school in which every child—and every teacher—is challenged and supported to produce his or her best work. While ongoing effort on the part of students and hard work on the part of teachers is the norm, there is no sense that all this work is just a grind. Rather, this work hums along in a calm, even joyful way. We touch on each of these aspects—respect and caring, hard work, and joy—a bit more fully below.

Care and respect.   Mrs. Davenport's first priority at Governor Bent was to create a caring environment. Yelling by teachers was banished. Students are also taught to behave in a caring and respectful way. This instruction begins concretely and early, and its impact can be felt throughout the school.

From the very beginning of the school year and the very earliest grades, children are taught that they must take care of the environment so that they and everyone else can have a good school. In most of the classrooms, each youngster is given a small space—perhaps one shelf, a small bookcase, or a bin of materials—to take care of. This helps the students to develop a sense of responsibility for keeping the physical environment orderly. It also reinforces the idea that children are capable of contributing to the school, and it is partly through such contributions that they come to feel competent.

Alongside this concrete instruction on caring for their physical space, children are continually encouraged and supported to act in a kind way. For example, Mrs. Hamner quietly reminded her students not to call out while another child was thinking, so that "Sarah gets more wrinkles on her brain," and thereby become smarter. Carolyn Chadwell relied on a small service-desk bell to keep the room operating at a low hum. However, she never used the bell. The bell was reserved for the students. If any student

At the Governor Bent School, individual students are taught to respect and care for their learning environments, in part by maintaining some part of their often-elaborate classrooms.

felt the noise level was interfering with his or her thinking, that student hit the bell and everyone else actually became quieter! Mrs. Davenport (like Mr. Lockwood, principal of Searsport Elementary, Chapter 11), occasionally makes morning announcements that she wants students to report the names of any children who were behaving nicely on the playground. She then tells those students how very much she appreciates their kindness.

During our classroom visits, we saw students behave with a good deal of kindness toward each other. For example, in Vanessa Stackpole's third-grade classroom, all but one of the children eagerly showed us their "squiggle books" (a notebook of detailed stories and drawings). The child who did not was new to the school and had Tourrette's syndrome, whose involuntary vocalizations often make the sufferer self-conscious and a target of unwelcome attention. As we went on to look at other children's work, we heard a boy next to the one with Tourrette's quietly ask, "Why didn't you want to show your work?" The new child responded, "It isn't any good." The old hand remarked, "You've only been here a few weeks, and look how far you've come already!"

As in any other school, there are children who misbehave. On very rare occasions, teachers may still have to send a child to "the blue couch" in Mrs. Davenport's room. This saves teachers from becoming angry and keeps a class focused on the curriculum. It gives the child time to cool off and to talk with Mrs. Davenport, who often takes them on a walk. Typically only children who are brand-new to the school wind up on the blue couch, because the other students have been socialized into the culture of the school. Another strategy for children who misbehave has been to involve them in activities that can give them a sense of their own competence and capacity to contribute. A common technique is to send some of the challenging older children to work with the little ones in kindergarten. There, the older children find a way of giving to others and sharing what they can do in reading, drawing, building, math, or some other area. The kindergartners look forward to these visits, giving the older children a sense that others need and want them. One teacher, Mrs. Sandy Lastra, purposely seeks out challenging children for her classroom, in which a service-learning curriculum is prominent. In various years, the students have learned about life in old-age homes, homeless shelters, homes for severely disabled children, and the daily life of native people on impoverished islands off the coast of Panama. They figure out what those people need to have a better life and then actually do, make, and deliver some of those things. (More detail on this curriculum appears below.)

Hard work.   Caring for others and the physical environment, and inculcating organization, competence, and a sense of belonging are all prominent features of the school culture at Governor Bent. These things are important in and of themselves. At the same time, Marilyn Davenport finds that they provide the foundation for carrying out high-quality, beautiful work. Producing such work is an essential task at the Governor Bent School.

High-quality work is a cause for celebration at the school. It is quite common to make a fuss over good work, whether it is by students or by teachers. In reading the example of Language Artists, you'll see that Nan Hamner talks about "celebrating" what children do well. Marilyn Davenport continually points out the good work that she sees from teachers and students. In this school, everyone is excited to see something well done and beautifully executed.

The teachers and students talk not only about fine work, but how it is accomplished: through persistence over time, learning from good examples, and revision. The idea of ongoing effort is shared throughout the school. It is expected that every night, every child in each classroom will do about a half-hour of "nightly reading" as well as some "nightly writing." Parents know about this and support it. Some rooms use posters on which children place stickers showing they made their nightly effort in each of these areas. In this school, it is cool for students to show that they do their homework!

Ongoing effort and revision is something that teachers model. They talk with children about how they think about problems, how they recognize when something is not just the way they want it to be, and how they tackle the problem again. Revisions, rather than first attempts, are the norm for teachers as well as students.

Children are taught to look at what they produce and to see if they can find ways to make it even better. One way that children come to understand what the qualities of good work are is through the widespread use of examples of student work from previous years. Teachers keep stellar examples of work from particular units and show these to students in their current classes. For instance, Carolyn Chadwell uses examples of the handmade books done by former students to demonstrate the qualities she wants: a fine story, and wonderful typography, grammar, illustrations, title page, cover, and binding. The quality of student work is continually going up at Government Bent. Several teachers mentioned that their supply of examples must be regularly updated, because newer students learn from, and then exceed, the exemplary work that is shown to them.

Hard work and high-quality work are also encouraged by connecting classroom activities to the world outside the school. For example, in Sandy Lastra's service learning curriculum, children made classroom materials for an elementary school off the coast of Panama that had none. Therefore, when Mrs. Lastra's students made charts of colors and shapes, diagrams of the body and the solar system, they knew it was important to carefully examine their work to make sure it was accurate. The materials also needed to be well drawn and beautiful, so that the students in Panama would have good information and a nice classroom. Because the Governor Bent School supports the development of Spanish as well as English in all children, these charts were correctly labeled in both languages. Other teachers throughout the school rely on public performances of work, from book report presentations to plays to dances so that the students understand and appreciate that their work matters.

There is no doubt that teachers work hard in this school. They put a great deal of effort into making their own rooms interesting places, and they put an enormous amount of thought into developing their curriculum. Yet, teachers do not leave the school exhausted and ground down each day. Because the school is an exciting place, where their colleagues and students do wonderful work, the teachers leave talking about what they saw that day and what they want to do tomorrow.

Arts

Many art forms are taught at the Governor Bent School and are integrated into many individual classrooms. The school has a general music teacher, but in some years it has had no art teacher. Despite this limited staffing, the entire school is infused with visual arts, music, dance, theater, and other art forms.

Dance can be found in several classrooms. For example, the physical education teacher focuses much of her work on helping children to become both fit and comfortable with their bodies by teaching movement choreographed to music. Frequently, physical education at Governor Bent is devoted to learning about the dance of other cultures. These dances are polished through practice and performed for parents and others in the community.

Visual arts and theater are commonplace. The library has a small amphitheater and children regularly perform plays there. A fourth-grade teacher, Terri Foote, built a small performance area in her room, which children sometimes use to perform book reports in the form of monologues, complete with props.

Marleyne Chula, who works with both special education and gifted students, integrates ideas from art, architecture, and design for all her students. For example, in some classes she fuses science and art, encouraging students to draw species as they morph according to evolutionary principles.

The arts play a prominent role throughout the Governor Bent School. These enable many different kinds of learners to engage, to represent their understanding, and to build memorable learning experiences.

Ms. Chula instills the idea of taking different perspectives on a given topic by first having students draw themselves from three different perspectives and consider how they, and other things, look from different angles. She also employs theater: her special education students developed characters for a play, made giant puppets for their characters, developed a script, and performed their play for their teachers and parents. Mrs. Davenport remarked that traditionally school provides few memorable experiences. So, the creation of performances—real work—is a way to engage diverse learners and produce powerful learning.

In Sandy Lastra's social-learning curriculum, students sometimes undertake learning folksongs and carols, which they perform at a nearby nursing home or a home for critically ill children. Several other classrooms use music as part of their bilingual learning program.

In both Carolyn Chadwell's and Nan Hamner's classrooms, the visual arts are widely employed. Chapter 6, Language Artists, provides an especially rich example of the integration of visual arts into the classroom.

In sum, the arts provide a powerful route for learning throughout the Governor Bent School. They engage students and give them multiple ways to learn and express their understanding. The arts provide concrete means for representing and building on concepts (e.g., "perspective"), and for creating high-quality work to share within and beyond the school walls.

Controlled Choice

While Mrs. Davenport insisted that teachers obtain quality work from students, she did not believe there was only one way to accomplish this aim. She encouraged teachers to learn new things and try them out in the classroom. At the same time, teachers were free to practice in their classroom in the ways that work for them. There were only two limitations controlling teachers' choice of practice: teachers had to make sure students produced high-quality work, and they could not be mean to students.

Given this, it is not surprising that across the classrooms of the Governor Bent School, teachers chose a wide array of practices. Mrs. Chadwell used monthly themes, which helped her to build bridges across the curriculum. For example, in March, she emphasized green. She decorated her room with frogs, used frogs in many of her math problems, outfitted her classroom with images of spring and St. Patrick's day, and provided green thinking caps for the class to wear. In contrast, Nan Hamner's classroom design remains largely unchanged throughout the year, and the ongoing, year-long activities and strategies of her Language Artists and other curricular units provided a cohesive learning environment. In Marleyne Chula's work with both learning disabled and gifted children, teaching and learning were structured around the steps of the process of design. That is, she asked students to identify problems, brainstorm possible solutions, generate an initial design, get feedback on the design, revise the design, and then produce a refined design. In contrast, much of Sandy Lastra's teaching focused on service-learning projects, some of which have been described above.

Teachers also gave students a good deal of choice in how they did their work, as long as the work was done well and was recognizably worthwhile not only to the student but to others. In Carolyn Chadwell's class, students are assigned research projects, within which is a fair degree of choice as long as high-quality work is produced. For example, in a unit on mammals, students had to produce a poster. However, they were free to choose any mammal and to incorporate into the poster whatever information they felt was important as long as the information was clear, correct, and attractively presented. Similarly, in Nan Hamner's room, students could develop illustrations and stories of their choice for their squiggle books. The control on this choice was that all their stories must go through the process of editing and revision, so that only their best work ultimately appears in the squiggle book. Similarly, during extended reading time, students could choose to read by themselves or with one or more buddies. They could read whatever they wanted and read it anywhere in the classroom (on couches, at their desks, in the meeting area). The major constraint was that they had to use quiet voices so that everyone could read and learn. In essence, students as well as teachers have a good degree of choice as long as they are doing good work and enabling others to do the same.

Collaboration

At the Governor Bent School much of the collaboration is informal. As Carolyn Chadwell explained it, teachers at the Governor Bent School, "have a wealth of knowledge and our principal encourages us to spread it around." To foster the sharing of good practice, Mrs. Davenport often covered teachers' classes so that teachers could spend time in each others' rooms. Mrs. Davenport sometimes suggested particular visits. For example, Jay Hamner, Nan Hamner's husband, is exceptional in his ability to keep students focused and engaged in learning. Any time a teacher needed ideas about keeping students on-task, Marilyn Davenport encouraged the teacher to visit Mr. Hamner's room and to watch him in action.

Such modeling might have created tensions in some other schools, but Mrs. Davenport genuinely sought and found strengths in every teacher and highlighted these strengths to help the staff as a whole develop. She then continually drew on individuals' strengths to boost the staff's knowledge. (As you read Developing Language Artists [Chapter 5], you'll see that Nan Hamner uses the same strategy with her students: she celebrates wonderful work and uses it to elevate the skills of the whole class.) Mrs. Chadwell echoed the same notion: "If you come up with a good idea, Mrs. Davenport will support you 100 percent, and then she encourages other teachers to try some of your ideas. . . . We love getting a good idea, because we can build on it and turn it into ours."

Teachers also used staff meetings as a somewhat more formal time for collaborating. Staff meetings at Governor Bent were entirely devoted to in-house professional development. During staff meetings, teachers shared their plans, ideas, and work. This gave the entire staff an opportunity to learn from each other, and it gave individual teachers the chance to get feedback on their work and strengthen their practice.

At Governor Bent, team teaching is sometimes used. For example, Mrs. Lastra (who runs the social-learning curriculum) and Mrs. Chadwell sometimes joined together to teach a unit. The technology teacher also worked with classroom teachers to support the particular curriculum of each room. However, the main form of collaboration comes in the informal sharing of curricular ideas and teaching strategies. In this school, teachers are collaborating by freely giving and receiving ideas that they can adapt for their own classroom. Encouraged and supported by the principal, they see each other as resources for getting new classroom ideas, for getting feedback on their practice, and for strengthening the education they provide to the students.

The Compass Point Practices provide a schoolwide scaffold for Governor Bent's teachers to build individual classrooms that enable diverse students to learn and produce beautiful work. Many of these practices are mirrored within individual classrooms. As you read Math Labs and Language Artists, you might want to think both about the particular activities and strategies used by Mrs. Chadwell and Mrs. Hamner, and also about how to include the Compass Point Practices in your own work.

CHAPTER

5 Math Labs

MATH LABS AT A GLANCE

Math Labs offer an engaging, hands-on format for teaching basic math skills and concepts to students working in small groups. In Carolyn Chadwell's third-grade classroom at the Governor Bent School, each "lab" is stored inside a rectangular plastic bucket. The bucket contains written instructions, called "task cards," which guide each group through a hands-on activity. During Math Lab time, one group's lab introduces a new concept or skill. The activities in the other labs entail practice using skills and concepts that have already been introduced. By rotating small groups through this mix of labs, the teacher can work intensively with one small group to ensure that new content is carefully explored while also ensuring that the rest of the class consolidates important concepts and skills. This format works throughout the whole year to help students grasp new ideas and ultimately master them.

Math Labs reflect a carefully conceived planning process. This process balances the demands of curriculum and standards with the learning needs of diverse students. No doubt, when you read more about Math Labs, you will think of many ways to adapt this planning process and design to math or to other subjects that you teach.

MI in This Unit

- MI helps the teacher to draw on a variety of materials so that many different kinds of students can master the same content.
- Task cards require students to use logical-mathematical intelligence, but they also involve the use of linguistic abilities to interpret the card's directions.
- Small-group work enables children to use interpersonal intelligence and to take on roles that engage their strengths.
- Many task card activities involve spatial intelligence needed to interpret figures and allow students to use bodily-kinesthetic intelligences.

Entry Points in This Unit

- Math Labs draw heavily on the logical-quantitative entry point as well as on the interpersonal entry point.
- Task cards employ the narrative entry point by incorporating a story related to the classroom theme.
- Math Labs incorporate the experiential/hands-on entry point by requiring students to set up and participate in math-based experiences.

While not every entry point is used in every set of labs, all are called on during the year.

Compass Points Practices in This Unit

- As the planning process for Math Labs shows, MI can be a tool for helping students attain high-quality work in a way that engages many children, not just those who are quick to find answers to abstract problem sets.
- Several other Compass Point Practices are prominently featured in Math Labs, particularly collaboration and choice.

WHAT ARE MATH LABS?

*All [Math Lab] tasks come with a task card. They all have a component of creativity. . . .
And then they also touch the mad scientist that you find in every child: They like to touch,
and try, and tear apart, and put back together again, sometimes paste, and transform any concept.
I find this allows the child to transfer their learning so that it is not just an activity.
It's something that they may be able to use in a different kind of setting.*

—Carolyn Chadwell,
Third-grade teacher
Governor Bent School
Albuquerque, New Mexico

Math Labs are the idea of Carolyn Chadwell, a third-grade teacher at the Governor Bent School in Albuquerque, New Mexico. Their format is very simple: A card of instructions (task card) is affixed to the front of a bucket of materials. Several buckets are set out at once. The number of buckets will vary

Math Labs in storage.

with the size of a class and the number of students in a group. (Mrs. Chadwell uses six labs at a time and prefers to have four students in each group.)

During Math Lab time students work in groups and follow the instructions on the task cards to do activities. Task cards list the steps for each activity and clearly specify what mathematical concept must be learned in each activity.

All but one of the labs that are put out at once are designed to reinforce a particular mathematical concept or skill in a number of different ways. The remaining bucket in a set presents material related to the new concept or skill. This makes it possible for the teacher to work intensively on the new material with a small group of students while other students review.

The theory of multiple intelligences is central to Math Labs. This theory reflects Mrs. Chadwell's belief that students will learn in different ways, because they vary in their relative strengths and weaknesses of intelligences. Some students will gravitate more to activities that allow them to use their linguistic abilities, while others will favor activities that use their spatial or logical abilities.

Mrs. Chadwell developed the Math Lab format to reach each of these diverse learners by using several intriguing activities all aimed at shedding light on the same mathematical concept. For example, during Math Labs students learn the concept of multiplication through many different hands-on activities. Therefore, students who might grasp multiplication by drawing scaled representations and other students who might grasp it by solving logical problem statements have an equal opportunity to learn. At the same time, all students have many different ways to practice the concept (and so, they are not bored by continually repeating the same activity). Because students approach the concept in many ways and on several occasions, they are also more likely to learn it and understand it. Because students eventually use all six Math Labs designed to shed light on a concept or skill, they have opportunities to work in their areas of strength, but they are also required to work in more challenging areas. This can help students to

Carolyn Chadwell and her students, in thinking caps, are engaged in a Math Lab task.

strengthen areas in which they are weaker. (A similar approach to working with strengths and weaknesses is described in the Schneider's Ink example in Chapter 7.)

Learning activities that approach a central concept in several ways are likely to help students who would otherwise struggle with a concept. In addition, because the task cards allow students to revisit the directions at any time, Mrs. Chadwell believes that Math Labs are particularly helpful for students who have learning disabilities. These students also see firsthand that not everyone in the group will complete the whole task card. This provides these students with a "tremendous comfort zone," particularly for students who need more time on-task to succeed.

Mrs. Chadwell tells of two experiences that led her to develop rich math curriculum for very different learners. One was her own experience with math. While Mrs. Chadwell clearly loves math now, that was not always the case. In fact, she hated math and considered this one of her weaker subjects prior to attending college. At college she purposely studied math because it was a weakness. In the process, she realized that teaching math differently would have benefitted students like herself. The second experience came through considering the varying abilities of her two daughters. Her older daughter was always in the top group in everything, while her young one always struggled. The distinct difference between the instruction the two received inspired her. As she recounts, "The remediation was tedious and designed solely to make my youngest feel that she was not as bright as her sister. And so I decided as a teacher I was going to make sure that children who were at the lower end of the rung felt as excited about what they were doing as children who needed enrichment. Because of this I have designed my Math Labs."

BOX 5.1 MOST MATH LABS REVIEW MATERIAL

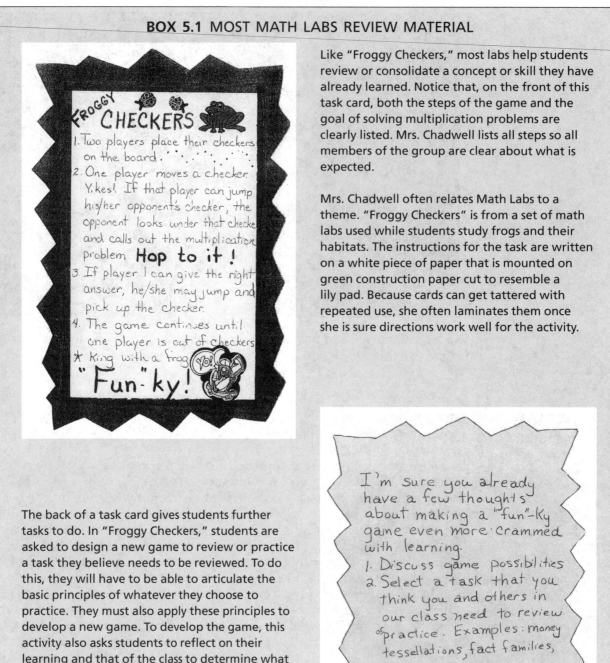

Like "Froggy Checkers," most labs help students review or consolidate a concept or skill they have already learned. Notice that, on the front of this task card, both the steps of the game and the goal of solving multiplication problems are clearly listed. Mrs. Chadwell lists all steps so all members of the group are clear about what is expected.

Mrs. Chadwell often relates Math Labs to a theme. "Froggy Checkers" is from a set of math labs used while students study frogs and their habitats. The instructions for the task are written on a white piece of paper that is mounted on green construction paper cut to resemble a lily pad. Because cards can get tattered with repeated use, she often laminates them once she is sure directions work well for the activity.

The back of a task card gives students further tasks to do. In "Froggy Checkers," students are asked to design a new game to review or practice a task they believe needs to be reviewed. To do this, they will have to be able to articulate the basic principles of whatever they choose to practice. They must also apply these principles to develop a new game. To develop the game, this activity also asks students to reflect on their learning and that of the class to determine what they think they have learned and what they still need to review or practice.

BOX 5.2 ONE MATH LAB PRESENTS NEW MATERIAL

Hop-Skip-Jump

Frogs can jump more than 17 times their body length. One species of tree frog can leap 40 times its length! Yikes!

1. Measure the height of 1 person in your group. Round it off to the nearest centimeter. Cut a piece of string the length of his/her body.
2. Measure the body string times 17. Compare the string with the space a classmate can jump. Write the total.
3. Students will take turns "helping" froggy to leap. Measure each leap with a meterstick or metric tape measure.
4. Keep a record of total jumped and distance to go.

The task card for "Hop-Skip-Jump" asks students to use metric measurement to solve a problem. The description also asks them to compare the "jump" of their classmate to their current study of frogs. This task shows that tasks need not be overly complex to provide students with many ways to engage with material. Within the constraints of solving this simple problem, students will be able to call on all but musical intelligence.

Because students are just beginning their study of metric measurement, Mrs. Chadwell spends much of her time working with this group.

The back of the "Hop-Skip-Jump" task card gives students more practice with the metric system. As a memory aid, there is even a handy review of metric conversion from centimeters to meters.

One addition, designing a game, is a familiar task for students in Mrs. Chadwell's classroom. A second addition asks students to connect their knowledge of frogs' jumping ability to what they have observed of their classmates' jumping ability. They are then asked to speculate about how a human's life would change if he or she could jump like a frog—a speculation that could open up lots of discussion back in science class!

10 mm = 1 centimeter (cm)
10 cm = 1 decimeter (dm)
10 dm = 1 meter (m)

★ Can you invent a game (with our hopping frogs) that will help teach about adding with metrics?

10 decimeters } = 1 meter
100 centimeters }

10 meters } = 1 dekameter
100 decimeters } (dam)

★ Can you imagine how the ability to leap 17 times your body length could change your life? Write about it

Over the years, Mrs. Chadwell has amassed a considerable collection to use in Math Labs. Her collection includes many materials she makes herself, because she loves to do this. She often reuses materials several times a year. A bucket for "Leap Frog Bingo," for example, has a game board, markers (tiny red and black plastic frogs), and a stack of cardboard cards. Each card contains a multiplication problem. Students play the game to review multiplication problems, but by adding a new stack of cards of division problems, the same game can be used over and over again.

The structure of Math Labs can be useful in teaching subjects other than elementary math. Teachers often collect materials to use in hands-on activities. The buckets and task cards of Math Labs are an efficient way to organize collected materials and a convenient means to convey instructions for hands-on activities to students. To meet the needs of many students, teachers often divide classes into small groups dedicated to one of several activities. Task cards of instructions that students can follow are a great way to structure how students work in small groups.

Regardless of the subject area, it is important to remember that just because an activity is engaging doesn't mean it is a worthwhile occasion for learning. Nor does the fact that an activity addresses significant disciplinary goals make it engaging to students or provide them with opportunities to learn. It's important to plan for both when designing activities. Math Labs are a good example of how activities can be engaging—even fun!—and at the same time address what must be learned in a discipline. For example, for the lab "Leap Frog Bingo" Mrs. Chadwell assembled an array of enticing

Math Labs provide engaging materials that foster math skills for many different kinds of learners.

materials and adapted a well-known game to provide practice in the basic disciplinary skill of multiplication.

Simple, well-planned activities like Math Labs can also show students firsthand that a discipline is complex. In the labs that accompany "Leap Frog Bingo," students do more than practice calculations and solve word problems. They also draw designs for their own gardens and contemplate the jumping abilities of a fellow student. When students engage a discipline in several ways, they see firsthand that any discipline has many aspects.

Meeting both disciplinary goals and the needs of students requires careful planning. The next section takes a close look at a planning process for Math Labs that can be adapted to many subject areas.

STRATEGIES: PLANNING FOR STUDENTS, CURRICULAR COHERENCE, AND STANDARDS

A Web seemed a concrete way to keep track of my thinking.
My Web connects core curriculum and pulls in MI to make a workable form for me.
I felt I was effective before, but when you see a corner of the foundation missing,
you have to shore it up. . . . The Web is a concrete checklist that helps find a specific
activity to catch children through their strength and give power to their intelligence.
—Carolyn Chadwell

Teaching any subject entails determining what it means to do high-quality work in that area. This is a goal to consider from the outset in any planning. At the same time, there should be opportunity for all students to attain that goal. The planning process for Math Labs shows one way to design activities with both goals in mind.

Before setting out to design engaging activities, it is often helpful to jot down ideas and diagrams. When she plans, Mrs. Chadwell draws a web to help her visualize her thinking. When she first began planning Math Labs, three questions guided her thinking and web building:

- How do individual students learn?
- What is required for the sake of curriculum coherence and grasp?
- What is required by the standards?

Planning Math Labs

When she designs activities for a new set of labs, Mrs. Chadwell takes into account what students have to learn and a class's progress so far in the curriculum. She also considers the goals that state and local standards set for all students. When she designs an activity to meet the needs of particular students, she also checks to see how that activity relates both to her curriculum for the year and to the standards for what students are required to know at the end of the year. Mrs. Chadwell focuses on all three points. To emphasize one direction over the others disrupts a very important balance. Such planning of activities is rarely a linear process. Instead, lots of refinements are apt to be generated as each question is contemplated anew.

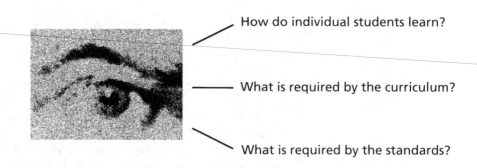

How do individual students learn?

What is required by the curriculum?

What is required by the standards?

Mrs. Chadwell's planning for Math Labs focuses on three questions.

How do individual students learn?

The theory of multiple intelligences is at the heart of this planning process. It is a tool for thinking about what will support the diverse student population of a classroom to do quality work. Knowing that students will learn in different ways means planning a range of activities. In her planning Mrs. Chadwell often incorporates a checklist based on the theory of multiple intelligences. In this way she makes sure to include activities that address several intelligences and offer students multiple ways to explore concepts and develop skills.

What is required by the curriculum?

Planning Math Labs also means attending to what is required for the sake of curriculum coherence as a whole. Math Labs give students both new and review material related to a given concept or skill. Because of this Math Labs can support both children who lack a firm grounding in the previously introduced skills or concepts and those who have mastered earlier material. In her classroom, Mrs. Chadwell is sure to include activities that address curriculum requirements for grade level, as well as below and above grade level. Because Mrs. Chadwell's labs relate to themes, these are also reflected in the activities she designs. For example, the set of Math Labs that students use to practice multiplication during the theme "It Isn't Easy Being Green" includes many references to frogs and their habitat.

What's required by the standards?

State and local standards require that students learn basic disciplinary skills and concepts. This is also the goal of Math Labs. However, it is the way Math Labs teach these that is special. Rather than learning basic mathematical skills and concepts in only one way, students are offered several ways to engage the required material. This insures that all students have an opportunity to attain the levels of proficiency required by the standards.

Designing Tasks for Math Labs

Before gathering materials for buckets and writing task cards, be sure to consider the preceding three questions. These questions can help maintain a focus both on what needs to be learned and how individual students learn.

Because several labs are set out together, they should be designed as a group. For example, during the time when students are also studying systems of the human body, a set of Math Labs might include one task card asking students to measure the circumference of their heads and calculate the ratio of the length of their body to the circumference of their heads. Another task may ask students to use their bodies to form a model of the digestive system, and then measure the length of the "esophagus" and "intestines" and calculate the ratio between the two. Although both tasks are experiential, the first may be more interesting to a student who is logical and quantitative and the second more interesting to a student who favors bodily-kinesthetic activities.

At the same time, any set of labs should be designed as part of an overall plan for the year. For example, task cards at the beginning of the year may ask students to simply measure the circumference of very basic things like rubber balls and compare circumferences. Later labs might ask them to find measurable differences among balls that have the same circumference but are made of different materials. (Because later task cards will also include a review of previous concepts as well as new material, students will also be asked to measure circumference in other ways throughout the year.)

The following general strategies are good guides for designing individual sets of Math Labs.

1. *Offer choice and activities that engage student interest.*

Math Labs reflect a belief that students are more likely to learn if they are interested and more likely to be interested in some activities than others. Math Labs offers students an engaging array of hands-on activities through which to learn. These activities can be modified in response to the particular class or time of year. For example, problems for practicing multiplication can be adapted to a special interest, like caring for a classroom's pet animal or a holiday like Halloween. Calculating what a pet hamster will eat that month might provide occasion to practice multiplication and parsing a group of pumpkins among students at Halloween prove an opportune time to practice division.

2. *Create math experiences.*

Math Lab activities are designed to create experiences for students to become immersed in math, or as Mrs. Chadwell says, "They are part of it, rather than just writing or reading about it." The math experiences Mrs. Chadwell designs relate to monthly themes. Theme-related activities on task cards instruct students to create games to practice multiplication or jump to determine what equals seventeen times their body lengths. At the same time, it is not unusual to see students wearing hats that they designed and constructed for the same theme. In fact, Mrs. Chadwell's classroom often appears to have the atmosphere of a clubhouse in which students are engaged in serious learning while also having fun.

3. *Include material that challenges and reviews.*

Math Labs have a flexible format. Usually the majority of material is review, with one lab presenting new work related to the same concept or skill. Yet, this format could easily be changed for a class that required less review. Additional materials and new task cards can give students more extended opportunities to review skills.

4. *Include connections to other parts of the curriculum.*

Math Labs provide many opportunities to connect math to other parts of the curriculum. For example, Mrs. Chadwell connects practice in measuring the volume of specific containers to science. She can draw on this measuring lesson when the class compares the dissected hearts of a cow and a sheep and determines how much blood each might pump.

5. *Use national and state standards to help determine what to include.*

State and local standards codify knowledge and skills that should be learned at a particular grade level. Because Math Labs include both new and review material, activities should address standards for below and above grade level. For example, the New Mexico standards require that students in grades 3 through 5 develop "process skills" through practice in several content areas. Therefore, Mrs. Chadwell's Math Labs build skills in three general areas: thinking (e.g., problem solving, learning to see relationships), communication (e.g., oral and notational ways to understand and communicate mathematical concepts), and connections (opportunities to relate what they are learning in mathematics to their own lives, other cultures, and societies).

These strategies for designing tasks can generate ideas for activities that support the development of skill and understanding in a wide range of learners. They can also serve as a guide when evaluating the success of activities that have been used in a specific classroom. In addition, they are a great way to ensure that you focus on the needs of individual students, curriculum requirements, and the state and local standards.

WHAT HAPPENS DURING MATH LABS?
ACTIVITIES, TASK CARDS, AND COLLABORATION

I have six Math Labs and the children rotate through the Math Labs. Each one of the Math Labs has a task card and an activity to go with the task that they are to perform. They have a facilitator and the facilitator changes every time I change the Math Labs. Their task as a unit is to decide what needs to be done.

—Carolyn Chadwell

Math Labs are a math curriculum used for building and consolidating mathematics skills and concepts throughout the school year. During Math Labs, students work in small groups to carry out a hands-on activity. Everything that a group needs for its activity, or "lab," is in a bucket. A task card affixed to the outside of each bucket gives students step-by-step instructions for the activity. Several labs are set out at a time, and all students eventually rotate through each lab. A set of labs provides several ways to learn a particular concept or skill. Because there are multiple ways to approach the same material, students are more likely to find a way that fits their particular strengths and interests. At the same time, because students rotate through all labs, they also have to stretch to use approaches that are less strong.

BOX 5.3 MATERIALS NEEDED

Materials for math labs will depend on the specific goals and activities of each lab. Often basic classroom materials are all that is needed. If you are so inclined, you can also make additional items with commonly available materials like paper, cardboard, glue, and markers. Don't forget that a cache of manipulatives and supplies can be recycled in several ways with the addition of new task cards.

Schedule: In Mrs. Chadwell's classroom, Math Labs run on a regular schedule, usually once a day for four days a week. Each group of students pursues one lab during a work period. The amount of time for a work period will vary, depending on the grade level, the students, and the complexity of the labs. Usually forty-five minutes to an hour suffices. Occasionally, it may make sense to run a longer session and have groups work on more than one lab. Sometimes a whole day can be devoted to nothing but Math Labs! Usually in one month a class will use several sets of labs. The sequence of the labs throughout the year will depend on the curriculum of individual classrooms, but it is helpful to use Math Labs regularly and at a specified time during the school day.

Assessment: There are lots of ways to assess how students perform the task described on each card. Mrs. Chadwell uses a combination of assessments. Some tasks give students a number of required steps to go through and contain a formal recording sheet to track the task. Others ask students to write down what they learned from the activity. Still others ask students to grade the activity. (In keeping with the humor that Mrs. Chadwell brings to her classroom, she grades Math Labs in reverse: A is for awful, B is for Bad, C is for cool, D is for Delightful, and F is for Fantastic.) In most cases, Mrs. Chadwell primarily relies on careful scrutiny of groups during labs. This informal assessment works well for her, because she will formally assess what students have learned in Math Labs in her more traditional curriculum ("Einstein Math"), which entails word problems and worksheets in a sequence of increasing difficulty.

Math Labs have three central elements:

1. group work to build a shared understanding;
2. task cards to guide students;
3. hands-on activities.

Group Work

During Math Labs, all but one group of students use labs that review material they have already covered. This allows them to consolidate their understanding. The remaining group does a new activity that extends the same topic to new material. When students work in groups, they get used to relying on each other for help. This helps them build interpersonal skills while, at the same time, freeing the teacher to work intensively with small groups of students who are learning the new material.

To assign students to Math Lab groups, Mrs. Chadwell puts numbers for four students on one of six hooks. Each hook reflects one Math Lab group.

Assign students to groups.   Before you start Math Labs, you will want to decide how many groups to have and how to assign students to groups. Students in Mrs. Chadwell's class each have a number. At the beginning of the month, Mrs. Chadwell makes up new groups and creates cards listing the numbers of the four students in the group. She posts these cards on numbered hooks at the front of the classroom. The number of the hook corresponds to the Math Lab each group starts with. When Math Labs begin, students check the hooks to see which lab will be their Math Lab for the day. The next time they do Math Labs, their number will be on a different hook. Mrs. Chadwell changes groups each month to get students used to working with a range of classmates. She typically has six groups of four students each because she finds that, within these groups of four, all children in each lab can be actively involved.

Specify roles in the group.   Each group should have a facilitator who is responsible for convening the group, retrieving the assigned Math Lab bucket from the shelf, and overseeing the group. Facilitators rotate, so all students get to perform this role. They quickly get used to these clear procedures and roles, which are repeated throughout the year.

Task Cards

A group of students follows the instructions on the task card for their bucket. Task cards guide the group through the activity and specify what is to be learned. Once written, task cards can be used year after year—a great way to save preparation time. Steps should be clearly stated and numbered on the task card.

BOX 5.4 STRUCTURING GROUP WORK

Clear procedures make group work much easier. In fact, once students get used to the procedures of a particular lab format, it might make sense to try a variation of that lab with other content at a later date. For example, rules for Mrs. Chadwell's lab, "Hidden Frogs," are very simple: Students gather around a tabletop filled with rectangular sheets of green paper. When turned over, each displays a single number or a mathematical problem. Students turn over another card on the table to find either the answer or the problem that goes with this card. Of course the trick is both to know the answer or problem and to remember where you saw that card on the table. The student who answers correctly gets to keep the cards "Hidden Frogs" and have another turn. The student who can't locate the answer loses the opportunity to continue. This simple format would easily keep students engaged in answering all sorts of problems, provided they were able to find something that was hidden and do this together at one table.

As they become more familiar with a format and working together, students will develop a better sense of the roles they might take on in a group. Students working on Mrs. Chadwell's review lab, "Tic-Tac-Toad," often remind the group to adhere to directions. For example, one girl reminds another that she needs to turn over two particular cards to get the answer, and thereby receive a small plastic frog on the board. When she calls out, "6 times 4," a girl to her right asks, "Wait, could I divide it?" She is told that, "It has to be times," but another girl checks the directions on the task card and says, "It says multiply or divide."

Students also take responsibility for teaching each other. For example, when a child absently asks, "What is divide again?" the girl demonstrating the cards explains that divide is when you see how many times six will go into twenty-four. To verify this, two students pick up calculators to see who can check this first.

BOX 5.5 TASK CARDS

#1 Leap Frog Bingo

Materials in buckets	Task card (front) instruction	Task card (back) instructions
1. a bag that contains laminated cards cut from green construction paper, each of which presents a multiplication problem (9×3, etc.) 2. a box of small plastic lady bugs and flies, a story ("An Unforgettable Frog Experience") mounted on green construction paper and laminated 3. ten gridded photocopies to serve as bingo boards	1. Choose any 24 of the numbers shown at the bottom of your worksheet. Write each number in its own square on the bingo sheets. 2. Shuffle the problem cards and pick the top card. Say the problem aloud. Any player with the product of that problem may cover the number with a token. 3. Continue picking problem cards until someone has five numbers, going across, down, or diagonally. 4. The winning player calls back each product to make sure each one of the problems called matches. 5. Play again. (*Be sure to check others' multiplication as you play.)	Help! I know there are probably a dozen ways we could change our bingo game to make it more challenging, but I'm going to count on you for ideas. Discuss ideas. 1. Invent (Choose) one of the ideas discussed. 　　Examples: decimals, fractions, polygons . . . 2. Try playing your game. 3. Revise the game if you need to. "Fun"–key!

#2 Hidden Frogs

Materials in buckets	Task card (front) instruction	Task card (back) instructions
1. a two-paragraph description ("What Frogs and Toads Eat") mounted on green construction paper and laminated 2. twenty problem cards and twenty answer cards, all printed on white paper and laminated after being mounted on green construction paper	The flat, round pads on the ends of the toes of some tree frogs are covered with thousands of small, fine hairs. A substance oozes from between the hair allowing the frog to cling to slick surfaces—like the bottom of these concentration cards. 1. The first player turns over two cards. If the math problem matches a math answer (insert drawing of problem on card), that player keeps the cards and takes another turn. If you turn over the tree frog you have an automatic match. 2. When all of the math problems have been matched, players count their cards. The player with the greater number of cards wins. 3. Play again.	Now that you have completed your task, it's time to use your incredible brain to invent a new game. 1. Examine the materials in the container. 2. Discuss game ideas. 3. Choose one idea. (Does it have a mathematical purpose?) 4. Try playing your game. 5. Discuss what worked and what didn't work. 6. Revise your game.

#3 Froggy Checkers

Materials in buckets	Task card (front) instruction	Task card (back) instructions
1. checkers with numbers added to the backs with marker 2. a bag for the checkers, a paragraph ("How Toads Keep from Being Eaten") to read 3. four rectangular sheets, each covered with black and white squares so that they form a checkerboard when put together	1. Two players place their checkers on the board. 2. One player moves a checker. Yikes! If that player can jump his or her opponent's checker, the opponent looks under that checker and calls out the multiplication problem. Hop to it! 3. If Player 1 can give the right answer, he or she may jump and pick up the checker. 4. The game continues until one player is out of checkers. 5. King with a frog.	I'm sure you already have a few thoughts about making a "fun"–key game even more crammed with learning. 1. Discuss game possibilities. 2. Select a task that you think you and others in our class need to review or practice. Examples: money, tesselations, fact families, etc. 3. Give your idea a try.

continued

Examples of Mrs. Chadwell's task cards show clearly written and numbered steps for each activity.

#4 Froggy's Garden

Materials in buckets	Task card (front) instruction	Task card (back) instructions
1. a box of rods (longest = purple, medium = green, shortest = pink) 2. several sheets of paper gridded with centimeter squares	1. Use 1 red rod, 2 light green rods, and 1 purple rod. Arrange the rods into a shape on centimeter squared paper in such a way that when you trace around it you only draw on the grid paper lines. Also you must be able to cut out the outlined shape and have it remain in one piece. Corners touching don't count. 2. Make several different shapes for froggy's garden. Trace each and record its perimeter. 3. Experiment to find out how to arrange the rods to get the longest perimeter and shortest perimeter.	**BRAIN BUSTERS** The area of a figure is the number of square units that fit inside it. Each ☐ = 1 square unit Count the square units of each item in Froggy's room. Read the "Way Cool Math Hint." Use this new information to answer the bonus frog work.

#5 Hop–Skip–Jump

Materials in buckets	Task card (front) instruction	Task card (back) instructions
1. a bag containing small plastic frogs, a cone of string for measuring, various kinds of tape measures, scissors, fuzzy toy frog 2. laminated green construction paper cut into frog shapes with the following questions written on the front and back of each: • 66 frogs came to the frog family reunion. 39 are boys. How many are girls? • Jumping Jeremiah jumped 12 times in the jumping contest. If he traveled 6 feet with each jump, how far did he jump in all? • There were 23 mosquitoes at the pond. Along came 48 more. How many mosquitoes in all? • Barry Bullfrog can croak 14 of the top 40 tunes. How many songs does Barry still need to learn? • There are 36 tadpoles swimming in the pond. Mrs. Chadwell catches 16 and puts them in a jar. How many are left?	Frogs can jump more than 17 times their body length. One species of tree frog can leap 40 times its length! Yikes! 1. Measure the height of 1 person in your group. Round it off to the nearest centimeter. Cut a piece of string the length of his or her body. 2. Measure the body string times 17. Compare the string with the space a classmate can jump. Write the total. 3. Students take turns "helping" froggy to leap. Measure each leap with a meterstick or metric tape measure. 4. Keep a record of total jumped and distance to go.	10 mm = 1 centimter (cm) 10 cm = 1 decimeter (dm) 10 dm = 1 meter (m) • Can you *invent a game* (with our hopping frogs) that will help teach about adding with metrics? 10 decimeters = 1 meter 100 centimeters = 1 meter 10 meters = 1 dekameter (dam) 100 decimeters = 1 dekameter (dam) • Can you imagine how the ability to leap 17 times your body length could change your life? *Write about it.*

continued

Specify the steps for an activity. The task cards on each bucket contain all the instructions for that activity. For the first Math Labs of the month, Mrs. Chadwell reads several task cards and displays the contents of the blue bucket that corresponds to each. This gives the class a preview of the materials and captures students' interest. Occasionally during Math Lab time, Mrs. Chadwell again directs students to the goals of each activity, but generally they follow the steps on the task cards on their own.

BOX 5.5 TASK CARDS *continued*

#6 Tic–Tac Toad

Materials in buckets	Task card (front) instruction	Task card (back) instructions
1. small brown toads, small green toads 2. 18-inch strips of black paper (44 in all), playing cards (only cards 4–9) 3. five frogs cut from green construction paper with shapes drawn on them (not to scale) and directions to find the area 4. one green construction paper frog with a "Way Cool Math Hint" that says "area = length × width"	1. Use the black strips of paper to make the tic-tac–toe game area. 2. Draw two playing cards. Multiply and divide the two numbers presented. 3. Place your frog or toad game piece on the board (if your answer is correct). 4. The first person to win five games wins.	A fact family is a group of math problems made from a limited group of numbers Example: $9 \times 6 = 54$ $$9\overline{)54}^{\,6}$$ $6 \times 9 = 54$ $$6\overline{)54}^{\,9}$$ You can even use fact family knowledge to check your math answers.

Explain goals, build connections. It is important to be explicit from the outset about the goals for activities. Mrs. Chadwell always takes time to explain what skills a particular Math Lab will help develop. She also asks students what connections they see to the monthly theme and previously studied math material. Mrs. Chadwell relates the activities in her Math Labs to other aspects of her curriculum, like science or language arts. For example, the task cards and activities for March are related to the themes of green (for spring) and Saint Patrick's Day. They also include activities that relate to the study of frogs underway in the science curriculum.

Hands-On Activities

Students are apt to find hands-on activities engaging, particularly those who do not readily grapple with abstract concepts. In addition, having them do several different hands-on activities can give students multiple avenues through which to understand a concept or master a skill. Therefore, it's always important to be sure that the activity is in service of learning—not just engagement!

Keep an eye on all the groups. Mrs. Chadwell spends lots of time with the group using the lab of unfamiliar material, but she also keeps an eye on the other groups to make sure they're on track. Occasionally students may need to be reminded of goals or how to act in their groups, or instructed to notice a particular material or set of instructions. Because tasks and activities for the individual labs vary, students are likely to find some labs more engaging than others. For example, one student might be more interested in the lab that uses a game to help students practice multiplication or division. Another might be more interested in a lab that incorporates practice of these by having students draw a design for a garden. Sometimes students may need extra encouragement to become engaged with a new lab if they previously used a lab that they really enjoyed.

Children whose labs enable them to practice previously covered concepts will ask questions if something is unclear to them. However, most of the time, these students will be able to work through and review the material without much assistance.

BOX 5.6 WRITING TASK CARDS

"Leap Frog Bingo"

Instructions on task cards must give very specific instructions and provide clear goals for an activity. Once you think of a task, the next step is to break the task down into step-by-step directions for students to follow.

Because students often work in groups, you may also want to include instructions that encourage interpersonal skills. For example, instructions can call on students to listen to their peers or discuss a solution with them. Oftentimes, the activity itself encourages such behaviors. In Mrs. Chadwell's math lab "Leap Frog Bingo," for example, students engage in sporadic conversation as they use an adaptation of a familiar game that pits knowledge against luck. Much of their conversation focuses on the task: to solve multiplication problems. However, at other times students remind each other to stay focused on the problem or to allow a peer to come up with the answer by himself. Students also take on group roles, like being responsible for running the game, pulling problems out of the bag, and calling out the numbers.

"Froggy's Garden"

Instructions for tasks derived from real-life problems should describe the skills you want students to apply to the task. Without that clarity, students are likely to find it hard to transfer skills they learned in another situation. Also, if the task substitutes a fictitious scenario for the real task, be sure to make clear the connection between the two. For example, for students to understand that the basic calculation and measurement skills they learn can be applied to construction and design work, they need to be encouraged to transfer this learning. However, they need not build an actual house. For instance, in Mrs. Chadwell's lab "Froggy's Garden" students use paper, colored rods, and colored pencils to design gardens on grid paper. They take measurements, calculate the perimeter and area, and write the answer next to the design. In this activity students clearly know that they are to use practiced calculation skills to take the same first step in the design process that architects go through to build a house or garden. As a related activity a class could even hold a contest for designs and then build a model of the winning design.

BOX 5.7 IF YOU ARE DOING MATH LABS FOR THE FIRST TIME

- Be clear about what you want students to get from the lab.
- Put this on the task card.
- Make sure that the material you present engages students in several ways.

- Start with a small number of groups (like 4 groups of 6–7 students) so that you can more easily observe the labs and help them, as needed.

BOX 5.8 DESIGNING HANDS-ON ACTIVITIES

"Froggy Checkers"

Thinking of things that students will like doing is one good way to start designing hands-on activities. Once you think of one task, try to think of another that will meet the abilities and interests of other, very different students. At the same time, think about the materials you have on hand or can make. Finally, remember to assess how well each activity works as a learning experience. Mrs. Chadwell uses several game formats because her students find games engaging. She then thinks of how a game can be adapted to serve learning. The game "Froggy Checkers" reviews multiplication and uses a checkerboard and checkers, each with a multiplication problem written with marker. A student who gives the correct answer to the problem retains her position; otherwise her jump does not count, and she must return her opponent's checker. If no one can give an answer, group members reach for their calculators to check computation.

Real-world applications are another good place to get ideas. For example, Mrs. Chadwell's math lab, "Hop Skip Jump," asks a group to calculate how far a classmate might jump if, like a frog, he or she could jump more than 17 times her body length. As part of their calculations, a group working on this lab lays down 17 lengths of string in preparation for a real-life test to see whether their classmate will be able to jump this distance. For the test, everyone in the class is invited outside to watch and silently "cheer" with only hand motions as the classmate lines up to take his or her jump.

The "Hop, Skip, Jump" lab introduces new material. Consequently, Mrs. Chadwell works closely with this group. Sometimes she explains some aspect of the material. Other times she reminds them of something, like being sure to convert inches to centimeters or to check a calculation.

Whether designing new or review activities, it's important to think of several things that students can do to help them understand a concept or develop a skill. So, for example, it's important to include both activities that make calculations with paper and pencil and by measuring physical objects.

"Hop–Skip–Jump"

Work intensively with the group using the lab with new material. One lab bucket contains instructions and materials that will challenge students to extend what they have previously learned. Students who are using that lab are likely to need the teacher working closely with them.

Have a regular schedule for Math Labs. This way all students can regularly practice math. At the same time, they will have regular practice working in groups. While it certainly is possible to use task cards and buckets sporadically, repeated use has the added benefit of establishing routines that will make group work go smoothly. Using the same procedures on an ongoing basis enables both students and the teacher to focus on content.

REVISITING THE FRAMEWORKS

Obviously, I am not going to reach every child every time, but I reach every child most of the time, and I don't think that could be said for the regular paper pencil tasks, the work books, the math books.
—Carolyn Chadwell

MI in This Unit

Each set of Math Labs always contains several different kinds of activities, because students will learn in different ways based on the relative strengths and weaknesses of their intelligences. Some students will be stronger in logical-mathematical intelligence, while others will gravitate more to activities that allow them to use their linguistic or spatial abilities. This means that the

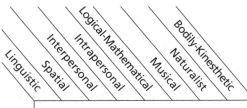

Linguistic	Spatial	Interpersonal	Intrapersonal	Logical-Mathematical	Musical	Naturalist	Bodily-Kinesthetic	ACTIVITIES
								Hands-On Activities:
	X			X			X	• Each lab is a hands-on activity that presents new or review material.
				X				• All labs in a set address a core mathematical concept or skill.
X	X	X	X	X		X	X	• Several labs are set out at a time so there are a number of ways to approach a concept or skill.
								Task Cards:
X				X				• Task cards of instructions clearly list the steps of an activity.
X		X		X				• Students can follow instructions on task cards with little assistance from the teacher, thereby freeing the teacher to work with students using the lab that contains new material.
								Group Work:
		X		X				• Explicit goals and expectations help students work effectively in groups.
		X	X	X				• Clear procedures help groups function efficiently.
X		X		X				• A regular schedule of math labs gives students ongoing collaborative time with their peers.

FIGURE 5.1   Multiple Intelligences Used during Math Labs

concepts that students are supposed to learn should be approached in several different ways. It also means that those with different profiles of intelligences are likely to find some labs more appealing than others labs. The intelligences that students will access in a given set of Math Labs will depend on the activities specified on the task cards. It is feasible for all the intelligences to be tapped within a set, but it is not necessary. The important thing to keep in mind is that each activity provides a genuine opportunity to work with mathematical concepts and skills.

Entry Points in This Unit

Entry points are routes into a topic or curriculum that enable diverse learners to engage the content. Math Labs offer students many different entry points to learn mathematical concepts and skills.

Logical-Quantitative: Math Labs focus on logical reasoning and calculation.

Experiential: Math Labs by definition are hands-on activities. They call on students to participate in activities that require mathematical problem solving.

Narrative: Many labs embed mathematical problems in stories or narrative related to themes or other areas of the curriculum.

Foundational: Any activity that encourages students to inquire about the nature of mathematics uses this entry point. The girl who asks, "What is division again?" during a Math Lab is asking a foundational question.

Interpersonal: Math Labs engage students in a social experience; they work in groups and often teach each other.

Aesthetic: Math Labs often contain a design activity, like "Froggy's Garden." Using tasks that involve geometrical forms and patterns can readily tap this entry point.

Compass Point Practices in This Unit

Math Labs provide a good example of the Compass Point Practices that support student learning.

Tool: Clearly the focus of Math Labs is on learning math, and MI is a tool for doing this in a way that engages many children, not just those who are quick to find answers to abstract problem sets.

Arts: In Math Labs the visual arts and design are incorporated as a way of learning math or to engage a student's interest. However, the arts are also an important aspect of the overall classroom environment in which Math Labs are used.

Choice: Students must participate in Math Labs, however the roles they take on in their groups are negotiable. Task cards direct students' focus while at the same time allowing for some choice in how the task is carried out.

Collaboration: Math Labs call on students to work in groups and collaborate in working through their task card activities.

Readiness: Mrs. Chadwell helps students work in Math Labs by thoroughly reviewing the concepts and goals involved in the set. She also prepares them to engage in this activity through a well-structured method of forming small groups.

Culture: Mrs. Chadwell's classroom mirrors the philosophy of the surrounding Governor Bent School: that all students should gain a sense of competence through good work and that all students should feel that they are part of the school community. Math Labs build on a belief in children's strengths. During Math Labs students are clearly focused on work, and working collaboratively and respectfully with each other, but they are clearly also enjoying themselves!

6 Language Artists

LANGUAGE ARTISTS AT A GLANCE

Nan Hamner's classroom

The Language Artists curriculum is a group of literacy-building activities used throughout the school year by Nan Hamner in her first- and second-grade classroom and other teachers at the Governor Bent School in Albuquerque, New Mexico. Language Artists includes writing and illustrating in "squiggle books," which encourage children to develop detailed, descriptive stories and build their understanding of narrative structure. It also entails nightly writing, which gives children regular opportunities to practice writing in different genres. A third component of this curriculum is the "morning message." These are engaging, whole-class language exercises aimed at developing language mechanics, editing skills, vocabulary, figurative language, and critical thinking skills. Like all other activities in Nan Hamner's class, the Language Artist curriculum is infused with a strategy of continually "elevating, celebrating, and evaluating" her students' work. Together, these strategies and activities enable students to understand and use language in skillful ways.

MI in This Unit

- Several different kinds of literacy-building activities engage students' multiple intelligences.
- Word puzzles used in morning messages draw on both linguistic intelligence and logical-mathematical intelligence.
- The production of detailed artwork in the squiggle books involves students' spatial intelligence and taps bodily-kinesthetic skills in the form of fine-motor activity.

Entry Points in This Unit

- In their squiggle books students develop detailed stories, which engage the narrative entry point.
- Producing, viewing, and describing artwork provide an aesthetic entry point into language arts.
- Word puzzles offer students a logical entry point for developing language skills.
- The experiential entry point is tapped by fostering students' own sense of themselves as writers: people who continually produce polished writing and who reflect on how language is used.

Compass Point Practices in This Unit

- The arts are a prominent feature in Mrs. Hamner's classroom as well as in the Language Artists curriculum.
- Multiple intelligences is used as a tool by Nan Hamner to engage diverse learners in building children's skills in language arts and other areas. The theory does not displace the curriculum.
- Choice is evident in this unit: Students can often choose what they want to write about or draw, but they must produce work that shows care and detail.

WHAT IS THE LANGUAGE ARTISTS CURRICULUM?

I want children to be able to express themselves clearly and comfortably and to be able really to express what it is they're thinking. I think it's important for every child, not just for the linguistic children, not just for the top group, or the group of children that will always do well. I want it to be true for every single child. I want them to feel they can express themselves in writing, using all the skills and tools they have, and it will make a difference.

—Nan Hamner
First- and Second-Grade Teacher
The Governor Bent School
Albuquerque, New Mexico

The Language Artists curriculum is an ongoing collection of activities and strategies that Nan Hamner uses to develop high levels of language skill in her first- and second-grade students at the Governor Bent School. Similar activities and strategies are also used by her husband and fellow teacher, Jay Hamner, with his fourth graders, and by several other teachers in this K-5 school. As these teachers reveal, this kind of curriculum can be readily adapted to suit students throughout the elementary grades.

Language Artists combines central elements of a traditional language arts curriculum, including reading, writing, grammar, punctuation, and vocabulary building with the making and appreciating of visual arts. The visual arts serve both as a means to advance language skills and as an end in themselves.

Through looking at and discussing art reproductions, and through drawing in their squiggle books, Mrs. Hamner helps children to understand fundamental elements of artistic composition: line, color, background, and foreground. Looking at art also builds cultural literacy around art forms, artists, styles, and various artistic periods. In addition, artwork helps children to observe carefully and to find a vocabulary to represent what they observe. For example, in a discussion of Andrew Wyeth's painting, *Christina's World,* Mrs. Hamner's students wondered if the young woman in the grassy foreground was "crawling" toward the barn in the distance or if was she "sprawled out," "crouching," or "lounging."

Mrs. Hamner also uses students' own artwork to promote their language development. She encourages them to produce detailed, colored-pencil drawings in their squiggle books, and students are also free to incorporate art into their nightly writing notebooks. These visual details challenge students to find words and create detailed stories that work well with the inventive, complex illustrations they produce. And, just as there are elements of visual artworks—for example, line, color, composition— Mrs. Hamner emphasizes there are elements of written works: for example, setting, characters, and a plot, with a beginning, middle, and end. Students learn that, just as there are different forms and styles of artwork, there are different genres of writing: fiction, nonfiction, and poetry.

Nan Hamner works with students to review drafts of their stories.

A student copies the final draft of his story into his squiggle book.

This combination of language arts and arts enables students with very different profiles of intelligence to engage and to learn. By involving this wide range of intelligences, Nan Hamner finds that Language Artists succeeds not only with "the group of children that will always do well" but with many kinds of students. She also succeeds in fully incorporating the state and district guidelines for language: fostering good listening skills, phonemic awareness, correct language mechanics, writing and revising skills, and comprehension of texts.

Alongside the Language Artists activities, Mrs. Hamner's teaching strategies (elevate, celebrate, evaluate) are continually in play. She is always evaluating her students' writing to understand the areas where their skills need to be elevated. She continually celebrates her students' writing, oftentimes choosing examples that might be useful to many members of the class. "Listen to this wonderful work," she'll say to the class, as she reads a child's metaphor, or vocabulary choice, or snippet of dialogue. "Isn't that the work of a true language artist!?" she'll exclaim with real delight. By celebrating good examples many times each day—by making such examples a notable classroom event—students become eager to listen for, and to use rich, expressive, and nuanced language. Through these strategies, even young students come to know and appreciate word play, metaphor, simile, alliteration, and other elements of language.

Because of these strategies and an ongoing set of activities that children really enjoy, Mrs. Hamner finds that, "I don't have to beg them to write—ever, ever, ever!" In fact, the very first thing children often ask in the morning is if they can write in their squiggle books that day.

STRATEGIES: ELEVATE, CELEBRATE, EVALUATE

> *Elevate and celebrate and evaluate. You can't leave any of them out.*
> *If you leave out the evaluation—well, that's your job as a teacher!*
> *If you leave out the celebrating, you're leaving out the most important part.*
> *That's where they learn from one another.... And you have to use every minute*
> *of every day to elevate language. It's an ongoing thing. I don't think you can*
> *do it once or twice or five times or ten times. It goes on all day, every day.*
>
> —Nan Hamner
> First- and Second-Grade Teacher
> The Governor Bent School
> Albuquerque, New Mexico

The activities that are used in the Language Artists curriculum are not the only reason for the success of this unit with a wide range of elementary students. As interesting and engaging as the activities are, the activities alone will not necessarily lead students to produce high-quality work. To produce such work, Nan Hamner asserts that it's essential to use three interrelated strategies. One strategy is to elevate children's capacities by helping them to become aware of the elements of good and interesting work and by having them practice using those elements in an ongoing way. The second strategy is to celebrate students' good work by sharing examples of it with the class. Finally, it's necessary to continually evaluate the work that students are producing. Evaluation enables the teacher to know what aspects of language need to be highlighted in the activities and clearly celebrated and shared in order to elevate students' skills.

Elevate

Elevating language is a primary aim of Mrs. Hamner's classroom, and of the entire Governor Bent School. Elevating language helps students to feel and become competent, another shared aim of the school. Mrs. Hamner remarked, "I don't know any children who don't want to do well. Sometimes they just don't know how. So, you have to give them some tools." Through the various literacy activities described in this chapter, Mrs. Hamner equips young students with crucial tools for using and understanding language: the elements of story structure, grammatical skills, a rich vocabulary of words and idioms, and an appreciation for figurative language.

Students acquire this knowledge in part because the strategy of elevating children's language goes on continuously and in many ways throughout the day and week. "We talk about writing and language all the time. It's just an ongoing thing. When we read, when we talk, when we write, when we share. All those times . . . Children will learn what it is you are the most consistent with in your teaching."

In addition to elevating language in the classroom, on Monday through Thursday students work on their nightly writing notebooks, which Mrs. Hamner collects and reads over the weekend. She responds to the good work that she sees in the notebooks by writing words of praise, and questions and ideas that the writing brings to her mind. At the same time, the students' notebooks yield information about the areas of language mechanics, vocabulary, or story structure that students are struggling with. Mrs. Hamner uses this evaluative information from nightly writing to select "morning message" texts. These are whole class exercises that are both fun and that

BOX 6.1 ELEVATING VOCABULARY VIA THE WORD BANK

The word bank is an active thesaurus that Mrs. Hamner created out of large laminated sheets of colored oaktag. The back of each sheet has a hook, so it can be hung on the chalk tray at the base of the blackboard.

Each colored sheet is a "word bank" of synonyms for words that children commonly use. Word banks have been created for many words, including *said* (e.g., *replied, gasped, whispered, added, exclaimed . . .*), attractive words (e.g., *beautiful, elegant, gorgeous, exquisite lovely, graceful . . .*), action words (e.g., *scurried*

slithered, scampered, raced, romped, stomped, scrambled . . .).

As Mrs. Hamner reviews drafts of children's writing, or as children speak, she'll ask them to come up with other ways to express the same ideas. To help them, she'll exclaim, "Let's bring out the word bank!" Then the children excitedly go to the word bank storage area, take out the sheets Mrs. Hamner suggests, and affix them below the blackboard. The word bank then becomes a resource for the rest of writing time.

The word bank builds students' vocabulary by providing synonyms for common words.

provide practice on needed skills. For example, if Mrs. Hamner sees quotation marks are missing from nightly writing, she will make sure that the next several morning messages incorporate opportunities to practice that kind of punctuation. As discussed in the following section, celebrating and sharing good work also elevates students' language.

Celebrate

Sharing good examples of student work with the whole class is vital to the success of language artists. Mrs. Hamner often stops the whole class to discuss something special that a student has done. "Class," she says, with a voice full of delight, "Listen to Nolan's fabulous metaphor: 'Her face was as green as an evergreen tree!'" Celebrating exemplary student work provides accessible models that elevate students' language skills. Nan Hamner observed, "Somebody is going to have beautiful handwriting. Someone is going to remember to indent. Someone's going to use an extraordinary word. They're your model. That's very important. That's really strong. It's really powerful."

Mrs. Hamner asserts that when students write for the teacher, they have an audience of only one person. However, when the teacher shares good work with the class, the class becomes the audience. This peer audience is extremely important, because "students learn so much from one another." Celebrating therefore also builds a classroom culture and a school culture geared toward appreciating excellent work.

Evaluate

In order to understand how students are progressing and to know what topics or problems to emphasize in teaching, it's essential to evaluate children's skills on an ongoing basis. "You can't just do it on page 24 and page 48, and in June," comments Mrs. Hamner. "[You need to] evaluate all the time. Whether it's when they're speaking, or when they're writing, or when they're doing their homework, you have to evaluate where that child is."

Ongoing evaluation reveals what aspects of language need to be elevated. It guides particular choices for morning message and nightly writing. It fine tunes the selection and celebration of particular kinds of model work from students. In short, ongoing evaluation is central to knowing students' current level of knowledge and skill and to elevating those levels.

Mrs. Hamner emphasizes that evaluation is "the hard part." It's fun to watch children develop detailed drawings and to elevate their language skill in part by celebrating the good writing that they do. But, keeping one's eyes and ears attuned to students' current levels and plugging in learning activities to move them forward requires a great deal of thought and attention. "It takes time to go through children's writing and to genuinely look for things that are going to cause the children to progress." However, the result of such evaluation, alongside celebration and elevation, is student work of remarkable quality.

WHAT HAPPENS DURING LANGUAGE ARTISTS?

The classroom has to be a special place. . . .
It should be an exciting place, and it should be a literate environment.
—Nan Hamner

Helping children to appreciate and acquire the means of expression is a goal that fills Nan Hamner's classroom. The room resembles a children's library. The walls are covered with posters of artists and reproductions of their work. There are also illustrations of the skeletal and muscular systems, a "mural" of construction paper that resembles the *Peaceable Kingdom* by Edward Hicks, and a life-size colorful, soft sculpture of an Egyptian mummy. There are display areas for all kinds of collections: children's dioramas of different artists, miniature shoes and glass slippers, book reports written on scrolls and stored in decorated cans, and children's drawings of ant tunnels. There are rotating bookshelves, terraced bookshelves, and regular bookcases filled with fiction, nonfiction, and poetry. And there are many different areas for reading and writing: clusters of desks, Mrs. Hamner's wicker chair which is big enough for two students to share, a platform covered in shaggy carpet. The room is organized this way for a purpose: to evoke the expression of ideas, to learn how ideas are expressed, and to support young students' capacity to express their thinking.

The Hamners and many of their colleagues (including Mrs. Chadwell, whose Math Labs are described in Chapter 5) have assembled collections of books and other materials over the course of several years. There is a storage area near the teachers' lounge where salvaged treasures are shared and where teachers can exchange materials with one another. Materials play an important role in most of the teachers' rooms. Mrs. Hamner explains why: There should be various materials and books about everything— "because everybody's not interested in just one thing."

Within this exciting environment, Nan Hamner offers a set of literacy-building activities that continue throughout the school year. This section details some of these activities, especially morning message, nightly writing, and squiggle books. When linked together with the strategies of elevating, celebrating, and evaluating student work, these activities help children to become language artists.

BOX 6.2 MATERIALS FOR LANGUAGE ARTISTS ACTIVITIES

The materials needed for Language Artists are largely simple and inexpensive. Most are readily available in schools. (Optional items are marked with an asterisk.)

For morning message:

- Chalk and blackboard.
- Morning message texts. These are readily developed at no cost.

For nightly writing:

- Wide-ruled spiral notebooks. Mrs. Hamner uses 60-sheet wide-ruled notebooks, and students may go through several in a year.
- Stickers.* (Mrs. Hamner uses these to highlight and comment upon student work and as a means of communicating joyfully with her students.)

For squiggle books:

- Wide-ruled notebooks. (Students may use several 60-sheet notebooks in a year.)
- Colored pencils.
- Stickers.*
- Plastic bins or other containers or shelving area for storing students' squiggle books in the classroom.

For the word bank:

- Colored oaktag or posterboard-sized sheets.
- Hooks to affix sheets to the chalkboard ledge or to a "clothesline" or other display area.

To support the development of language artists it is also useful to have:

- A wide selection of reading materials in the classroom: fiction, poetry, and nonfiction on a broad range of subject matters.
- Posters, prints, and reproductions of artwork. These provide opportunities for children to learn about art, to acquire art concepts and vocabulary, and to be challenged to use language descriptively and expressively. These prints can sometimes be borrowed from libraries.

Morning Message

Morning messages are brief texts—usually six or seven sentences—that are prepared by the teacher. The text is the focus of a 15–20 minute daily lesson that gives the whole class opportunities to learn grammar, figurative language, and thinking skills. Mrs. Hamner notes that because of morning message, "The [student's] paper doesn't have to go home with red marks on it." Instead, "We all sit side by side. We all feel successful." Daily practice throughout the year makes it possible for children to acquire new language skills and use language correctly.

Morning Message Texts

There are many different kinds of morning messages. For primary-age students at the beginning of the school year, it's helpful to use messages that have a "frame." In these messages, most or all of the lines start out the

---

BOX 6.3 MORNING MESSAGE TEXT

The text for morning message is short—typically five or six sentences.
Here is a typical example:

May I have your eyes on the board?
Did you know I only have eyes for you?
Did you know I've got my eye on you?
Did you know I can pull the wool over your eyes?
Did you know we can see things eye to eye?
I'm all ears gasped the class.

The middle lines of this morning message have "a frame," an opening that remains consistent across several sentences. This assists early readers, helping them to feel confident and to participate in the reading. The little line drawing also provides a bit of help for young readers. The last line remains unpunctuated to provide the class with ongoing practice in editing and punctuation.

same way. This structure helps beginning readers to participate, elevates their word-recognition vocabulary, and builds their confidence. The morning message also incorporates a few, very simple line drawings. Together with the frame, these "little picture cues" support and engage young readers (see Box 6.3).

The content of a morning message may teach about language itself, like the example below, or about art, music, science, or other subjects. The content may also present problem-solving skills, such as analogies or brainstorming. Alongside such content, the lines of the message are used to teach grammar, punctuation, and other essential language skills to elevate students' language.

> It's time for hilarious hyperbole!
> "I'm so hungry, I could eat a bear!" said Ryan.
> "I must have walked a million miles!" puffed Sara.
> "I almost died laughing!" giggled Talya.
> "I have tons of baseball cards!" boasted Adam.
> I didn't sleep a wink yawned Rip Van Winkle.

This morning's message text focuses on hyperbole (other language-based morning messages explore similes, metaphors, antonyms, alliteration, onomatopoeia, and homophones). At the same time, the example helps to build vocabulary by introducing alternatives to the word *said*. Finding synonyms for common words, partly through the word bank (Box 6.1) is one way of elevating children's language. In this example, the last line is intentionally left without punctuation. Every morning message leaves out several punctuation marks to give the class practice in editing, grammar, and punctuation.

In the next example, the content is quite different. It opens with two Spanish sentences. This supports one of the school's goals: to foster Spanish–English bilingualism among all children. After those sentences, the content is aimed at fostering children's critical thinking skills. It does so by drawing their attention to similarities and differences in the paired objects included in each line.

> Buenos días clase!
> Hoy es martes magnífico.
> Think about it! a pencil and chalk
> Think about it! a comb and brush
> Think about it! soap and toothpaste
> Think about it! a magazine and newspaper
> What about a bird and butterfly _____ Stephen

Because morning message is done every day, the children encounter and review individual topics many times. By the end of the second year in Mrs. Hamner's class, the children know how to punctuate. They also have a storehouse of synonyms, vocabulary, and figurative language, and they have worked on a range of critical thinking skills.

Using Morning Message Texts

Morning message is written on the board before the students come in each morning. After coats and backpacks have been put away and greetings exchanged, the whole class gathers in front of the board. In line with her method of using good examples and celebrating student work, Mrs. Hamner picks a relatively strong reader to read the whole message aloud. Hearing the message read well celebrates good work. It also elevates reading and speaking skills by modeling these for the whole class.

Then the whole class and Mrs. Hamner read the message aloud with expression! Mrs. Hamner then leads a discussion about the text. For instance, if there is a message about hyperbole, Mrs. Hamner asks, "Who knows some other hyperboles?" and "Who wants to share a hyperbole that you have made up?" She will talk about what it means to exaggerate, and the children ask questions and give examples in response to Mrs. Hamner's questions and to each others'. In the morning message text that contained paired items, such as pencil and chalk or comb and brush, the teacher and class discuss the similarities and differences of each pair. Through this and other morning messages that incorporate similarities and differences, children come to see and use such comparisons as a way of thinking and problem solving.

Mrs. Hamner also points to other aspects of language that are notable in the message. For instance, in the above example on hyperbole, she highlights the many words that were used instead of *said*. This helps to build children's vocabulary, and they learn to choose words that really express their thoughts and convey their ideas.

Next, Mrs. Hamner draws the students' attention to the line that needs to be punctuated: "How many mistakes are in that line?" Children silently answer by holding up fingers for the number of mistakes they believe the line contains. The number varies across the children. "Who wants to try it?" She then calls on a child to punctuate the last line. The rest of the class is reminded not to correct the mistakes for the student at the board. "Don't steal the wrinkle from anyone else's brain," Mrs. Hamner tells them. "Let Sara do the work so she can get smarter." The children observe closely to see how Sara punctuates the line on the blackboard. When she finishes, Mrs. Hamner asks, "Did she get all the mistakes?" If there are mistakes, the other youngsters will suggest what still needs to be corrected in the last line, and the student at the board puts in the corrections. When the line is perfect, Mrs. Hamner asks, "Who thought six mistakes?" Hands go up. "You were right!" Then, at Mrs. Hamner's prompting, the class zestfully acknowledges the work of the student at the board, "Good for you, Sara!!!"

After the text is corrected, the class spends time building phonemic awareness. Mrs. Hamner may use the morning message to point out some letter blends. She may note patterns in silent *e*'s or point out other unusual silent letters. She may draw attention to a combination of vowels and how those combinations are pronounced. She may talk about root words and endings, such as *-ing* or *-er*. Her choice of examples is guided by her own ongoing evaluation of student work. This helps her to know where students' current knowledge is, where they are experiencing difficulty, and what information will foster progress. Because morning message is a daily event, and one that the children pursue with enthusiasm, the teacher can continue to address decoding and grammar challenges, while also expanding vocabulary, figurative language, and critical thinking skills, until the students have grasped them.

Nightly Writing

In Nan Hamner's class and throughout the Governor Bent School, students write every night, Monday through Thursday, in their nightly writing notebooks. Nightly writing, like morning message, helps build their literacy through regular practice. In fact, the two activities work together in a very systematic way:

- Nightly Writing enables children to apply some of what was learned during morning message and other parts of the day.
- Mrs. Hamner evaluates nightly writing notebooks over the weekend to inform the following week's instruction. This evaluation helps her to highlight specific information during morning message, and during other times of the day, that will elevate the students' literacy skills.

Nightly Writing Prompts

Originally nightly writing was very open-ended. Students could write about anything they wished, as long as they spent about fifteen minutes writing in their notebooks. Some children would make lists, and others would write long journal entries. To enhance expectations and to give

---

BOX 6.4 NIGHTLY WRITING PROMPTS

Here are a few of the thought-provoking nightly writing prompts that Mrs. Hamner has used:

1. Imagine you are a successful author. What advice would you give students to help them to be successful writers as well?
2. Most American children watch about three-and-one-half hours of television each day. A typical American child goes to school for six hours a day. If suddenly there were no more TV, what would you do with your time?
3. If you could be an animal for a day, which one would you be? How would you spend the day?

- If you could be an animal for a day, which one would you be? How would you spend the day? *Lovely!*

If I could be any animals in the would I would be a bird so I could fly. I would sor across the plans. Beautiful! Then I would rest for a while. Then I guss I have to eat? So I will. Then I would fly somerore *I'm hungry!*

children some focus, the teachers began to send children home with "little ideas" for nightly writing that would help them build specific skills. For instance, students have been asked to write five different story beginnings.

Most recently, Nan Hamner explained, the teachers started "giving things that went just a little bit further. We started giving things that were just difficult enough—right there on the edge of what they could do on their own in terms of critical thinking—that the students would almost have to talk to their parents about it." By bringing parents into a discussion with their children about the nightly writing topic, students are more likely to grow in their knowledge.

As with morning message, the topics used for nightly writing are wide-ranging. Some, like the assignment on story beginnings, focus directly on the topic of writing. Others draw from science, social studies, and other subject areas. This range of topics addresses students' different interests and strengths while still giving them practice in writing. (Box 6.4 gives examples of some of the nightly writing prompts used in Mrs. Hamner's class.)

Running a Program of Nightly Writing

Each student has a spiral notebook especially for his or her nightly writing practice. The writing assignments for an entire week are given out on Mondays. Sometimes students cut and paste the night's assignment on the top page of the notebook before they begin to write.

Mrs. Hamner collects the students' nightly writing notebooks each Friday. She reads through each student's work between Friday and Monday. Among the things Mrs. Hamner notices in her review:

- Is language being used expressively?
- Is the student using a varied and interesting vocabulary (e.g., are there synonyms used for common words, such as *big, nice, pretty,* and *said*?)?
- Is the student using descriptive language?
- What patterns of difficulties are present in the students' language mechanics, spelling, punctuation, and grammar?

BOX 6.5 STARTING NIGHTLY WRITING

It's helpful to give each child a notebook for nightly writing.

- Explain that using this notebook every night will help them to become writers who can say exactly what they're thinking in a powerful and interesting way.
- Discuss with the children the qualities of good writing that you want them to develop, such as using a varied vocabulary. Brainstorm examples of varied vocabulary (What are some of the many ways to say someone is "happy"?) and share examples of interesting vocabulary from students' work or children's literature. Ask the children what they think of the examples and emphasize that this kind of vocabulary makes writing more intriguing and expressive.
- Explain that you are going to give them some ideas to write about Monday through Thursday and that your own homework will be to review and respond to their work over the weekend.

The evaluative information gleaned from this review helps Mrs. Hamner to select morning message texts that will help build particular kinds of skills. This evaluation also helps her to know what to emphasize within a particular morning message. For example, if she sees that children are misspelling short vowel sounds, she will emphasize those sounds during the next week's morning messages.

Alongside this evaluation process, Mrs. Hamner responds in the nightly writing notebooks to the work that the student is doing. She has a variety of ways she responds to the work:

- She underlines things that she really feels are well done and remarks in writing to the student, "Beautiful," "Interesting," "Wonderful," "Lovely!" "Excellent ideas!"
- She indicates when she agrees with the student by writing things like, "Of course!" "Absolutely," "I feel that way, too!"
- She responds to students' ideas with ideas of her own. For example, after a student provided a long list of alternatives to watching television, Mrs. Hamner wrote: "I don't think you are going to have any time left to watch TV!"
- She also adorns the students' notebooks with an array of stickers related to their writing, and she very occasionally affixes a coveted Super Writer Award sticker!

Perhaps controversially, Nan Hamner does not underscore mistakes in spelling, mechanics, or other areas. Instead, as the example in Box 6.4 illustrates, Mrs. Hamner focuses on what the children have truly done well. "The things that are written [in response to the students' work] are all very honest. I don't say 'your handwriting is beautiful,' if it's not. I don't say 'this is extraordinary work,' if it's not."

Instead of highlighting the mistakes or falsely praising work that needs improvement, Mrs. Hamner uses information from the students' nightly writing notebooks to select particular morning messages and to build particular language arts skills that need developing. The key is to "Evaluate all the time. . . . You have to evaluate where that child is. And you have to plug things in that will elevate his or her skill."

By celebrating and sharing what the students do well, Mrs. Hamner keeps them engaged in writing, and builds their appreciation for good language. By providing many different kinds of topics, she keeps a variety of learners engaged. By evaluating the ways the students are using language, she can select activities and emphasize information to elevate their skill and knowledge.

Squiggle Books

Squiggle books are spiral-bound notebooks that contain detailed, colored-pencil illustrations and stories that represent a student's best work. The books take their name from the "squiggle," a black line drawing that Mrs. Hamner places on a right-hand side page of a child's notebook. Each squiggle serves as an inspiration for a student to create a more elaborate illustration and to develop a detailed story to accompany it. This leaves room on the facing left-hand page onto which the student will copy a final, edited version of a story.

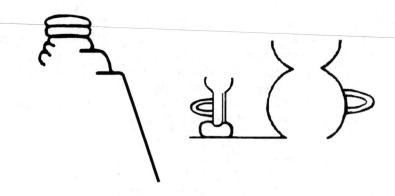

FIGURE 6.1   Examples of Squiggle Drawings

Some squiggles are almost representational, suggesting particular objects, such as pumpkins or bows. Others, like the examples in Figure 6.1, are more abstract and open-ended. Squiggles range in size, but generally fill a space smaller than a 3″ × 3″ section of a page.

In the course of the squiggle book activity, students learn about story elements: setting, characters, and the plot. They learn that story plots have a beginning, where settings and characters are often introduced, and a middle, where characters encounter a problem, and about endings, where the problem is resolved. Moreover, they learn about the writing process of drafting, editing, and revising, and they use this process to develop and orchestrate their own story elements during squiggle book time.

Creating Squiggle Books

Mrs. Hamner uses the squiggle book activity three times a week, typically for an hour each session (and never less than forty-five minutes). A student continues to work on the squiggle drawing and story for as many days as necessary to do a good job on the assignment. This is in line with the notion that the squiggle book is for best work, and best work takes time, effort, and lots of practice.

Children typically elaborate the squiggle into a detailed illustration before they draft the story. In Mrs. Hamner's classroom, the children employ "magic coloring" in their illustrations. This is a technique Mrs. Hamner learned from one of her students. In magic coloring, the students color small sections at a time using small strokes with a colored pencil. All the white space is filled in this way. This technique helps students to avoid hasty scribbling and enables them to produce beautiful illustrations that they feel proud of.

Creating a detailed illustration helps the student to conjure up a detailed story. However, the story itself is not begun in the squiggle book. It is first drafted on other paper. The draft is reviewed, edited, and reviewed again by the student and Mrs. Hamner. Only when the story reflects the student's best work does he or she copy it into the squiggle notebook to accompany the drawing.

BOX 6.6 CREATING SQUIGGLE DRAWINGS

Squiggles provide the inspiration for drawing. When a student is ready to start a new squiggle, Mrs. Hamner draws a squiggle in the students' spiral bound squiggle notebook. Mrs. Hamner has a special technique: She uses the right-hand page and the page behind it for the squiggle. She puts dots of white glue on the edges of the page behind the right-hand page and seals the two pages together. This gives the child a stronger surface on which to do the drawings and prevents any color from bleeding through. Also, by using the right-hand page, if a child feels that she's made a mistake that "she can't live with," then she can remove that illustration without damaging any other part of the notebook.

As children work on their stories and illustrations, a great amount of celebrating goes on. Mrs. Hamner will call the class's attention to strong examples that individual children are producing. She'll note details in the illustration, for example the use of a horizon line, or the placement of characters below the horizon. (Highlighting these details draws in students' naturalist intelligence and requires them to think about the objects in the world and how to represent these.) Mrs. Hamner will also read with great expression the opening of a particular story, or note appreciatively how a child is using dialog.

All of this celebrating provides models for students and helps guide them toward producing strong work. "I think the most important thing, and I know we keep coming back to this, is celebrating and sharing of their work. It is the thing that is the most powerful, because they see other children doing it. . . . Someone has wonderful coloring, wonderful detail. And you just have to find who that child is, and they're your model."

A great deal of preparation enables children to write good stories in Nan Hamner's class. At the beginning of the year, Mrs. Hamner seeks to elevate their capacity for storywriting by helping them learn the elements of the

---

BOX 6.7 TWO DRAWINGS BY CHRISTINA, A SECOND GRADER

Halloween   The Three Fluffy Rabbits

Christina drew the first squiggle, "Halloween," early in the fall at another public school in Albuquerque. The second was done about one month later, after Christina had transferred to Governor Bent because her parents believed she was capable of much better work.

The second squiggle, produced at Governer Bent, is rich with detail. Its blue sky background has clouds and a smiling sun. Its green foreground has several trees of different shapes (including the tree-shaped squiggle), three rabbits, two of which are speaking to each other, and carrots. Appropriate to a story about rabbits, there is also an underground. It incorporates, among other things, tunnels, insects, and some furnishings for the rabbit inhabitants. The accompanying story has a vivid setting, uses dialog, and uses a rich and varied vocabulary.

story: "You have to tell them what those things mean: Setting, what does a setting mean? Where the story takes place. What are some different kinds of settings that you can use? The same with characters, and names for characters. I think the hard part is trying to do it all at once. Approach it a small amount at one time, rather than trying to do the whole story, because [initially] that can be too frustrating."

In Mrs. Hamner's class, children learn how to develop each part of the story. For example, in class they brainstorm many types of settings ("At a nuclear power plant, one day in the spring . . ." was the opener offered by one little boy), and they consider how places and times can be described. In their nightly writings, they practice writing only the beginnings of stories. Then they tackle the difficult work of story problems and solutions. With a great deal of elevating, celebrating, and evaluating all the children can orchestrate these elements into high-quality stories by the end of their second year in Mrs. Hamner's class.

Nan Hamner notes that this approach to writing, using squiggles or "illustarters," has been used for quite some time with elementary students. However, the quality of work that the children at Governor Bent produce in response to squiggles is truly remarkable. It is important to understand that the activity, the squiggle, does not make for this quality. The emphasis on quality work throughout the Governor Bent School, and the strategies of celebrating, evaluating, and elevating are crucial to the students' achievement.

These emphases are powerfully demonstrated in the work of Christina, a second-grade student whose work appears in Box 6.7. Christina's work helps to highlight how the same child given the same curriculum (squiggle books) can perform in markedly different ways. The differences in Christina's performance were spurred by teaching strategies exemplified by Nan Hamner and also by the school culture, in which hard work (such as daily and nightly practice) is the norm and beautiful student work is shared and celebrated.

REVISITING THE FRAMEWORKS

> *Marilyn Davenport did for me what all of us as teachers should do for children,*
> *and that is look for and nurture strengths.*
> —Nan Hamner

MI in This Unit

Multiple intelligences provides a tool for thinking about students' intellectual strengths and the different ways they can learn. Language artists readily engages different intelligences, especially students' linguistic and spatial intelligences. This combination provides a route into language that may prove especially fruitful for youngsters with spatial strengths who are often poorly served in school (Winner, 1996). In addition, though less obviously so, there is a strong interpersonal component to this work (and, we would argue, to most effective classroom teaching!). Celebrating and sharing work serves as an ongoing opportunity to understand others' strengths and learn from the good work that other students exhibit. Fine motor skill, needed to produce detailed drawings, taps students' bodily-kinesthetic intelligence, and the naturalist intelligence is integrated as well in close observation, and production, of visual artwork. Through morning message and nightly writing exercises that emphasize problem solving, analogies, and syllogisms, there are regular opportunities for students to use logical-mathematical intelligence. A range of other intelligences may be employed as well, depending on the nightly writing assignments that are used and on individual students' choices for squiggle books. Keep in mind that there is no point in using every intelligence, if doing so requires superficial activities that do not strengthen skills or enable students to produce quality work.

Entry Points in This Unit

The Entry Points Framework provides a tool for thinking about curriculum and the ways that a discipline or topic can be made accessible to different learners. Language Artists is a curriculum that can be accessed through several entry points.

Linguistic	Spatial	Interpersonal	Intrapersonal	Logical-Mathematical	Musical	Naturalist	Bodily-Kinesthetic	ACTIVITIES
								Morning Message:
X								• Students learn new vocabulary, language, concepts, decoding skills, and language mechanics.
X	X							• Students use pictures as cues to help make sense of text.
X				X				• Students learn critical thinking and problem-solving skills.
X		X	X					• Students learn from hearing and celebrating others' good work.
								Nightly Writing:
X								• Students learn new vocabulary, and practice story elements.
X			X			X		• Students often write about their own activities, thoughts, feelings, and observations.
X				X				• Students are often given brain teasers or other writing prompts that draw on problem solving.
								Squiggle Book:
X								• Students practice story elements and use detailed vocabulary.
X		X	X					• Students learn from hearing and celebrating others good work.
	X					X	X	• Detailed illustrations and magic coloring require observational, spatial, and fine motor skills.
X	X					X		• Students view and discuss visual arts.

FIGURE 6.2   Multiple Intelligences Used During Language Artists

Narrative: Students are encouraged to write stories and to understand story structure, especially in their squiggle books but also in their nightly writing.

Aesthetic: The celebration of detail and beauty, both in students' writing and drawing, reflects the aesthetic entry point.

Experiential: In their squiggle books, students undertake the same experience as a professional writer: drafting, reviewing, editing, revising, and producing a final version.

Logical-Quantitative: The nightly writing assignments often ask students to deal with logical problem solving and numbers. Analogies and other problem-solving approaches used in morning message also access this intelligence.

Interpersonal: Throughout the classroom, students look at and consider others' strengths and learn from their exemplary work.

Compass Point Practices in This Unit

The Compass Point Practices serve as a tool for building and understanding organizational practices that engage multiple intelligences in ways associated with benefits for students. Mrs. Hamner's classroom is an organization that incorporates several Compass Point Practices.

Tool: In Language Artists, MI serves as a tool to help students understand and produce high-quality work in art and language arts. The students engage in this curriculum through several intelligences, but MI theory is not the focus of the curriculum.

Arts: Squiggle books involve students in the process of developing rich and detailed drawings. Developing an imaginative drawing spurs children to undertake a detailed and imaginative story. Looking at and discussing artwork also helps children to learn about art and find words to express what they see.

Choice: Guided or controlled choice is used to support student engagement as well as the development of their skill. In Language Artists, all children are expected to produce squiggle books. However, they are free to develop their own illustrations and stories. Free choice may be constrained in order to advance students' skill. For example, Mrs. Hamner decided to give her students specific questions for nightly writing to build their problem-solving and critical-thinking skills.

Collaboration: Collaboration in the Language Artists curriculum happens in part because all the teachers in the Governor Bent School use nightly writing (as well as nightly reading), and many also use squiggle books. These schoolwide activities encourage teachers to learn from each other (much as Mrs. Hamner celebrates students' good work). A key collaborator for Nan Hamner is her classroom aide, Bobbi McCuddihy, and also her husband, Jay Hamner, who teaches fourth grade at Governor Bent. These close collaborators are essential sources for feedback on her classroom. Collaboration also occurs as teachers visit each others' classrooms and share materials.

Readiness: Mrs. Hamner supports students to do challenging tasks through preparatory processes. For example, she gives them practice in writing story openings and in drafting and revising before she expects them to produce a final polished story. Through daily practice in figurative language, spelling, grammar, and punctuation, she prepares them to use and appreciate nuanced language.

Culture: Nan Hamner's classroom is one in which there is a belief that all students have strengths, where different strengths are shared and appreciated, where joy and hard work—effort and practice over time—are the norm, and where beautiful work is celebrated.

CHAPTER

7

The John F. Kennedy School

The curriculum example from the John F. Kennedy School is called Schneider's Ink. The unit was developed by Donna Schneider, who teaches in a full-inclusion class of twenty-five third graders. Schneider's Ink is a hands-on, publishing business. Students get sales orders, lay out text, design materials using computer software, handle the finances, and generate printed materials that are actually used for school performances, banners, and other purposes. This real-world unit draws on many different intelligences to help build students' skills in language arts, mathematics, computing, graphic design, planning, and teamwork. Before starting the detailed description of Schneider's Ink, this chapter provides an overview of the school in which the unit is taught. Using the Compass Point Practices as a framework, the chapter describes schoolwide practices that support this unit and other high-quality work by students and teachers at the JFK School.

OVERVIEW OF THE JOHN F. KENNEDY SCHOOL

The John F. Kennedy Elementary School is in Brewster, New York, a town about fifty miles north of New York City. Brewster was historically an agricultural community. More recently, because it is the last stop on the Metroline Rail from Manhattan, it has attracted many city commuters, including

The John F. Kennedy Elementary School, Brewster, New York

firefighters and police officers, as well as professionals and their families. The area surrounding the school reflects this history, with its mix of older, worn farmhouses, suburban homes, and shopping areas. The JFK School is set off a winding road, which still has a country feel to it. It is a sprawling, one-story brown brick structure, built in the 1960s, with an enormous parking lot in front. In back, playground equipment of various eras occupies large grassy tracts. Just inside the main door is the school's office, with a secretary's station fronting the corridor behind a glass wall, something like a bank teller's window. Nearby there's a large picture of John Kennedy, with his young daughter Caroline, and other images of the president for whom the school is named. Beyond that, classrooms are spread out over many long and wide cement-block corridors.

Until the 1998–1999 school year, the John F. Kennedy School had classes for students in kindergarten through grade 4. It then became a school for kindergarten through third grade. The school population remains large, about 800 students, and typically has twenty-five students per class. Almost all the students are from white, middle- and upper-middle-class families. There is a very small percentage of students on free and reduced lunch, and there are a few students whose families have immigrated and who are enrolled in bilingual education. Depending on enrollments, there are about seven classrooms per grade. In addition to about thirty-five regular classroom teachers, there are full-time teachers for art, music, physical education, and library. There is also an enrichment teacher who supports the development of students' gifts and talents throughout the school. Each of the kindergarten classrooms has a full-time aide.

About three classrooms at each grade level have fully-included students who have a wide range of physical and/or learning disabilities. In each of the full-inclusion classrooms, there is also a full-time aide. In addition, there are sometimes full-time aides for individual students with profound mental or physical challenges. An occupational therapist and a speech and language teacher also work part-time with students and teachers in these classrooms.

JFK's principal, Natalie McKenna, grew up near Brewster. Although she has traveled and worked in other areas, she served in the Brewster Public Schools for twenty-two years, including ten years as a principal. Brewster's school district emphasizes equal educational opportunity and preparation for the future. However, Ms. McKenna's goes beyond the district's mission to emphasize the value of providing strong, inclusionary classrooms for students with special needs. Ms. McKenna remarked that, in her school, "we have no resource rooms and no self-contained special education classes."

This full-inclusion approach is reflected in Schneider's Ink, the rest of the work that Donna Schneider does in her classroom, and in other classrooms at each grade level that serve special needs students together with other students. Students are educated to their fullest possible potential alongside all the other students in the school. The result of this approach is that the JFK School was named one of four model inclusion schools for the state of New York in the early 1990s. The school also shows strong results for all students, regularly scoring in the top few percentiles for the state's test of reading and math. Many of the school's special needs students exceed state averages on these same assessments.

COMPASS POINT PRACTICES

Clearly, the JFK school is enabling a great variety of students to learn at a high level. It is also supporting teachers to do extraordinary work. The approaches and qualities that enable teachers and students to draw on their strengths and produce such strong work can be understood in terms of the Compass Point Practices, described below. We review the Compass Point Practices in an order that lets the John F. Kennedy School's experiences be clearly told.

Readiness

The JFK school began drawing on MI in 1991–1992. Given the school's emphasis on, and success with, inclusion of students with disabilities, it was somewhat surprising for us to learn that the initial motivation to incorporate MI came first from the school's part-time teacher of the gifted, Rochelle Kaplan. Ms. Kaplan, who also served as a part-time art teacher, attended a summer institute in 1991, called Confratute, which is held each year at the University of Connecticut. The institute advocates a schoolwide enrichment program developed by Professor Joseph Renzulli (Renzulli & Reis, 1997). At that institute, one workshop focused on the theory of multiple intelligences. The theory resonated strongly with ideas that Ms. Kaplan, Ms. McKenna, and other teachers at the school had. As Rochelle Kaplan put it, MI offered "a good extension" of the staff's existing ideas about the diversity of students' strengths and its emphasis on inclusion.

When Rochelle Kaplan returned from Confratute, she shared what she had learned with Ms. McKenna, who decided to have a series of additional workshops around MI for the entire staff. Ms. McKenna and Ms. Kaplan agreed that it would be useful to introduce the whole school to the theory. To do so, Ms. McKenna brought in the Confratute workshop leader, Dr. Susan Baum.

Susan Baum has a particular way of introducing the theory: She first groups teachers according to areas in which they say they are weak, for example, building, art, acting, music, writing, and dancing and then has each group develop and present a project. After this, she asks them to form groups according to their strengths, and has each group again carry out and present a project. This approach had an electrifying impact on the JFK teachers. They *felt* as well as deeply understood the fear and sense of incompetence experienced by students who are compelled to work over and over again in areas where they struggle. They also felt the sense of accomplishment and pride in good work experienced by students who excel in doing what is asked of them. From this, the staff came to recognize more strongly the importance of providing learning experiences that enabled all students to work on their weaknesses but also to work in and support their areas of strength. (In line with this understanding, Donna Schneider says that the way she moves students forward is to "work with their strengths, and expose them to their weaknesses.")

Bringing a workshop to the whole school was important, Natalie McKenna argued. "Everybody heard the same message. I really believe that's important to hear the same message at the same time. Then . . . the staff can have common conversations afterward that will feed on each other and feed on and build ideas." The message was clearly taken up: Teachers of inclusion students, as well as regular classroom teachers, clearly felt that the theory offered a helpful framework for working with students and for enabling them to use their strengths to learn. MI supported the overall goals of the school; it was an idea that was welcomed. In addition, Ms. McKenna, like the other school principals in this volume, have gained the trust of their staff about which ideas matter: "I've been in this system long enough that people know who I am and what I'm about. I don't think I've brought anything frivolous into the building."

After the first, schoolwide conversation, Sue Baum and Rochelle Kaplan worked with teachers at their grade levels to help them identify constructive uses for the theory. Whole school conversations continued at faculty meetings. These provided opportunities for exchanges across the building and for new staff to learn. They also underscored that MI is "a very big item in this building."

MI Is Used as a Tool

At the JFK School, MI didn't create the philosophy or structures needed for inclusion, but, said Ms. McKenna, "MI was a great extension of that." It "gave people more skills with which to deliver [curriculum and services] to children." In essence, the theory acts as a tool to help teachers understand the range of individual students strengths, and to find opportunities for them to become engaged through their strengths and to work on their weaknesses.

How the teachers used the tool varied from classroom to classroom. Teachers were encouraged to put the theory into practice in ways that made the most sense to them and to share their experiences and learn from them. Nevertheless, some common approaches emerged. For example throughout the kindergartens and in other classrooms in the early grades, many teachers developed MI-influenced activity centers. The centers have different emphases: building, art, nature, music, story, numbers, and drama. In each of these centers, children can draw on one or more cluster of strengths while also working to develop skills in disciplinary areas.

The centers served at least two purposes. First, by rotating through the different centers, the children had opportunities to participate in activities in which their strengths were drawn on and to work in their areas of need with the support of the teacher and classroom aide. Second, centers supported assessment and planning. Following center activities, teachers, aides, and students reflected on and assessed the learning that took place. The students were encouraged to review what they did and how they did it, and to represent this verbally and in pictures in kindergarten, and in writing once they entered first grade. Through these reflections and the teachers' and aides' observations, the educators gained a clearer understanding of how each child learned and could use that information to plan other activities to advance their skills and knowledge.

In the older grades, activity centers gave way to classroom-wide projects-based curricula, such as Schneider's Ink. In these units, students do high-quality work and come to an understanding of the topic at hand, while using their strengths and addressing their weaknesses.

Sometimes centers specified tasks that needed to be accomplished. A nature center might require observing different leaves under a magnifying glass, drawing them, and discussing how they are alike and how they are different. In other instances, centers gave small groups of children a chance to work on a child-directed activity using different materials, such as legos, blocks, storybooks, rocks, and minerals. Centers could also be linked together to support understanding within an overarching class topic, like spring or butterflies. (Centers that are used to support themes are described in the Rivers Study, Chapter 3.).

Along with MI, other tools were important to the school. One key tool is assessment. Ms. McKenna explained that once educators begin to teach and access the curriculum in multiple ways, it's important to incorporate assessments that fairly reflect these broader approaches. (Howard Gardner [1991a] has elsewhere referred to this as "intelligence-fair assessment.") In the kindergarten learning centers, for example, teachers assess students by using center-related evaluation forms. At regular intervals, teachers, working with volunteers and aides, observe and help children in the different centers and, using the evaluation form, record how individual students carried out their work and what individual students had to say about their experiences in the centers. In this way, teachers have information from their own and others' observations to help them understand how students are performing in a range of different learning experiences.

At the JFK School, many teachers of students in older grades make use of rubrics to support and assess students' efforts to do high-quality work in a range of areas. For example, as we'll see in the next chapter, Mrs. Schneider has students use rubrics to assess their publications. Rubrics are tailored to fit the qualities that matter in a particular piece of work. For instance, in a publishing business, it's important not just that all the words are spelled properly and the text is nicely displayed, but also that images are executed well and orders are delivered on time. A rubric can assess and support the salient elements of actual work. Actual work, such as a publishing business, in turn draws on many different strengths.

Another important tool for teachers at the JFK School was Joseph Renzulli's Talent Development Model (Renzulli & Reis, 1997). This model is aimed at promoting students' and teachers' active engagement and enjoyment in learning, and moves teachers away from the more traditional "chalk and talk" presentation. Given its emphasis on more hands-on and real-world problem solving, this model is one that works well with MI.

Culture

> *We have a very energetic staff here, a risk-taking staff. . . . One of the things you have to give people is the freedom to make mistakes and to be risk takers . . .*
>
> —Natalie McKenna

The culture of the John F. Kennedy School shares features that are common across the schools we studied. There is an emphasis on caring, kindness, and respect for others. There is hard work, especially among teachers, and a belief in children's strengths. Yet, there is also enjoyment, even playfulness, in the work by both teachers and students.

Care and respect. At the JFK School care and respect for others are fundamental. It is a school in which every kind of strength and disability are found shoulder to shoulder in the hallways and in the inclusion classrooms. The expectation is that *everyone* will need help to do his or her best work and everyone will be helped and respected. The level of care, though, exceeds typical notions. For example, in Donna Schneider's room, there was a girl with multiple physical disabilities who had difficulty with the regulation of her body temperature. Without any to-do or complaints, students put on or removed their sweaters as the girl's aide opened or shut windows to the cold March air, and the classroom discussion of new vocabulary proceeded uninterrupted. Living with physical and cognitive differences appears to be a natural part of the JFK School culture, both for adults who work with children and among the children themselves. In the hallways, there is a great deal of comfort and acceptance among students and little, if any, social distinctions made by students of disability or nondisability status: Students with different kinds of needs and strengths appeared to cluster together in classrooms and to interact, to work together, and to play.

Alongside this high degree of caring, there are high expectations that everyone will produce strong work. Ms. McKenna sets the tone for this. She expects teachers to be risk takers, to reach for things beyond their grasp. When teachers come to her to talk over new ideas with her, they are almost always encouraged "to go for it. Try it. You can tweak it if it doesn't work, but try it." Like other principals we spoke with, Ms. McKenna will secure materials and technology to support these ideas to the extent that her budget allows.

Hard work. Hard work is as intrinsic to the JFK culture as care, respect, and high expectations. The high expectations and support provided for teachers is mirrored in teachers' work with students. This work sets an example for the students' own efforts. Ms. McKenna commented that Donna Schneider gives "200 percent to those students and to her job. And she expects 200 percent back. Students give it willingly because I believe they know how hard she tries to make things exciting and interesting for them."

Sue Chamberlain, a speech and language teacher who often works side by side with Donna Schneider in the classroom, noted that she and Mrs. Schneider are frequently on the phone together at nights and on the weekends. They are excited by the ideas they've had for a particular unit and want to share them with each other and figure out how and when they can put them into practice.

The teachers' efforts are mirrored in their students' focused engagement. Whether they were working in small groups or individually, youngsters across different classrooms were eager to pursue their learning activities. For example, when we talked to a group of students about their work in producing a sequence of drawings, they were quite polite but clearly eager to get back to the task at hand.

Teachers noted that hard work was involved in launching the use of MI theory. In order consciously to make classrooms and curricula accessible to the range of intelligences required more planning and time. A number of teachers commented that in the past, when they directed the instruction from the front of the room, they felt it was easier to plan. However, with their efforts to develop group work and a wider range of activities, teachers found that the "kids are very excited." "It keeps their attention focused for a lot longer than the typical (of old) lesson," and they "were completely engaged."

A belief in children's strengths. JFK teachers' belief in children's strengths is demonstrated through the high expectations that they have for students to produce exceptional work. Donna Schneider emphasized this when she asserted that it may take some students longer to do such work, but they are all held to high standards for the work they produce.

One of the things that helps students to produce high-quality work are clear expectations. Teachers at JFK widely employ rubrics, which detail the kinds of characteristics that they are looking for in student work and specifies what these characteristics look like at various levels of quality. By giving rubrics at the beginning of an assignment and discussing these, students have a clear understanding of what's expected and they have explicit guidelines for what they need to do to produce quality work. The upshot of high expectations, high support, and clear guidelines turns out to be a great deal of strong student work. (Rubrics are also used by teachers at the McCleary School, Chapters 2–3, and in Glenridge Elementary, Chapters 9–10).

In real-world projects, such as Schneider's Ink, students have many different roles and therefore many opportunities to engage different strengths. For example, some will rely more on linguistic skills, others on spatial skills, but through the course of the project, students will tap into areas that are strong as well as those that need strengthening. Even in curriculum that is not based on a real-world project, teachers build learning through different areas of strengths. Lorraine Major, a second-grade teacher, noted that to foster students' success she continually is "searching for and creating lessons that can be learned through various intelligences." Another JFK teacher noted that the students themselves are "more willing to take a risk, knowing that we all use different strengths to learn."

Expectations for students to do work involving a wide range of intelligences may seem at odds with increasing demands by state policymakers for "standards." We asked Natalie McKenna how the New York State standards influence the work and expectations at the JFK? Ms. McKenna replied, "You have to reflect upon what's being done [in the school] and how this can be integrated into the standards. . . ." Reflecting on the state standards occasionally indicates a need for "assimilating and integrating" some of what the state sets forth. However, where there is already good teaching and curriculum, "You don't throw the baby out with the bath water."

Enjoyment in the classroom was evident at the JFK school. As at several other schools we visited, students were happily engaged in their activities. There was a good deal of steady, humming concentration, and seemingly little frustration, even among students with disabilities. Everyone seemed to understand that they could find ways to succeed and would be helped to succeed. One teacher said that students, "seem to enjoy what they are good at and can show the other children their strong points."

In sum, the culture at JFK includes hard work, but students enjoy doing the work that they're focused on, state and district standards are exceeded, and teachers' efforts are validated by the results.

Collaboration

The JFK School involves teachers in many formal and informal collaborations. Formal collaboration often takes the form of paired classrooms: There are several such classrooms in which two teachers and their students work closely together throughout the year, doing joint planning and projects. Classroom teachers can choose to get involved in these long-term classroom collaborations. Common planning time for grade-level teachers is another formal structure that helps teachers share ideas and get feedback.

In addition, the emphasis on inclusion at the JFK School fosters a general spirit of teacher collaboration throughout much of the school. As Donna Schneider's classroom demonstrates, full-inclusion rooms mean that there will often be more than one teacher in the room for at least part of the day to support the special needs of a wide range of learners. These teachers orchestrate lessons, and sometimes co-teach lessons, to emphasize skill building for particular students as well as foster engaging lessons for the class as a whole. For example, in one unit, Donna Schneider and Sue Chamberlain devised a lesson that involved students using papier mâché and focusing on building vocabulary from this concrete experience (e.g., *gooey, slimy, wet, cold, disgusting, sticky*). The whole class enjoyed both the vocabulary and the opportunity to do 3-D modeling. In the process of this kind of collaboration, the teachers also gained skills from observing each other in action and talking about how they work to develop and assess students' skills and understanding.

Controlled Choice

At the JFK school, there's an emphasis on enabling students to work with their strengths and pushing them to "go beyond their comfort zone." One of the ways this happens is through the kinds of activity centers that are common in the kindergarten and first-grade classrooms. In these rooms, students are often allowed to choose the kind of activity they want to pursue. However, after they have had their initial choice, they are asked to rotate to a center that may be farther down their list. In this way, students who are comfortable with language may start in the drama center or book area, but then move on to other centers that emphasize math or three-dimensional modeling or music.

Similarly, in the theme-based work that happens in the older grades, students may select activities in areas of their strength. However, in the course of this work, they will still be required to undertake activities that build needed skills. So, for example, in developing a play to be performed for the rest of the school, students who enjoy being in front of the curtain may get larger parts to perform. However, they will still be required to work with the set crew to do some design and painting. At the same time, the students who prefer to work behind the scenes may be drafted into presenting brief introductions or transitions, so that they get some public speaking skills. In Schneider's Ink, the same principle operates: While some children really enjoy the design work, they will still be required to undertake tasks that draw on language and math skills.

The choices students have are further governed by a single requirement. Whether they are working on their first choice or the one they tend to find frustrating, they need to produce the best work possible. Producing high-quality work is not a choice. Students learn that through extra time, reflection, revision, and support of multiple teachers, they can generate the kind of work that's required.

Arts

The John F. Kennedy School provides many opportunities for students to work in a variety of art forms, both in the classroom and in separate classes devoted to art and music. Within classrooms, students are also engaged in the arts. As noted above, several activity centers in the early grades incorporate music. In the older grades, a number of teachers have students writing and performing plays for the rest of the school. Teacher collaboration has helped this process. Rochelle Kaplan, who served as both art and enrichment teacher, worked closely with many classroom teachers, especially to bring the visual arts into the classroom. One classroom teacher commented that, "I brainstorm often with all the special area teachers!"

Oftentimes, a visual arts component was brought into literacy work. For example, students across all grade levels developed their own books, with detailed covers and page illustrations (pictures of these appear in the Schneider's Ink example (see Box 8.8). Also see Chapter 6, Language Artists, for a detailed description of an arts-infused language arts curriculum). For students who had few difficulties with decoding and comprehension, these required illustrations sometimes helped to stretch them into areas where they could develop other skills. Howard Gardner has also argued that the process of translating ideas into more than one symbol system entails transfer of knowledge and builds understanding (Gardner, 1999).

For students who struggle with language, the opportunity to represent their ideas visually can provide a vehicle for representing their thinking. For example, a student may not initially be able to create a detailed story, but may be able to represent rich and colorful visual detail. Teachers can then work with the student to build a vocabulary that reflects the images he or she has drawn. Working from the student's area of strength provides a way to develop new strengths in other areas.

As you read Schneider's Ink, you will find many ways that teachers build from areas of strength to support areas of weakness. You will also see powerful examples of how collaboration and real-world work can serve a great diversity of learners. As you read this example, you might think about opportunities in your own school or classroom to incorporate some of these approaches.

Schneider's Ink

SCHNEIDER'S INK AT A GLANCE

Donna Schneider, third-grade teacher and president of Schneider's Ink

Schneider's Ink is a practical, real-world publishing company operated by third graders in Donna Schneider's full-inclusion class at the John F. Kennedy School in Brewster, New York. Schneider's Ink relies on printing technology—just as any modern publishing company does—to provide banners, programs, flyers, and certificates for school events that happen throughout the spring term. This real-world focus, along with teacher collaboration and MI, allows the company to draw on the strengths of every student.

Publishing ventures like Schneider's Ink are a good way for students to enhance their understanding of language arts, mathematics, computing, and graphic design. At the same time, this real-world experience helps them acquire organizational skills, to understand how publications are produced, to learn how businesses are run, and to contribute to the community. Overall, the unit enables Mrs. Schneider to meet one of her central goals: to have students transfer classroom knowledge and skills to other situations. Transfer shows Mrs. Schneider that the students understand and can use what they have been taught.

MI in This Unit

- This project gives students many opportunities to engage linguistic, logical-mathematical, spatial, interpersonal, and intrapersonal intelligences. Bodily-kinesthetic and naturalist intelligences can also be incorporated.
- Like real-world businesses, Schneider's Ink relies on the orchestration of different individuals' strengths.
- To match children's strengths with the work that needs to get done, students formally apply for jobs that call on their strengths.

Entry Points in This Unit

- The activities in Schneider's Ink are designed to provide students with many routes to understanding how publications are produced and how businesses operate.

- Schneider's Ink draws heavily on the interpersonal and experiential hands-on entry points. The narrative, aesthetic, quantitative, and logical entry points are also well represented.

Compass Point Practices in This Unit

- Mrs. Schneider's classroom and Schneider's Ink as a business organization draws strongly on all the Compass Point Practices.
- Compass Point Practices are in place throughout the John F. Kennedy School.
- These organization-wide practices enable MI to be used in ways that advance students' knowledge and skills.

WHAT IS SCHNEIDER'S INK?

Via technology, we established a publishing company that provides practical, real-time avenues to transfer knowledge learned in the third-grade curriculum.

—Donna Schneider
Third-Grade teacher
The John F. Kennedy School
Brewster, New York

Schneider's Ink is a real publishing company that is operated by third-grade students under the watchful eye of the company's president, classroom teacher Donna Schneider. The company is in business during the spring of the year, when the school has a number of performances and other activities that require programs, banners, announcements, and other printed material. The company's hours of business are usually two forty-five-minute blocks of time each week.

Outside of company hours, the class is involved in other activities and lessons devoted to learning and applying knowledge from the range of

Work done during Schneider's Ink company time.

Language arts work that takes place outside of company time (and includes reading, vocabulary building, and finding tricky spelling words).

subject areas. For example, students may be reading stories and studying new vocabulary words encountered in the stories. Or, they may be constructing objects that they read about in their stories, such as hot-air balloons or piñatas, and learning more about these objects using the Internet.

During company time, Schneider's Ink follows the same kinds of procedures that grown-up businesses do. The business posts classified ads to attract qualified staff. Students write résumés, get letters of recommendation, and interview for jobs. Once they are hired, students sign job contracts, keep track of their hours, and get paid with classroom currency that can be used in the class store. The students also make sales calls to other classrooms to solicit orders. They design and compose the print orders using desktop publishing software. They edit and proofread the publications, deliver the work, and follow up with customer satisfaction surveys. The range of activities in Schneider's Ink allows students to find jobs that draw on their strengths and develop in areas that are less strong.

Like most real businesses, Schneider's Ink relies on knowledge and skills from several disciplines. In this case, language arts, mathematics, visual arts, and computing play important roles. Through Schneider's Ink, students practice skills and develop knowledge in these disciplines. They also get opportunities to transfer these skills to real-world situations. For example, students take basic computation skills that they learned in class to calculate how much money they should be paid for their work. They apply rules of spelling, grammar, and punctuation from their language arts lessons to produce and proofread printed materials. Such work helps the overwhelming majority of students to meet and exceed the language arts and mathematics standards that have been put forward by the state of New York and the local school district.

Alongside meeting these academic standards, students develop an understanding of how publications are produced and how businesses are run. Because each printing job requires input from many students and cooperation among them, students also gain important organizational and teamwork skills.

This kind of unit can succeed in classrooms that serve many different kinds of learners. Donna Schneider developed and runs the company in a full-inclusion class. Of twenty-five students, typically one-quarter to one-third have special needs, including attention deficit disorder, physical challenges, and language, speech, or reading difficulties. In this class, the company's success is partly due to the collaboration among the classroom teacher, the occupational therapist, and the speech and language pathologist. These educators work closely together for several hours each week in the classroom. They also map out ideas together during common planning times and in many informal conversations throughout the week. These exchanges help the teachers match students' strengths to the work that needs to be done. These ongoing exchanges have also played an important role in developing teachers' practice and enabling them to support children's learning. For example, because Donna Schneider and Sue Chamberlain, the speech and language teacher, have worked closely together for four years, Mrs. Schneider now feels like she can truly support the speech needs of her students even when Mrs. Chamberlain is not in the room.

Because youngsters with learning disabilities have important responsibilities in carrying out the company's work, Donna Schneider notes that they take a very active role. Working from their strengths enables these students "to do the job to the best of their ability" and to meet the high expectations the classroom teachers set before them. In this class every student is engaged and participates, and everyone learns important skills and lessons.

Sue Chamberlain, the speech and language teacher, and Donna Schneider collaborate closely to meet the needs of a wide range of students.

STRATEGIES: WORKING WITH STRENGTHS, FOSTERING TRANSFER

My goal . . . is transfer. Students may read in my classroom, but can they read when they leave my classroom? Can they go home and read something? Can they go home and read a recipe? . . . Can they generalize what they're learning here to other areas? Or is it just restricted in this little, little, circle here [in the classroom]? And that is my biggest push. It is the hardest part. 'You might be able to do x, y, and z with me, but that doesn't mean you've got it. Can you do it when you leave me? Can you do it in a different situation?' That's our ultimate goal.

—Donna Schneider

Donna Schneider and her colleagues work hard to ensure that students both acquire and apply knowledge and skills. For many researchers, the sound application—or transfer—of knowledge and skills to new situations is the essence of understanding (Perkins & Salomon, 1989; Resnick, 1987). To enable children to acquire and transfer knowledge, the teachers in this classroom rely on several strategies, among them:

- working with students' strengths
- providing hands-on learning and real-world work
- supporting quality work

Each of these strategies overlaps with the others. Together, they help a wide variety of students to engage, to learn, and to apply what they've learned to produce good work.

Working with Students' Strengths

MI is an integral part of my everyday curriculum and instruction. I have found that the students succeed best when exposed to material in a variety of ways.

—Donna Schneider

For many children, especially children with special needs, school involves working on weaknesses, with occasional opportunities to use and enjoy one's strengths. But the strategy in Mrs. Schneider's room is just the opposite: "We work with their strengths and expose them to their weaknesses."

The focus on strengths helps students to become engaged in the curriculum—a necessary prerequisite to learning what's taught. Throughout the classroom, engagement is evident. (We could hardly get students to look up from their work to talk with us about their classroom!) Children remain on-task, whether it is whole-group instruction or small group work. The same holds very largely true for the children with attention deficit disorder.

"My expectation," says Mrs. Schneider, "is that whether they're inclusion children or not, they're going to do the work. They might do it in a different way, but they're going to do it. And they can do it. If you give them the opportunity to succeed and a way to succeed, they will!"

The teachers in this room oftentimes support opportunities for children to engage and succeed by creating roles and jobs that both draw on children's strengths and help them to work on their weaknesses. For example, in Schneider's Ink, students apply for positions such as illustrator, proofreader, or customer service rep. A student with good spatial skills but weaknesses in reading or speech may decide to apply for the job as an illustrator. But to get that illustrator's job, the student will still have to put together a written job application and use spoken language in a job interview. A stu-

BOX 8.1 ENGAGE CHILDREN THROUGH STRENGTHS BUT EXPOSE THEM TO WEAKNESSES

Both large-scale simulations (like Schneider's Ink) and small units can allow students to take on roles that engage them through their strengths and expose them to their weaknesses. A small-scale example comes from Book Travelers, another unit in Donna Schneider's classroom. In this curriculum, students are members of a four-person book club. Each student in the club has a job. The "discussion driver" keeps the group on task using a set list of questions; the "vocabulary tracker" notes unusual or unknown words, looks them up, and brings back the definitions for the group to discuss; the "scribe" records notes from the discussion, and the "story mapper" provides the illustrations.

Each group generates a book review. Students can choose to produce these in typed or handwritten form or using PowerPoint. These reviews can be presented to students in other classrooms.

Initially students are assigned jobs according to their strengths. However, when the group takes on a new book, the jobs rotate. In that way, students start with jobs that are aligned with their areas of strength. They only take on more challenging work after seeing how other students carry out those tasks. For example, a child can choose to be a "discussion driver" after seeing how another child has handled this task. Or a child might choose to try PowerPoint publishing after the group has figured out how to produce reviews in a handwritten format. Through such techniques, children engage through their strengths, their talents are recognized, and their learning needs are addressed.

In Donna Schneider's class, book reviews can be produced in different formats that engage students and address their learning needs.

dent with strong interpersonal skills and weakness in math may decide not to apply for the accounting position, but the student will still have to keep track of his hours and calculate how much he is supposed to be paid.

Fostering Transfer through Hands-on Learning and Real-World Applications

> *We really look at hands-on learning and what occurs in real life.*
> —Donna Schneider

Hands-on learning

As in most classrooms, Donna Schneider's employs traditional, teacher-directed lessons in math, language arts, science, and social studies. Yet, these forms of teaching and learning are complemented by hands-on learning activities, such as Schneider's Ink. The hands-on experiences are not meant as a substitute for more traditional forms of instruction. Instead, each approach works side by side to engage the students and to foster their skills, knowledge, and understanding. As Donna Schneider put it, "Students need a math time" as well as "concept time" in other curricular areas. "But they also need a time to apply what they learn."

Hands-on learning benefits students who struggle with written notations as well as those who do not. Students who readily acquire information by reading it are challenged to apply the information and produce something from it. For example, students who read and write well may be challenged to put their language skills to use in a job interview. Students who are good at math might be asked to set up an accounting system to keep track of the Schneider's Ink payroll.

Children who have difficulty reading and writing can also gain knowledge and skill by hands-on work. Hands-on work can help to build vocabulary and concepts from concrete activities. For example, in Schneider's Ink children use computers to make business cards for themselves in their own jobs. This hands-on work provides an opportunity to learn many new words, such as: *alignment, centering, serif, stock, logo, typeface, bold.* Donna Schneider and Sue Chamberlain constantly work with the class to connect vocabulary that is learned through hands-on work to other contexts. For instance, they might ask the class to consider whether a person can be bold, if they themselves were ever bold, or if they can remember a character from a story that they would describe as bold. Building connections among hands-on work, the students' own experiences, and the written/represented world fosters deep understanding of words and how they are used in different contexts.

For children who are struggling with reading and language disabilities, the opportunity to learn and demonstrate understanding through hands-on approaches is especially important. These youngsters can show you what

More traditional forms of learning, such as reading time, complement hands-on experiences in Donna Schneider's classroom.

they know and understand oftentimes far better than they can write it down or tell you. A child who cannot write a paragraph can nevertheless show you in his sales pitch that he can organize his thinking and make a persuasive argument. Donna Schneider told of one boy who could not organize his ideas on paper, but who could persuasively describe the benefits of doing business with Schneider's Ink. ("He could get rich selling freezers in the Arctic!" remarked Mrs. Schneider.) Furthermore, helping students to produce some good work in at least one way gives them a can-do sense of themselves. So, though some children may struggle in particular areas, "We're able to give them success in one area, and then that actually motivates them." The students then become more willing to work in ways that do not come as easily to them.

Hands-on learning also helps students learn to follow directions, to plan, and to grasp sequences and relationships between events. For instance, in Schneider's Ink orders first have to come in, then orders need to be reviewed and understood, the pieces of the job need to be assigned to staff members, the text needs to be copyedited, and the completed job needs to be inspected and then delivered. Learning about sequence and relationships is important for all children. Doing so in a hands-on way is especially useful for inclusion students. Students are motivated to grasp sequence, relationships, and directions in this project, because they are producing something that is real and useful for the school community.

Real-world Work

In Schneider's Ink, children are learning about how a business operates by doing the work of a real business. They are also learning about how printed materials are produced by making real banners, programs, and other publications. The real-world emphasis of this and other units advances learning in several ways.

- *Transfer*

   In Schneider's Ink, or other real-world units, there's a very clear need to transfer academic knowledge and skills to new situations. For example, it's important to apply knowledge of numbers and measurement in order to lay out a page or business card. It's apparent that spelling and proofreading lessons need to be applied, because real programs and banners have to be grammatically correct.

- *Practice*

   A real-world emphasis encourages practice. Students (and their customers!) want to see the work done right. Sometimes this means doing the work over, or revising it several times. Sometimes practice happens by bringing the same skill—for example, measuring or making presentations—to somewhat different situations. By practicing what they've learned and applying it to new settings, students are also more likely to have command over what's been taught.

- *Engagement*

   Real-world work engages students in part because the work is seen and used beyond the classroom. In addition, it engages them because it oftentimes entails a degree of imaginative play. For example, for their job interviews or sales pitches, students often dress up in business clothes. Once they're "employed," the students carry around their own business cards. Sue Chamberlain, the classroom's speech and language pathologist, says that because the activities are fun, they motivate students and teachers to reflect on the work. A willingness to revisit and reflect on one's work in this way is essential to improving it (see Schön, 1983).

Supporting Quality Work

Work that is done in the real world has known standards and processes that help to ensure quality. Mrs. Schneider draws on this aspect of the project to help support the production of quality work for students. She also supports quality work through rubrics and high expectations.

- *Real-world standards of quality*

  Like most real-world publishing companies, Schneider's Ink builds quality control efforts right into its production process. For example, the staff of Schneider's Ink is carefully selected. The staff includes an editor or proofreader. This person must review all the typed material for spelling and punctuation. The staff also includes a quality control manager, who inspects the completed job to make sure every detail is right. In addition, the staff conducts customer surveys to make sure that their products meet their clients' expectations. When a product falls short, the work is done again until it is right.

- *Models*

  In curricula based on real-world work, there are existing models of high-quality products that can be brought into the classroom and studied in a hands-on fashion. For Schneider's Ink, students can look at wonderful examples of brochures, programs, and announcements and consider what makes them so good. They can also learn about the processes for producing them through reading and research. Through these and other approaches, students gain an understanding of the qualities that matter and how to get these qualities into their own work.

- *Rubrics*

  Donna Schneider and her collaborators draw on "friendly" rubrics. Rubrics are assessment tools that specify qualities that are important in a given piece of work and the degree to which a student has incorporated those qualities. Rubrics can be used to support work in process (formative evaluation) and also to evaluate completed work (summative evaluation). (See Goodrich, 1997; Goodrich Andrade, 2000; Wiggins, 1998. Also see Chapters 3, 10, and 12 for other classrooms that use rubrics.)

  In Mrs. Schneider's room, sometimes the teachers hand out the rubric at the beginning of the assignment, so students know what they should be aiming for in their work. At other times, the students and teachers work together to produce a rubric for a particular project. This might be done in part by looking at models of real work (or thinking about models seen in and outside of school) and then by articulating the qualities that are important for the work. Issues of accuracy, neatness, color, composition, and overall interest might be some of the qualities that the children and teacher specify. The degree to which these qualities are actually produced in a given work range on a scale. For example, 0 might indicate the quality was lacking or barely met, 1 indicates that the quality was partly met, and 2 indicates the quality was met at a high level.

FIGURE 8.1   Rubrics help students to understand, develop, and evaluate good printed materials.

Take a Close Look at Your Publication			
	0 POINTS	**1 POINT**	**2 POINTS**
Format	Missing several parts. (For example, missing all or parts of text or illustrations.)	Missing one part.	Contains all parts.
Spelling	Three or more words are misspelled.	Less than 3 words are misspelled.	All words are spelled correctly.
Grammar	Punctuation and capitals are missing.	Most items are correctly punctuated and capitalized.	All items are correctly punctuated and capitalized.
Illustrations	Illustrations are not appropriate or well done.	Most illustrations are appropriate and well done.	Illustrations are appropriate and well done.
Neatness	Words and illustrations are not as legible or neat as they could be.	Most words, and illustrations are as legible or neat as they could be.	All words, and illustrations are as legible or neat as they could be.
Accuracy	Information is inaccurate in several places.	Information has one minor inaccuracy.	All information is accurate.
Maximum = 12 points			

Expectations

Setting high expectations is a key part of the quality control strategies in this, and many other, classrooms. Together with the many other supports and strategies described above, high expectations act as "a self-fulfilling prophecy," says Donna Schneider. The students will produce high-quality work because it's expected, and because they are given the means to do so.

WHAT HAPPENS DURING SCHNEIDER'S INK? ACTIVITIES TO START AND RUN A PUBLISHING COMPANY

We really look at hands-on learning and what occurs in real-life.
—Donna Schneider

It's so real, the kids buy into it.
—Natalie McKenna, principal of the John F. Kennedy School

To start a company, you need people to do the work. Once the staff is in place, you need to get orders, produce the work that's been ordered, make sure the work meets the customers' expectations, and keep the company's financial house in order. The activities described below show how Schneider's Ink goes about accomplishing these tasks.

BOX 8.2 TIMING

It's important to run the business when demand for services is high. Often this is in the spring of the year. This timing also allows teachers to have gathered lots of information about students'

strengths and interests. Teachers can then create jobs that suit many different students and enable them to contribute productively.

BOX 8.3 MATERIALS NEEDED

Here are materials that the Schneider's Ink teachers have suggested:

- markers and/or other drawing materials
- colored paper, and paper of various sizes for banners or other special orders
- Access to copiers

- computers
- computer printers
- software for graphic design, desktop publishing, and word-processing
- scanners for digitizing students' illustrations and other visual materials

---

At the same time, these activities are a snapshot. Donna Schneider emphasizes that Schneider's Ink, like real-world businesses, is responsive to changes in the environment, including changes in materials, technology, leadership, the students/staff involved, and the staff's prior knowledge. So, as you read this "work in progress" (or other examples in this book), you might want to think about how it can be adapted to your own classroom or school. Toward the end of this section, we'll discuss the changes that the Schneider's Ink teachers are considering.

Staffing Schneider's Ink

The Classifieds

To secure the company's staff, Mrs. Schneider gives each student a copy of the "Help Wanted Classifieds." The classifieds list an array of jobs, including customer service, distributor, editor, illustrator, layout designer, sales manager, secretary, advertiser, typist. Each job posting has a specific description. Reviewing the job listings with the students accomplishes several things.

VOCABULARY   As you can see from the classifieds in Box 8.4, the job listings use sophisticated language. So, reviewing the classifieds provides an opportunity to strengthen students' vocabulary and comprehension. To understand what different jobs require, students need to know what it means to be *motivated, congenial, reliable,* and *detail conscious.* To help students grasp the meaning of these words, this discussion includes considerations of characters from real life and books who have demonstrated such qualities.

EXPECTATIONS   A conversation about each of the classifieds helps to make the qualifications and responsibilities for each job very clear. This sets out the expectations for each job and for each print order.

QUALITY CONTROL   The review of the classified ads supports quality control. In the review Mrs. Schneider emphasizes that the customers, who are

BOX 8.4

Classifieds

❖   ❖

Volume 1, Issue 2

Help Wanted Classifieds

Customer Service

Self-motivated, dependable person should possess congenial manners, organizational skills, and ability to work as a team member. Individual should possess good problem-solving skills and should be able to handle complaints from customers.

Distributor

Seeking reliable, organized, and on-time person to deliver customer orders. Must be neat, and knowledge of JFK delivery area is a must.

Editor

Printing company is seeking individuals with effective editing and proofreading skills. Must be able to correct documents for capitalization, grammar, and spelling.

Illustrator

Looking for individual who is good at free-hand illustrations. Must have creative problem-solving skills. Need someone who is organized and extremely detail conscious. Must also be good at working with graphics on a computer. Art sample must accompany application.

Layout Designer

Highly organized and motivated person needed to help printing company design and prepare customer documents. Must enjoy working with others on a team. Person should possess some computer knowledge, although some training will be provided.

Sales Manager

Leading printing company seeking qualified sales managers. Super people skills are needed. Must be willing to talk in front of adults. Must show enthusiasm and be dramatic in presentation of sales pitch.

Secretary

Applicant must be organized, be a team player, have good interpersonal skills, and possess a knowledge of written language. Must be able to take and file orders. Some computer knowledge is necessary.

Advertiser

Local company is seeking creative individuals with lots of ideas. Person must be able to "sell" their ideas to potential customers through written advertisements. Sample of an ad is required with application.

Typist

Top, local corporation needs accurate typist to enter wording for documents, flyers, cards, and banners. Must be detail oriented. Some computer experience is necessary. Some training will be provided.

Accounting Manager

Leading printing company seeking organized, neat individual with excellent math skills. Must be able to compute numbers accurately. Some experience with a calculator is necessary.

Reviewing the Classifieds with students helps to build their vocabulary and understanding of the project and its expectations.

the other teachers at the school, want each publication to meet professional standards. (After all, the printed materials are going to be handed out around the school, and to parents, grandparents, and other members of the community!) To help students understand what the standards are, the teacher and students talk about the qualities of a good printed job. For example, the work must be accurate, neat, eye-appealing, and finished on time. This discussion also helps to support the development of a rubric.

SEQUENCING   The classifieds help to build students' understanding of the sequence of events that needs to take place to make the business run. Some students will be responsible for bringing in publication orders from teachers. Once the orders come in, other students will be responsible for reviewing the order and distributing parts of the work to other staff. Some staff will make sure that the text is typed. Others will design illustrations and arrange the text and graphics. After this, a staff member will edit the text. Later, other staff members will inspect the job, deliver the order, and make sure that the customers are happy with the work. The sequence can be complex, because several print orders may be happening all at once. Therefore, it's expected that different staff members will have to cooperate about when to do particular work and plan how to get the jobs done on time. It is also expected that staffers who are not busy in their Schneider's Ink jobs can help busier staff members, or they can work on other assignments to extend or reinforce recent class lessons.

Job Application Process

After the classifieds have been reviewed, students begin the job application process. Students circle three jobs that they'd like to do and number their choices from 1 to 3, with 1 being the job they'd most like to do. Then, they prepare for their interviews by drafting a résumé, writing up a job application, getting a letter of reference, and, if the job calls for it, putting together samples of work or a portfolio.

RESUME   One session of Schneider's Ink is devoted to understanding what a résumé is and how to draft one. The first drafts are done in class, beginning with a template that Mrs. Schneider provides. In the section of the template called "skills," students write information that is relevant to the jobs that they want to do. For example, students who want the job as illustrator can write about the artwork they've produced, their experience with computer graphics, or provide other details that may be important and persuasive, based in part on the classified ad. After the class session, students edit and proofread their individual drafts either in small groups or individually. They then revise their résumés and, using word-processing software, polish the résumés into final form.

INTERVIEW NOTIFICATIONS   After reviewing the students' choices, teachers match the students' choices with the work that needs to be done. Then, each student receives a letter to congratulate him or her on getting an interview for a particular position. The letter also lets the students know when the interview is, and the materials they'll need to bring to the interview. (NB: In general, each job is filled by one student. Occasionally, students are paired for certain jobs, depending on the students' skills, the amount of work to be done, and the amount of support a child needs. It's important not to have too many children in a single job, because they will not have enough work to do.)

BOX 8.5 HOW TO APPLY FOR A JOB AT SCHNEIDER'S INK & CO.

Students write a résumé in which they answer the question: What can you bring to the job in the way of skills?

Joe Smith
127 High Street
Brewster, NY 10509
(914) 279-xxxx

Objective:
To obtain a job with a printing company

Education:
1991 to Present, John F. Kennedy Elementary School, Brewster, NY

Skills:
(list skills here)

References available upon request.

They receive a letter inviting them to interview for the job.

Schneider's Ink & Company

Dear Miss/Mr. [Student's last name]

Congratulations! We are pleased to inform you that you will be interviewing for the position of Illustrator.

Your interview will be on Monday, March 4. At that time, you will need to bring with you your application, résumé, art sample, and letter of reference. You will be notified as to the exact time of your interview. If you cannot make your interview, please contact me, and we will reschedule it.

I look forward to meeting with you and discussing this position.

Sincerely,
Mrs. Schneider

LETTERS TO PARENTS   To involve parents in supporting their children, and to inform parents about the class's work, Mrs. Schneider sends home a short letter about the project. In the letter, Mrs. Schneider tells parents that students will be interviewing for jobs of their choice the following week. In preparation for the interviews, she asks parents to help their child "to dress appropriately for an interview." She also asks parents "to write a *brief* letter of reference." The letter should be supportive and mention qualities that show how the child is best suited for the job he or she has chosen (see Box 8.6).

JOB APPLICATION ESSAY   Students prepare written responses to the job application questions in advance of their interview. These responses help them organize their thinking for the interview and practice persuasive writing and other language arts skills.

The application has five questions:

1. Use three adjectives to describe yourself.
2. What do you think this job involves?
3. What do you think you will have to do?
4. What skills will you bring to the job?
5. Why should we hire you over someone else?

The job application also provides another opportunity to prepare students to do high-quality work by making clear what the expectations are.

THE INTERVIEW   Students bring their written application, résumé, letter of reference, and any samples of their work to the interview. Mrs. Schneider or her collaborating teachers individually interview the students using the five questions that the students have responded to in writing. The interview gives students a chance to make oral presentations, to communicate their ideas directly to the teachers, and to use evidence in their presentation from their letters of reference, résumé, or other sources. The students can also bring their own questions or extend the conversation into areas that the teacher has not asked about. So, for instance, some children take the interviewer through their portfolios of artwork. Some describe their collection of baseball cards to show that they attend to detail and organization. The interview also gives the student and the teacher a chance to review the job qualifications, and this helps to ensure quality work from each child.

HIRING   Following the interviews, the teachers meet to decide how to allocate the jobs among the students. Once the decisions are made, students receive an "employment contract." This highlights the need for staff members to do their best work and the conditions for continuing their employment (see Box 8.6).

Running the Publishing Business

When each student's job is assigned, and the students clearly understand their work, they operate their business like a well-oiled machine!

Marketing   The sales staff visits classrooms to announce the start of the printing business. They explain the kinds of work the printing business does and field any initial questions from the teachers. Mrs. Schneider will often pair up children for this work. One may be very outgoing and articulate, the other more reserved, but still interested in sales. In this way, one student helps to model the work for the other.

BOX 8.6 REFERENCES AND AN OFFICAL CONTRACT ARE REQUIRED

Parents write a letter of reference.

To: Personnel Director, Schneider's Ink

I would like to recommend John for the job of quality control manager. John has assisted me in several building projects and has learned the importance of accurate measurements. He has an excellent sense of detail and precision. He has a devotion to order, which can readily be seen in his baseball card collection. These books are organized accurately by year and team. The contents are handled with extreme care. John would certainly be a welcome addition to your quality team.

Sincerely yours,
[John's Dad.]

cc: JES

Once they get the job, students agree to an employment contract. The contract specifies what they must do to fulfill their job and what they will receive in return.

Schneider's Ink & Company Employment Contract

I _____ , accept the position of _____ with Schneider's Ink & Company, beginning on _____ . In accepting this position, I agree to fulfill my job responsibilities to the best of my ability. My salary will be $2.00 (classroom money) a week plus $2.00 for every hour worked. If I cannot fulfill my job, I will be reassigned to a new position in the company without interruption of pay. I can be terminated from employment for the following actions: fooling around instead of working (2 warnings), excessive tardiness and incomplete, unacceptable work (2 warnings).

_____

Employee

_____

Donna M. Schneider, President

_____

Date

Customer Reps   When teachers have an order to place, they contact the customer service rep, whose business card has been left by Schneider's Ink staff with the classroom teachers. The child in this job has the teacher fill out an order form with the exact information that should appear on the printed product (see Box 8.7). Oftentimes, the teacher just provides some text and leaves all the design work up to Schneider's Ink. The customer service rep brings this information back to the secretary.

Production   The secretary, who acts more like a production manager, examines the order and sees what sorts of work will be involved in producing it. She delegates the various pieces of the job to other students and follows up with the students, "to make sure that they're on time with the project." Some work may go to a layout designer, who makes the general plan for the print job. Pieces of the job then go to the illustrator and the typist. When the text has been entered into the computer, the editor reviews it to make sure that the spelling and punctuation are correct. Illustrations are scanned in and set alongside the text. A sample of the order is printed and then folded, if necessary. Then the whole thing is sent to the quality-control inspector. (Mrs. Schneider has found that among her students are some who may not be strong in entering the text or layout, but who are nevertheless capable of quality-control inspection: They can stand back from the product and see if there are problems with it.) If the sample is approved, the rest of the work order is fulfilled. The order is delivered to the teacher, along with a customer survey (see Box 8.7). The completed survey helps the staff find out whether their work meets the customer's expectations.

Handling Business Problems

Two kinds of problems occur in this business. One kind entails the product, the other involves the staff and their work process.

Problems with the product   When a problem with the print product appears, the quality-control people or the teacher report this to the students, and the students fix it. For example, one program had too many graphics squeezed into it. The students had a lot of ideas for the program and tried to represent all of them. Mrs. Schneider helped the students to review the information that needed to be conveyed in the program, to prioritize the information, and "then go back to the drawing board and do it again." The rubric can also be used to pinpoint problems and guide the students toward better-quality work.

Problems with the staff   Sometimes problems occur with the staff of the printing company and their work process. In some instances, workers fall short of their job contract. For instance, on one occasion, the accounting managers were found to be "cooking the books," to make extra wages! In this case, the students were removed from their job, but rather than firing the students, the students met with the company's president for a lesson on ethics and honesty. After this, the students had to reapply for a new job, and go through the job process again, including getting new letters of recommendation.

Another staff problem that occurs is that students turn out not to enjoy their job, or they find that they have skills in another area. In these cases, students write to the president to request a job transfer and the reasons for it. These requests are typically granted.

BOX 8.7 THERE ARE FORMS FOR ORDERS AND CUSTOMER SURVEYS

Upon completion of the job, they evaluate the quality of the job.

**Schneider's Ink
Customer Survey**

We would like to know how satisfied you were with the work we completed for you. Please rate us on the following, using a scale of 1 to 10. (1 being the least satisfied, 10 being very satisfied). Also, please feel free to comment on anything we have done for you. Thank you.

The job was completed in a timely manner:
The job was completed as ordered:
The materials were neat and presentable:
Our employees were polite and helpful:
Overall, how satisfied were you?

Comments:

Customers use an order form to specify the kind of job and special instructions.

**Schneider's Ink
Order Form**

Teacher's Name: _____
Grade: _____
Date Submitted: _____
Date Requested: _____

(Please submit a sample, if necessary)

Job Description	Size and Amount	Special Instructions (text, format, font, paper)
☐ Banner		
☐ Invitations		
☐ Cards		
☐ Announcements		
☐ Play Program		
☐ Other		

BOX 8.8 PRINTING TECHNOLOGIES

Publishing units can be launched using a wide range of technologies. From its beginning, Schneider's Ink has been a unit that draws heavily on technology, but a unit like Schneider's Ink can be adapted to technologies that can be as basic as the human hand or as high-powered as the most modem computer and software. What's key is to determine the technology appropriate to a particular use and class. For example, handmade work is appropriate to publish one-of-a-kind materials. Students can publish illustrated books that can be bound and used by the school library. In fact, Mrs. Schneider's students produce illustrated books like those shown below, although they do not do so in the context of a classroom business.

With the availability of a copier, handmade work can also be duplicated and used as the basis for programs, certificates, or other widely-circulated materials that the school community needs. Students' experience with different kinds of software may also shape the sort of publications they can undertake. For example, students in Mrs. Schneider's class began to generate PowerPoint book reviews once that software became available. A range of other variables, such as student interests and teacher demands, may also affect both the kind of technology that is used and the form of publications (e.g., paper vs. electronic, book reviews vs. programs).

It's also possible to draw on other software to support the development of children's skills, knowledge, and understanding. For instance, to build mathematics knowledge and skill, spreadsheet software could be used for accounting work or for analyzing customer satisfaction surveys. Students might also use page layout programs to incorporate graphics and text. These technologies are akin to what is used by real printing companies.

Alongside all the other elements of Schneider's Ink, working through such problems gives students the opportunity to apply knowledge and skills, to gain new skills, and to learn how real print jobs are produced and how real businesses are run.

A Note about Change

The world of publishing has changed a great deal since Schneider's Ink first began, and so have a number of other variables that can affect the business, or classroom curriculum. For example, the fourth grade was relocated from the John F. Kennedy School to another building. Because of this, the number of performances has gone down and the demand for printed programs has declined. As a result, Mrs. Schneider is finding new ways to generate business. She is looking for business from other schools in the district and from the PTA. At the same time, while business is slack, the students are using their Book Travellers reports (see Box 8.1) as the basis for Power Point book reviews. These reviews, like other contemporary publications, can be published using many different media or technologies. Mrs. Schneider's students can also present their reviews to younger children to build younger students' interest in books and to increase their own presentations skills.

Donna Schneider underscores that "things have to change. You cannot take the same project and implement it in the same way every year. The kids change, the materials change, the dynamics in the classroom and the school change. And if those change, other things have to give." The important thing is to adapt to change in ways that allow students to be engaged through their strengths, exposed to their weaknesses, and to apply what they're learning.

REVISITING THE FRAMEWORKS

MI in This Unit

In Schneider's Ink, you can see that not every intelligence is used. Musical intelligence isn't used. And, while some fine motor skills are needed, there is little call for bodily-kinesthetic intelligence. Mrs. Schneider has chosen to stick with meaningful activities that are central to the publishing business, and to look for other opportunities during the day or week to involve intelligences not central to Schneider's Ink. This is a wise choice!

Entry Points in This Unit

There are many routes to understanding how publications are produced and how businesses operate. Because Schneider's Ink is such a multifaceted unit, it can draw on all the entry points. Through these different entry points, a wide variety of learners can foster their skills, while gaining an understanding of how publications are produced and how businesses are run.

Narrative: In reviewing the classifieds, Mrs. Schneider walks children through the story of running the printing business. In addition, there is some amount of imaginative role playing: As the students apply for jobs and carry them out, they are acting out roles in the printing business.

Linguistic	Spatial	Interpersonal	Intrapersonal	Logical-Mathematical	Musical	Bodily-Kinesthetic	Naturalist		ACTIVITIES
									The Classifieds:
X									• Students learn new vocabulary.
X			X						• They consider their own strengths and job preferences.
		X		X					• They are exposed to sequencing and think about the relationships among jobs and the team that are needed to produce the work.
									Job Applications:
X			X						• Students prepare a résumé and write job application essay.
X		X	X						• Students participate in a job interview and explain their qualifications for the job.
									Running the Business:
X		X							• Students make sales calls.
X	X			X					• Students produce their own business cards.
		X		X					• The parts of the job are distributed.
	X					X			• Students design the product and produce illustrations.
X	X			X					• The text is set on the page.
		X							• Students coordinate their efforts to produce the job.
X	X	X							• The job is inspected, and revised.

FIGURE 8.2 Multiple Intelligences Engaged During Schneider's Ink

Aesthetic: Depending on their role, students have the opportunity to attend to the aesthetic dimensions of publishing, including the layout of text, the overall composition of text and graphics, and the creation of illustrations.

Quantitative: Students calculate their hours and wages. They use measurement in the process of centering business card text and designing printed materials. In the classifieds and in the course of producing the products, students deal with logical sequences and relationships.

Experiential: Schneider's Ink takes students through the experience of running a publication business and producing printed materials. It encourages them to apply math, language, and other skills to real-world activities.

Existential: The fundamental nature and principles of business, publishing, and printing are not specifically addressed during Schneider's Ink. This entry point could be employed in this or a similar unit, depending on teachers' and students' interests.

Interpersonal: Students have the chance to work with and learn from each other in many ways in this unit. For instance, pairs of salespeople can visit a prospective customer. Other jobs readily call for students to work together and complement each others' strengths. For example, the layout person needs to work with the illustrator and graphic designer to produce the overall composition.

Although it's not essential to use every entry point for each topic, rich topics, like this one, allow many different ways for students to explore and learn.

Compass Point Practices in This Unit

Compass Point Practices are organizational practices that allow multiple intelligences to be engaged in ways that advance students' learning. These practices are in place both throughout the John F. Kennedy School and in the smaller organization of Schneider's Ink.

Culture: In this caring and respectful classroom, every child is seen as having strengths and high expectations are held for all children. Hard work is evident in both students and teachers. At the same time, both the children and their teachers are enjoying the work.

Readiness: The timing of Schneider's Ink is important. The unit takes place in spring, when several preconditions have been met. Students have had many experiences working in groups and collaborating in hands-on work. The teachers have a good grasp of their students' strengths and interests. This helps them to develop jobs that accommodate many different kinds of learners. The timing also coincides with many school performances, which helps to keep the company going.

Choice: Students have choices in the ways that they participate in the work. For example, they can choose particular roles for Schneider's Ink or in the Book Travellers work. However, the choice is controlled. For example, in Book Travellers, the jobs rotate, so that students are engaged through their strengths and exposed to their weaknesses.

Collaboration: Donna Schneider collaborates closely with colleagues in her classroom, especially the speech and language teacher, Sue Chamberlain, and the occupational therapist. These collaborations include formal planning time, shared teaching time, as well as many informal exchanges.

Arts: The visual arts are clearly a part of Schneider's Ink. Students can choose to do free-hand illustration or work with images in a digital medium. Depending on the unit, music, dance, and various visual art forms are employed to support and demonstrate learning.

Tool: MI is a tool for helping to ensure that many different kinds of learners are engaged and learn. However, the theory stands in the background and the curriculum in the foreground. For example, in Schneider's Ink, the classifieds were organized by job type, rather than by intelligence.

Glenridge
Elementary School

The curriculum example from the Glenridge Elementary School is the Heritage/Traditions Unit, which was developed by Mrs. Marge Staszak for her looped classroom of fifth to sixth graders. The unit is aimed at building students' understanding of both their own family heritage and, through that, an understanding that the United States as a whole is comprised of people from many lands and cultures. The Heritage/Traditions Unit enables students to explore this content through many different intelligences, and requires them to undertake work in several disciplines: history, language arts, visual arts, and math. Portions of this unit can readily be incorporated into many elementary or middle-school classrooms. This chapter provides the school context for the work Mrs. Staszak does. It first gives a brief overview of the Glenridge Elementary School, then, through the framework of the Compass Point Practices, it illustrates the ways that the school as a whole enables both teachers and students to draw on a range of intelligences and to learn at high levels.

OVERVIEW OF THE GLENRIDGE ELEMENTARY SCHOOL

Glenridge Elementary School, Renton, Washington.

Glenridge Elementary is a K-6 school in Renton, Washington, a suburban area in the Kent School District outside of Seattle. Glenridge occupies a new, one-story building made of earth-toned masonry blocks with narrow borders of blue on a site surrounded by towering evergreen trees. Although the school was built in the late 1990s, a few portable units were soon added behind the main building, near the large playground area. The school's main entrance is at the middle of the building and the main office is just inside. Immediately to the right of the office is the school's "gallery," in which the best examples of framed student artwork are displayed. At the center of the gallery is a portrait of Christopher Columbus by fourth graders.

The gymnasium, orchestra room, and multipurpose room are off to the left. To the right are three hallways, distinguished by classrooms at two separate grade levels and by the color of their carpets: burgundy, blue, and green. Each hallway has floor-to-ceiling bulletin boards and several glass-enclosed shelves. All of this is used to display abundant amounts of student work.

Glenridge replaced an existing school, the Spring Glen School, which had been awarded a Blue Ribbon School of Excellence. Spring Glen had been a magnet school that parents throughout the district could choose. Glenridge "grandfathered" Spring Glen students and their siblings, but was opened to serve a much larger, neighborhood-based student population. In the transition, the student population grew from 320 in 1996–1997 to 635 in 1997–1998. The student population remained 85 percent white, with the great majority of students coming from families with middle-class incomes. The percentage of Asian students grew from two to eight percent. African Americans comprise four percent of the school population. Latino and Native American students together constitute three percent. Class sizes in the upper grades range from 26 to 28 students. To accommodate the greater number of students, the staff nearly doubled, growing to 23 classroom teachers and 10 specialized staff (including administrators, a librarian, special education/resource teachers, a physical education teacher, music teachers, and a technology specialist). This kind of transition and growth is challenging. Yet, in the change from Spring Glen to Glenridge, the school, its staff, and students continued to thrive and move forward.

Glenridge's success builds on the groundwork laid at Spring Glen. All the Spring Glen parents enrolled their children at Glenridge, even though they now had to provide their own transportation. The principal, Sheryl Harmer, and all of the staff moved to the new building. Just as important, Ms. Harmer reported that, "the philosophies and the programs came with us."

The Glenridge Elementary School is focused on working with individual strengths, and it uses the idea of exploration as an overall metaphor for learning in the school. In line with that metaphor, students—and their teachers—see themselves as "voyagers" on a mission to acquire greater knowledge and skill. The school's motto reinforces this idea: "Learning is our voyage. Knowledge is our quest. The world is our classroom."

To facilitate such exploration, Glenridge employs many mutually supportive tools: multiple intelligences; extended blocks of time for rich, project-based curricula; inclusionary and heterogeneous classrooms; inquiry-based learning; connecting students to the school, involving parents, and working with other organizations to bring in learning opportunities in the arts and other areas.

The logo for Glenridge Elementary School describes learning in terms of exploration and adventure.

The results of these efforts are impressive on many levels: from the quality of student work to the joyful spirit of the classrooms, from the many requests to place student teachers there to the fact that Glenridge produces scores at or near the top of the district on the Comprehensive Test of Basic Skills (CTBS), the fourth-grade Washington Assessment of Student Learning (WASL), and the Six-Trait Writing Assessment for third and sixth graders (an assessment that looks at ideas, organization, voice, word choice, sentence fluency, and conventions).

COMPASS POINT PRACTICES

The success of the school overall can be understood through the framework of the Compass Point Practices. This framework of organizational practices shows how the school enables those within it to draw on their strengths in order to learn at high levels. This framework also provides a way of seeing Marge Staszak's Heritage/Traditions Unit in the context of schoolwide practice. We describe the Compass Point Practices in an order that allows Glenridge Elementary's story to be clearly told.

Readiness

> *Philosophically, we were very vested in . . . looking at students and their individual strengths.*
>
> —Sheryl Harmer
> Principal
> Glenridge Elementary
> Renton, Washington

The incorporation of multiple intelligences into Glenridge Elementary began in 1992, when a parent shared an article about MI with the principal, Sheryl Harmer. Ms. Harmer noted that, because of extensive parent communication and outreach efforts, the parent understood that MI would be of interest. "She knew that, philosophically, we were very vested in . . . looking at students and their individual strengths." Given that there was "quite a link" between the school's philosophy and the theory, Ms. Harmer introduced the theory to the staff as an idea "we might want to look into." Ms. Harmer supplied articles about the theory from journals, and she and the teachers discussed these at staff meetings. After these early discussions, they decided to devote more time to see "how MI fit with . . . the way we were trying to meet children's needs." The next school year, 1993–1994, the entire staff read and discussed *Frames of Mind,* and several teachers from across grade levels went to a staff development meeting with Linda Campbell, an early proponent of MI based in Seattle.

The readings and staff development were exciting to the teachers. They saw that the theory clearly meshed with the school's existing beliefs about individual learners and inclusionary classrooms and also with its focus on inquiry and exploration. Yet, the school did not adopt one, comprehensive method of putting the theory into practice. Nor was there a top-down demand that everyone incorporate MI. Instead, implementation proceeded "step-by-step in terms of the teachers' comfort level." It was important to "allow people to get into it at whatever interest level they have and . . . wherever it seems to fit the most." (A similar notion was expressed by Searsport's principal, Doug Lockwood. See Chapter 11). In line with this approach, teachers were encouraged to think about the ways that the theory might serve their students, to share the things they tried out in their classes at staff meetings, and to work through ideas and experiences with their peers. Trying out ideas, reflecting on the experience and revising practice are the norm at Glenridge, as it is at the other schools profiled in this book. Ann Reed, a fourth-grade teacher, underscored this point: "The administration always encourages the staff to be creative and try things. And if we fail, or it's not quite what we wanted as an outcome, then that's okay. . . . We do something different until we get it right."

When Spring Glen was being transformed into Glenridge, Ms. Harmer held numerous meetings with the existing and newly hired teachers to develop strategies for structuring a learning environment that served all children. In these sessions teachers shared approaches for incorporating MI, expanding students' knowledge through research-based inquiry, and extending the classroom learning opportunities through community partnerships. Through these strategy sessions, the strengths of Spring Glen were expanded throughout Glenridge Elementary.

Ms. Harmer believes that financial resources are not an obstacle in implementing MI. She argues that it does not cost much money to incorporate the theory, but, like other principals, she notes that there is a cost involved in "time to communicate, to talk, to research, to study, to plan. It takes extra time." She does, nevertheless, devote professional development dollars on implementing MI and other, complementary efforts, because "it's really important to bring in consultants occasionally. You need to hear from the outside. You need to send people for visitations to other schools." However, she is careful to make sure that staff development money is not fragmented or spent on "the flavor of the month." These funds flow to support building-wide goals for staff development that she and the teachers have chosen.

Culture

We work so hard here, and yet we have so much fun.
—Katy Henderson, sixth-grade teacher

The culture of the Glenridge Elementary School includes qualities found across the schools that we visited. Relationships are marked by caring and respect. Teachers work very hard, students are challenged, and there is a commitment to producing high-quality work. At the same time, students and teachers enjoy being there. We consider the qualities of Glenridge's culture in greater depth in this section.

Care and respect.   At Glenridge Elementary, caring and respectful interactions are essential to the school's operation. As Ms. Harmer put it, "We try to make sure that kids have lots of ways to be connected with their school, to contribute to their school, to have meaningful relationships with other kids. That needs to be pervasive, and then you see it in the quality of work that the kids produce." At Glenridge, these kinds of relationships are forged in many different ways. One way is through classroom looping. In looped classrooms, students move with their teacher and classmates across two consecutive grades. Looping creates a longer-term relationship among classmates and between students and the teacher. It also facilitates transitions at the beginning of the second year. The teachers found that students don't "feel like they have to reestablish themselves and kind of make their own turf in the fall." Students know their teachers' expectations, and teachers can build on their existing knowledge of individual students and the dynamics among them.

Sheryl Harmer models the importance of student–adult connections. "I want to make sure that I know every child in this school." One way she does this is by eating lunch with every child and a friend of the child's choice at least twice each year. She also reads every child's report card and makes comments on each one. This personal attention both builds and supports high levels of expectations for each child: No one is slipping through the cracks, either in the classroom or in the school as a whole.

"Positive discipline" is yet another way of helping youngsters to feel connected and respected among their peers. Under the schoolwide "positive discipline" policy, students are expected to be respectful, to take responsibility for their actions, and to become increasingly capable of making good choices. They are also taught to apply "the Voyager problem-solving steps" when they are having difficulties with themselves and others. This begins with "stop and calm yourself" and progresses through identifying problems, brainstorming and evaluating helpful ideas, and evaluating and implementing them.

To reinforce the positive discipline policy, one teacher remarked that "we catch kids being successful and we talk about it in the classroom." Similarly, Mrs. Sandy Molnar, a teacher who coaches special needs and other students intensively during pullout sessions, rewards students each day for "getting caught for doing something good. It is a central part of the school to note when students are helping others, contributing ideas, cooperating, and caring." Ms. Harmer's daily announcements also include the names of students who've been "caught" in these acts. The school also makes sure that "everyone really is validated and truly a part of all of the activities." As a result, there are no in-groups and out-groups: "there's not a hierarchy here" among students. Given these efforts to create a positive, respectful, and inclusive culture, disciplinary problems are very rare.

Hard Work. Strong and positive social interactions provide a groundwork that enables students and teachers to work hard and pursue high quality work. Perhaps in the spirit of voyagers, there is value placed on going the extra mile in one's efforts. Adults model this for students. In whatever they do, from a dedication ceremony for the new school's library to the quality of the classroom handouts, teachers "put the extra polish on it." Ms. Harmer believes that attention to the aesthetics helps to set an environment of and for high-quality work. (This view is shared by Mrs. Davenport, the Governor Bent School's principal.) It creates an environment that people find interesting and enjoyable (see the Arts Compass Point, below).

Teachers are also explicit with students about teachers' own efforts. The culture is pervaded by demonstrations of good work, reflection about the characteristics of particular pieces of good work, and self-assessment. Teachers critique their own work in front of students: the work they put into it, what they like about it, what they don't, and what they think they need to do to improve a particular piece of work. Students are supported to acquire the same habits of self-assessment and reflection. They critique their own and other students' works in class. "We use a lot of examples, and so we show exemplary work for children and allow them to learn from their peers in that way." The teachers ask not only, "What was good about this?" but also, "What can we do to make this even better?"

A central tool for reflecting on work and fostering quality is the extensive use of rubrics throughout the school. Ms. Harmer believes that the adoption of rubrics was "a direct result of our MI studies." The school has developed rubrics for a broad range of student work: writing in various genres, presentations, graphs, diagrams, posters, maps, dances, musical compositions, dioramas. The rubrics describe the characteristics of work at various levels of quality and encourage students to draw on a variety of strengths. For example, on a rubric for a map, a work that is "not yet quality" shows few landforms, doesn't attend to scale, does not provide a key or the key has few symbols, and it shows little creativity or sense of design. In contrast, a map of "excellent quality," includes all the important land forms, is drawn to scale, uses a complete and clear key, and makes strong use of color and design.

The rubrics are shared both with students and parents. Each grade level produces a weekly parent newsletter, which describes the following week's major projects, themes, activities, assignment due dates, and rubrics. Such rubrics not only set expectations. They also guide students toward the production of high-quality work and are used by teachers and students to assess work (see Andrade, 1997; Goodrich Andrade, 2000; Wiggins, 1998).

What happens to students with special needs or learning disabilities in this school, where high-quality work is such a central part of the culture? These students and their families are also encouraged to exceed expectations. This expectation is accompanied by ongoing school–home communication. Mrs. Molnar, who works with students who need extra support, noted that "often special needs students . . . are only challenged to a certain level that is often much lower than that of other students in a school. I think that all students must be challenged and that, by raising the level of expectation, students often respond to the challenge."

Mrs. Molnar works to maximize, but not overwhelm, her students. To maintain this balance, she "makes sure that parents openly communicate any pressures that the children are feeling." If need be, she wants the parents, to tell her "Look, I've worked with my child and . . . at this point we are saturated." She and the regular classroom teachers may modify assignments and deadlines, but they continually provide the support to get special needs students—and all students—to do the best work possible. Relatedly, because the school works to foster high-quality work from all students, parents of youngsters who have been selected for programs for the gifted typically opt to keep their children at Glenridge.

The students' and teachers' effort and wonderful work is celebrated throughout the school. During these twice-a-month gatherings, called "Fab Fridays," teachers spend an hour after school to share their recent classroom successes, and sometimes also seek input on how to work through some difficulty. Throughout the school year, teachers display the best work of every one of their students on the bulletin boards and in glass cases near their classrooms. There, others can see it, reflect on it, and consider new ways to develop their own teaching and learning. As she travels around the classrooms, Ms. Harmer praises high-quality work each day, leaving notes for teachers and for students about what she sees them doing and the strengths of it. (And she may also suggest ways for doing things even better.) Alongside all this, there are school wide assemblies to take note of students' best work and to reward extra effort and improvement. In addition, many classroom curriculum units, such as the Heritage/Traditions Unit described in Chapter 10, have a culminating celebration of student work, which parents, peers, and others in the school community can attend.

In short, the school culture at Glenridge is one characterized by respectful and caring relationships, hard work, beliefs that all children can use their strengths to exceed expectations, and a good deal of joy. The upshot is an abundance of work that is well worth celebrating.

Collaboration

Informal and formal collaboration are pervasive at Glenridge. A collegial environment throughout the school makes it possible for the staff to learn from each other in an ongoing, informal way. "The staff is so willing to share," said Tammy Westrick, a first-grade teacher. "We all basically get along. We are open and caring. And we know that every lesson that we do is always a draft." Teachers often exchange ideas about current lessons and projects in their lunchroom, where they can also consult the latest educational journals and the school's substantial collection of educational resource books.

Collaboration is also formally structured into the schedule of the school. One of the main ways that collaboration is structured into the school is through "team meetings": common planning time for teachers at the same grade level. These take place for one hour each week during the school day. In team meetings, teachers plan, refine, and share ideas about curricula. This spurs the broad adoption of useful ideas. For instance, as a result of these meetings, the Heritage/Traditions Unit was adopted by other sixth-grade teachers. Team meetings also provide opportunities to brainstorm new ideas for project-based curricula, to get suggestions on practice, and to develop plans for co-teaching.

The commitment to working constructively with one's team members begins with the hiring process. New teachers are essentially hired by the team. Ms. Harmer participates, but she gives the final say to the team. As a result, no one is forced to work with an unknown teacher, and new teachers are welcomed warmly as colleagues.

Collaboration in grade-level teams is complemented by exchanges about curriculum and pedagogy across grade levels. This happens at least twice a month during Fab Fridays. In addition to sharing their successes and seeking feedback during these meetings, teachers also bring back ideas from professional development meetings they have attended outside the school. For example, two teachers who had recently attended a professional development seminar on real-world science projects underscored the usefulness of employing the scientific method (i.e., generating a hypothesis and using data to test it). They conveyed information about twelve different in-class activities, and demonstrated some of them, in order to improve science instruction and students' understanding of scientific concepts.

Collaboration is also evident in teachers' work with special needs students. All students are taught together in heterogeneous classrooms. Mrs. Molnar, the special needs teacher, holds pull-out coaching sessions for students diagnosed with learning disabilities and others who need extra help. To ensure these students get the support they need, Mrs. Molnar consults almost every day with the classroom teachers of her students. She is fully aware of their current and future lesson plans. This ongoing collaboration allows both teachers to share their observations of the student and to coordinate their efforts to enable each child to succeed in the classroom.

Arts

Glenridge Elementary School has a strong commitment to the arts and gives them a prominent role in the school. The school has band, orchestra, and general music teachers. Although the school has no art teacher, the visual arts are present throughout the school, as are drama and other artforms. The school environment is overflowing with student work and images. Ms. Harmer commented, "I think the aesthetic environment that we create, whether it's in the classroom or within the school, gives a lot of unspoken messages to children about how we value art and their efforts."

Educators at Glenridge encourage an aesthetic approach to the work of their students. One powerful way they do this is through their rubrics. For example, in the map rubric mentioned earlier, quality work required a strong use of design and color. In the rubric for the production of a book, the components for excellent quality include "aesthetically pleasing illustrations" and "a creative cover."

Despite the absence of an art teacher, visual art is taught as a discipline within the school. All the teachers have undertaken professional development in Discipline-Based Arts Education (DBAE), a program designed by the Getty Foundation. DBAE offers teachers a way to expose students to art history, aesthetics, the compositional elements of visual arts, and art making (Eisner, 1992). In addition, Glenridge collaborates with a local college to train parents to serve as art docents. Together with the classroom teachers, these parents help to develop lessons in visual arts for every classroom. "It's a wonderful partnership between the teachers and the parents,"

Art and aesthetic considerations have a prominent place at Glenridge Elementary School.

Ms. Harmer notes. Parents can also serve in artist-in-residence programs, working with children before and after school on a range of different art projects, each one lasting about ten hours.

Visual arts are also clearly integrated into the classrooms, where they fit well with project-based curriculum. As we'll see in the following chapter, students in Marge Staszak's Heritage/Traditions Unit use the visual arts in producing several elements of their scrapbook and in the design of the scrapbook as a whole. Other artforms are also employed. For example, Mr. Koenig, a fifth- and sixth-grade teacher, has small groups of students translate short stories into plays, which they rehearse and then perform for the rest of the class. As an interim step, he has the students draw storyboards for five to seven scenes from the story. In a third-grade unit on Folk Tales, teacher Dotty Watson helped children to transform a folk tale into a drama, which was then staged. Because there is no drama teacher, the school draws on outside expertise, including local theatre groups and a week-long theatre workshop offered each year by the Missoula Children's Theatre.

Controlled Choice

At Glenridge there is no one approach to teaching that pervades the school, and there is no one way that things must be done. Ms. Harmer likens her job to that of an orchestra conductor or theater director. Her aim is to "find a way for everybody to shine in their own particular way." Teachers say that Ms. Harmer's leadership—especially her willingness to let them practice teaching in ways that serve many different learners—is vital to the school's success.

In line with Ms. Harmer's approach to leadership, teachers have a great deal of choice in their classroom practice. There are shared emphases and tools, including multiple intelligences, project-based curriculum, and inquiry-based learning. At the same time, teachers are encouraged to use these tools flexibly and to try out new ideas. Because of the collaborative and collegial aspects of the school, teachers reflect on and assess their choices in an ongoing way. Through team meetings, staff meetings, Fab Fridays, and daily conversations, teachers are continually exchanging ideas about their existing practice and innovations, getting feedback on their work, and making their work better. If an idea is tried out and doesn't work, it is dropped and everyone learns from that experience as well. In essence, while teachers have a great deal of choice in their classrooms, that freedom is inevitably pointed in one direction: toward best practice.

Just as teachers have choices in the way they go about doing their best work, so do students. Teachers include choices for students in their project-based work. Yet, as Marge Staszak's Heritage/Traditions Unit stresses, students' choices are controlled: some elements of the project are required, other elements allow students to select from a range of different choices. Teachers often encourage students to reason about and explain their choices. For example, Ann Reed, a fourth-grade teacher, always asks her students to talk about why they chose to do a particular piece of work, why they chose to do it in the way that they did, and how they would choose to make it even better. In essence, through choice, students as well as teachers are encouraged to reflect on what they do and how to improve it.

Tool

I don't think that you can look at MI just to say this is an instructional strategy that you . . . just sort of layer onto a school. It has to be a part of the culture, and it has to have tendrils that reach throughout.
—Sheryl Harmer

Glenridge began incorporating MI in 1992. According to Ms. Harmer, the theory has helped everyone to understand that "There are lots of different ways to know and to demonstrate that knowing." To support this understanding, teachers do talk with students and parents about the theory. The point of this talk is not to teach the theory, but rather to help youngsters to draw on the many ways that they can learn. The theory doesn't displace the curriculum—everything isn't taught in seven or eight different ways—and the staff is careful to avoid labeling students as spatial, or kinesthetic, or verbal. Instead, teachers use MI as a tool to open up the curriculum so that more students can gain knowledge and skill in math, language arts, science, social studies, movement/physical education, and the arts.

Although MI is important at Glenridge, the theory is used together with several other practices that are aimed at enabling a broad diversity of learners to succeed. Another driving force in the school is "research-based inquiry." At Glenridge, this means that students' questions are central to the classroom activities, and students undertake research to get the information they need to answer their questions. (The "KWL" approach used in the McCleary School is another way of putting students' questions at the center of instruction. See Chapters 2 and 3.) Another tool that's common across Glenridge's classrooms is an integrated, project-based curriculum. This curriculum brings together learning in language, math, visual arts, social studies, and other areas to support meaningful work, such as the production of a play, or developing a history of one's own family. As students conduct research and produce meaningful work, they get many opportunities to draw on a variety of intelligences. For example, in the Heritage/Traditions Unit, students draw on linguistic, interpersonal, intrapersonal, spatial, logical-mathematical, musical, and bodily-kinesthetic intelligences. These approaches—MI, inquiry-based learning, and integrated, project-based curricula—work together to enable diverse learners to engage the curriculum and to develop knowledge, skill, and meaning.

Together, the Compass Point Practices enable teachers to engage multiple intelligences in ways that advance students' learning. They provide a supportive environment for teachers to launch such work in their own classrooms. In light of your own schoolwide practices, how might you adapt the activities and strategies described in the Heritage/Traditions Unit that follows?

CHAPTER 10

Heritage/Traditions

THE HERITAGE/TRADITION UNIT AT A GLANCE

What's a tradition?

A special thing my family does every year.
My brother and I get one early Christmas present
I go to my grandma's house and open presents
I go to my other grandma's to open more presents.
That's a tradition!

This poem was written by a student during the Heritage/Traditions Unit that Marge Staszak developed for her sixth-grade class at the Glenridge Elementary School in Renton, Washington. The unit incorporates activities from social studies, as well as language arts, mathematics, and the arts.

The Heritage/Traditions Unit has a dual focus. It's aimed at enabling students to learn about their own family history, about America's history of immigration, and about the different cultures present within their own classroom and in the wider society. At the same time, it helps students advance their language and math skills, and develop the organizational skills needed to carry out a multipart project.

As part of this curriculum unit, students interview family members between Thanksgiving and the winter holidays, when students often have more access to their extended family. Writing a poem is one of many activities that personalizes the unit for students, while at the same time helping them to learn particular skills.

Marge Staszak teaches a looping fifth- and sixth-class. Because students stay in her class for two years, she does this unit every other year. Each time she does it, Mrs. Staszak chooses from the many activities that she has developed over the years, but each year, two activities remain the same: Students organize the work that they produce during the activities into their own Traditions Scrapbook, and present one or more pieces from their scrapbooks at a Traditions Banquet, a celebration attended by their classmates, family members, and other members of the school community.

Mrs. Staszak looks over a student's draft work for the Heritage/Traditions Unit.

MI in This Unit

- Heritage/Traditions incorporates several different disciplines and a variety of activities to enable diverse learners to engage the topic.
- The Heritage/Traditions Unit engages intelligences through activities that are substantive.
- Students can draw on linguistic, logical-mathematical, bodily-kinesthetic, spatial, interpersonal, intrapersonal, and musical intelligences.

Entry Points in This Unit

- The Heritage/Traditions Unit enables students to learn about their own family history, immigration, and various cultures through each of the entry points.
- The narrative, quantitative, aesthetic, and interpersonal Entry Points are the most frequently used.

Compass Point Practices in This Unit

- The Compass Point Practices in place throughout Glenridge Elementary allow the school to engage multiple intelligences in ways that advance students' learning.
- Most of the Compass Point Practices are also in place within Mrs. Staszak's own classroom. Most notable are arts, readiness, and a culture that is hardworking but joyful.

WHAT IS THE HERITAGE/TRADITIONS UNIT?

It's a unit that invites students to delve into their past, their heritage, their ancestors, their family customs and stories—their traditions.

—Marge Staszak
Fifth- and Sixth-Grade Teacher
Glenridge Elementary School
Renton, Washington

The Heritage/Traditions Unit involves a sequence of assignments that take place over a three-week period of time. During this time, students work on a range of activities that combine the study of immigration with a study of the diverse heritage in their own and others' families.

Students compile many assignments from the unit into a Traditions Scrapbook, which they display during a banquet held before the winter holiday break each year. As parents, grandparents, and other guests circulate to look at the scrapbooks, the sixth grade students in Mrs. Staszak's class share food, music, and stories that reflect each of their families' heritage and traditions.

In Marge Staszak's looped class, the Heritage/Traditions Unit takes place in sixth grade, after the required fifth-grade topic of Colonial America.

Students' Heritage/Traditions scrapbooks capture their classmates' interest.

This sequence helps the students to see how the country evolved from its native people and early settlers to the complex, multifaceted society that now exists. At the same time, as Mrs. Staszak notes, this approach allows students "to discover the importance and joy in learning about their history."

In the Heritage/Traditions Unit students develop subject area skills in social studies, language arts, mathematics, and art. For example, in one language arts activity students write about and share a story that has been told and retold in their family. As part of this activity, students learn interviewing skills, hone their writing skills, and practice their presentation skills. Several of the activities are aimed at helping students to develop their skills and knowledge of mathematics. In one, students are asked to create a graphical representation of their own heritage, using information gathered from interviews. In art activities, such as drawing an object valued within their family, students learn specific production skills at the same time they learn about artistic traditions of a culture.

In addition to subject area goals, the Traditions Scrapbook also has another larger aim: To help students develop the organizational skills needed to complete a large project over an extended period of time. This skill becomes increasingly important as students move toward middle school.

Strategies for helping students produce an extended project, like the Traditions Scrapbook, as well as descriptions of some of the individual activities undertaken for the Heritage/Traditions Unit, are described in the next sections.

STRATEGIES: BUILDING READINESS, MODELING, AND CULMINATING ACTIVITIES

You know you can tell children, 'I want you to plan this out,' and 'Be sure you do a little bit at a time.'
But kids at that age just don't know how to do that. I've found that, over the years of teaching,
you have to structure it for them. For a long-term project like this, it's much better if you force them
to be structured, because it's not the nature of a twelve-year-old to be able to plan all that.
That's a difficult process. It's even hard for us sometimes.

—Marge Staszak
Fifth- and Sixth-Grade Teacher
Glenridge Elementary School
Renton, Washington

The Heritage/Traditions Unit aims to build both organizational skills and students' knowledge of their own family history, of immigration, and of the many cultures that have become part of American society. These aims are supported by three key teacher strategies:

- building readiness in school and home;
- modeling good work;
- holding culminating activities.

These strategies can be adapted to any extended project work with students in a variety of grade levels and content areas. As you read these strategies, you may want to think about how they might be included or adapted in your own curriculum.

Building Readiness in School and at Home

To participate successfully in the Heritage/Traditions Unit, students need to be supported both in school and at home. Right from the start of the unit, Mrs. Staszak encourages parents to be involved.

One way Mrs. Staszak builds readiness is by giving students a packet of materials to share with their parents the week before the unit's actual start. The packet includes a letter to parents about the unit, a rubric detailing the qualities needed for a good scrapbook, and a project calendar. The packet also includes a list of required and extra-credit activities for students to do during the unit.

Letter to Parents

The letter to parents helps to introduce the Heritage/Traditions Unit to each student's family. It describes some of the activities that will take place and it suggests ways that parents or other family members can help their children during the unit. For example, the letter includes a survey and other work that is convenient to undertake during the coming holidays. Information collected during family holidays will be used in several different activities and products during the Heritage/Traditions Unit. A copy of the letter appears in Box 10.1.

Project Calendar

As Marge Staszak developed the Heritage/Traditions Unit, she realized that "the more involved the unit became, the more difficult it was for students to complete their tasks on time." To help students develop skill in

BOX 10.1 LETTER TO PARENTS

Dear Parents:

For the next several weeks (until the start of winter break) we will be studying the diversity of each of our family's heritage. During this exploration students will be asked to interview their relatives so that they might learn about their past and that of their ancestors. Each student will then produce a scrapbook that will contain a personal history of his/her family.

The scrapbook will contain such items as favorite family recipes, favorite family stories, family rituals, unusual or funny things that happened in one's family, and a family tree. Most the work for the scrapbook will be done in class; homework will consist of editing and polishing various parts of the scrapbook and designing an unusual or interesting cover for the scrapbook.

Because we realize that many families see relatives during the Thanksgiving holiday, attached you will find a short survey that students may use to help them learn about their family's history. It would be helpful if the children took the questionnaire and family tree worksheet with them if they visit relatives. With the questionnaire completed, the children may find it easier to complete their scrapbooks.

Thanks for your help in this project.

A letter to students' parents explains the Heritage/Traditions Unit and prepares them to support their children in the project.

FIGURE 10.1

A calendar for the Heritage/Traditions Unit includes dates that assignments are due. This helps students to manage their time, and it helps to keep parents informed and support their child's success.

Monday	Tuesday	Wednesday	Thursday	Friday
	Handout Traditions Scrapbook Information		Thanksgiving	Thanksgiving
	Name Page	Family Rituals		Family Tree
	"What's a Tradition?" Poem Family Recipe	Family Memorabilia	Dedication Page Ethnic Graph	Family Stories
Penny Time Line of My Life	Front Back Cover, Title Page Table of Contents Venn Diagram About the Author	Scrapbook Due! Traditions Banquet		

managing their time, Mrs. Staszak now includes a project calendar in the introductory packet. The calendar helps students and their parents to track when all the Heritage/Traditions Unit assignments are due. This helps students complete their work in a timely way. To provide additional structure and support for time management, Mrs. Staszak also keeps a large calendar at the front of the classroom. Every morning students have time to report on their progress and to discuss any questions they might have.

The clear timetable of the project calendar helps both Mrs. Staszak and parents keep track of students' work as they progress through the unit. This is a simple way to build in support for their success, to identify those who are having trouble producing some part of the scrapbook, and to take steps to meet their individual needs.

Rubrics

Rubrics are tools for assessment and instruction used throughout Glenridge Elementary School. A rubric generally includes two things: characteristics important for a particular work to include and indicators showing the extent to which students fulfilled that quality (Goodrich, 1997; Goodrich & Andrade, 2000; Wiggins, 1998).

Mrs. Staszak sends home rubrics for the overall scrapbook, as well as for individual pieces of work that will go into the scrapbook. She uses a five-point scale that shows the degree to which students meet each of the important characteristics (0–1 indicates "not yet quality" work; 2–3 is "almost quality"; and 4–5 is "excellent quality"). The rubrics help the students and their parents understand the kind of work students are expected to produce. This can help students to work toward those expectations and help parents to support them.

By providing students and their parents with a packet of materials about the Heritage/Traditions Unit, Mrs. Staszak paves the way for students to be successful. The packet's letter, calendar, rubric, and other materials enable families to get ready to support students' efforts in the unit. The packet helps parents, students, and educators to share an understanding of what's needed to produce strong work.

FIGURE 10.2
A rubric helps students and their parents to know the characteristics of a good scrapbook.

Content	All scrapbook components are complete and finished with accuracy and great attention to detail.
Format/Mechanics	Entire scrapbook is laid out in the correct format. Attention is given to correct grammar and paragraphing.
Quality	All sections of the scrapbook reflect superior quality.
Creativity	All components of the scrapbook show signs of creativity; extra touches have been added to create outstanding, eye-catching appeal.
Presentation	Scrapbook is presented to audience in a clear, enthusiastic manner. Plenty of eye contact, poise, and confidence.

Modeling Good Work

While the rubric describes the characteristics of a strong piece of work, modeling lets students see concrete examples of such work. For the Heritage/Tradition Unit, several kinds of modeling are used: modeling of high-quality scrapbooks, the process for producing parts of the scrapbook, and modeling of the scrapbook presentation.

Modeling the Scrapbook

On the first day of the Heritage/Traditions Unit, Mrs. Staszak reviews scrapbooks that her former students have created. (The scrapbooks have to be borrowed for this purpose; Mrs. Staszak finds that "no one, of course, wants to let me keep their scrapbooks, and their parents don't either!"). The caring and respectful culture of the school supports this kind of student-to-student learning. Modeling these scrapbooks against the dimensions of the rubric gives students a clear and concrete illustration of the work they are expected to do. The model scrapbooks are kept in the classroom to provide handy references whenever students want to see them.

Modeling the Process

Current students also model how strong work is developed. When students in the class are in the process of creating good work for their scrapbook, Mrs. Staszak suggests that other students "go over and see" how this work is being done. (Note: In Chapter 6, Language Artists, you'll see that Mrs. Hamner also uses good student work to model the qualities she seeks. She refers to the sharing of this work as "celebrating.")

Modeling the Scrapbook Presentation

Each student needs to present one or more pieces from his or her scrapbook at the Heritage/Traditions Banquet. To support good presentations, Mrs. Staszak invites former students to present their Traditions Scrapbook for current students. This gives her current students the chance to see a high-quality presentation in action.

BOX 10.2 PAGES FROM A STUDENT'S HERITAGE/TRADITIONS SCRAPBOOK

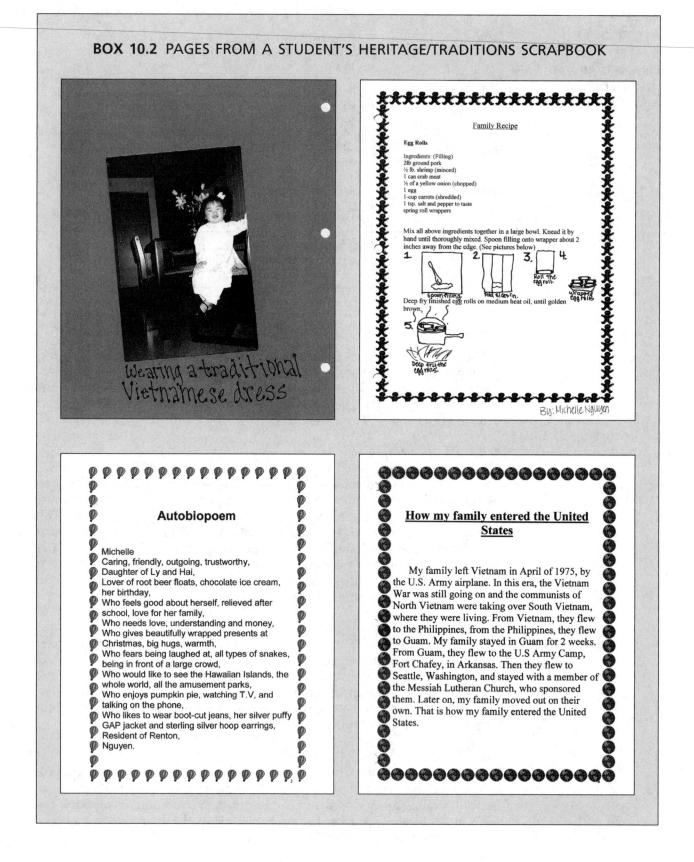

wearing a traditional Vietnamese dress

Family Recipe

Egg Rolls

Ingredients: (Filling)
2lb ground pork
½ lb. shrimp (minced)
1 can crab meat
½ of a yellow onion (chopped)
1 egg
1-cup carrots (shredded)
1 tsp. salt and pepper to taste
spring roll wrappers

Mix all above ingredients together in a large bowl. Knead it by hand until thoroughly mixed. Spoon filling onto wrapper about 2 inches away from the edge. (See pictures below)

1. *Spoon filling.* 2. *Fold sides in.* 3. *Roll the egg roll.* 4. *wrapped egg rolls*

Deep fry finished egg rolls on medium heat oil, until golden brown.

5. *Deep fry the egg rolls.*

By: Michelle Nguyen

Autobiopoem

Michelle
Caring, friendly, outgoing, trustworthy,
Daughter of Ly and Hai,
Lover of root beer floats, chocolate ice cream, her birthday,
Who feels good about herself, relieved after school, love for her family,
Who needs love, understanding and money,
Who gives beautifully wrapped presents at Christmas, big hugs, warmth,
Who fears being laughed at, all types of snakes, being in front of a large crowd,
Who would like to see the Hawaiian Islands, the whole world, all the amusement parks,
Who enjoys pumpkin pie, watching T.V, and talking on the phone,
Who likes to wear boot-cut jeans, her silver puffy GAP jacket and sterling silver hoop earrings,
Resident of Renton,
Nguyen.

How my family entered the United States

My family left Vietnam in April of 1975, by the U.S. Army airplane. In this era, the Vietnam War was still going on and the communists of North Vietnam were taking over South Vietnam, where they were living. From Vietnam, they flew to the Philippines, from the Philippines, they flew to Guam. My family stayed in Guam for 2 weeks. From Guam, they flew to the U.S Army Camp, Fort Chafey, in Arkansas. Then they flew to Seattle, Washington, and stayed with a member of the Messiah Lutheran Church, who sponsored them. Later on, my family moved out on their own. That is how my family entered the United States.

Modeling helps all students, but it can be especially helpful for students with learning differences. Mrs. Staszak tailors how she models work to accommodate the needs of children with learning differences. She begins modeling by working with students' strengths. For example, with students who have writing or language difficulties, Mrs. Staszak begins by modeling visual work from the scrapbooks and pictures of completed scrapbooks. She then encourages students who struggle with writing skills to dictate the story first to her or to a parent. While accommodating their needs, she supports their efforts to produce good work by "raising the level of expectation for the student as well as involving the parent." Students with special needs are also helped by close cooperation with the special education teacher, Mrs. Molnar. For example, Mrs. Molnar brings in additional picture resources pertaining to immigration, various cultures, and family trees, and helps students practice their presentations.

Holding Culminating Activities

Culminating activities are another strategy for helping diverse learners to produce high-quality work. Because students know that their work is going to be shared at a public event that includes their family and other members of the school community, they are motivated to do their best.

The Traditions Banquet that concludes the Heritage/Traditions Unit is also a way to involve the community and enables the students' work to be publicly appreciated by the school and family. Each year, students, their families, and the school community eagerly await the banquet at which students and their families share the students' scrapbooks while enjoying food and music from different cultures. As guests stop to look at their work, students make presentations about one or more pieces of their scrapbook. For instance, they might explain their family tree, or the origins of their name, or why they drew a particular object that's treasured in their family. A rubric helps the students focus on important qualities of a good presentation (e.g., eye contact, clarity) and both the presenter and the class audience evaluate the presentation against the rubrics.

The Traditions Banquet is also a time when the learning of different generations is shared. "Parents often start sharing stories about when they were in sixth grade or about their family background. . . . Grandparents love to tell what school was like when they were in fifth or sixth grade. It's so much fun, and they get so excited. I actually got thank-you letters from grandparents telling me what a wonderful unit it was."

WHAT HAPPENS DURING THE HERITAGE/TRADITIONS UNIT? LANGUAGE ARTS, MATHEMATICS, AND THE ARTS

> *I just think MI makes this unit come to life for the kids.*
> —Marge Staszak

During the Heritage/Traditions Unit, students undertake a variety of individual and small-group activities involving language arts, mathematics, and the arts. These activities enable them to draw on their multiple intelligences to understand their family history, immigration, and the diverse

---

BOX 10.3 MATERIALS NEEDED

Activities in the Heritage/Traditions Unit use many common classroom materials such as:

- markers and/or other drawing materials
- colored paper, and paper of various sizes
- computers

- computer printers
- software for graphic design, desktop publishing, and word processing

In addition, students bring photographs and other scrapbook materials from home.

---

nature of American society. These activities also support the development of time-management and public speaking skills. At the same time, the activities result in final products that can be included in their Traditions Scrapbook.

Mrs. Staszak holds children to high expectations for each of the activities, "If you don't set high standards for students, and you let them get away with the least amount that they'll do, that's what they are going to produce for you. The more you say, 'No, that's not acceptable. We're going to do this over, but I'm going to help you,' . . . the more they know that that's the quality that I expect." This expectation, along with her strategies of building awareness, modeling, and holding culminating activities, fosters strong student work.

The activities are scheduled to take place between Thanksgiving and the December holiday break, about one week after the packet of preparatory materials is sent home. During this time of year, students are likely to have more opportunities to gather information and do research with members of their extended family.

The amount of class time dedicated to the Heritage/Traditions Unit can vary. Some or all of the regular classroom time for language arts, math, and social studies can be devoted to the unit. Some art and music classes can also be devoted to it. It depends in part on the number of activities that are incorporated and the kind of work that students are expected to produce.

Some of the activities are described below. They illustrate how a range of different students can be engaged in this unit through substantive disciplinary work. As you read these, it's likely that many other engaging and substantive activities will come to mind.

Language Arts Activities

Reading, writing, and public speaking are skills that are needed for, and developed in, the Heritage/Traditions Unit. As part of the unit, students are asked to produce a variety of written products, to read different genres, and to learn how to communicate with peers and other audiences. Through these activities students learn about their own family, immigration, and the many cultures that make up the United States. These activities also help them meet the state and district learning objectives. These objectives call for children to be able to recognize and generate different literary forms, to proofread and edit, and to analyze information encountered in reports, presentations, and visual displays.

Among the writing activities are a Traditions poem, a brief autobiography, descriptions of family memorabilia, and stories that have been told and retold in the students' families.

The Family Story

The family story is an essay in which students capture an event that has been told many times in their family. To support diverse learners so that they can produce a strong essay, Mrs. Staszak uses several preparatory events:

- To gather information for the essay, students learn about how to do an interview. For example, they learn about asking open-ended questions. These are questions that invite people to provide detailed responses, so that students can get a richer story. ("Tell me about when you were little, . . ." "tell me about how you managed to come to America . . ."). They also learn that to be a good interviewer, they have to pay attention to the other person's ideas and to notice if the person is tired or needs to take a break.
- In preparation for these interviews and essays, students read fiction, nonfiction, and poetry about different immigrants' experiences and about their family history. Through readings in these various genres, students learn that their own writings, like their readings, can take on a variety of forms and styles.
- Students begin to organize information from the interviews and readings into an essay through a structured writing process. This same writing process is used across many different written assignments in Mrs. Staszak's room. The process begins by brainstorming ideas. The students then connect their ideas through a writing web. Mrs. Staszak finds that the writing web provides a "really good way for children to become focused" and to organize their thinking before they do their actual writing. It also provides a visual structure to support the organization of written compositions (see Figure 10.3).
- The connections made in the web help students produce their first draft of the family story. They share their draft with a student partner who provides feedback on particular points, such as word choice and organization, and then decide whether they want to use their partner's feedback.
- Students revise their family story until it is at least well organized and grammatically correct.

FIGURE 10.3
Brainstorming with a Writing Web

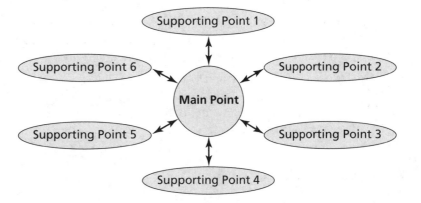

BOX 10.4 A QUESTIONNAIRE HELPS STUDENTS COLLECT INFORMATION

Name_____

Below is a list of questions that will be helpful for you to use to ask relatives questions about your family's heritage. Since many of you see relatives over the Thanksgiving holiday, we are providing this survey so that you can take notes that will help you write items for a family scrapbook, our December project.

The information you get can be written in note form; it does not have to be in complete sentences. Include enough details in your notes so that you can write your required scrapbook parts in paragraph form when we begin our writing next week. Have fun!!! This will result in a great scrapbook for you to keep.

Heritage Questionnaire

1. What are two favorite family stories that have been passed down in your family? These may include things that happened to grandparents, parents, uncles, aunts, cousins, etc.

2. What special recipes are served at family gatherings? (You must have at least two recipes with all ingredients: you may have more than two if you choose). Also, tell where you got the recipe or how it originated.

3. What funny or unusual things happened to someone in your family? (List two incidents). Be sure to get details so you may explain them fully in your scrapbook.

4. What funny family words originated with someone in your family? For instance someone may have called hamburgers, "hannaburgers" when they were young because they couldn't pronounce the word correctly.

5. What do your grandparents remember most about their year in school as a sixth grader? What about your parents or aunts and uncles? What was the school day like? What type of clothes, food, and music were popular then? What did kids do for fun outside of school?

6. When someone was sick in the family, what did their parents do or use to help them get better? Did they concoct homemade remedies for the sick person to take? If so, what were these concoctions or remedies?

7. Please fill out the family tree worksheet to the best of your ability. It is helpful to do this ahead of time (before we begin the scrapbook) so that you will have the necessary information to fill out a clean copy of the family tree to include in your scrapbook.

Mrs. Staszak wants each child to develop writing that is "imaginative, clear, and concise." As the family story activity reveals, she provides a range of approaches and structures, including various reading materials, interaction with others, a visual organizer, and a clearly outlined writing process. This variety of structures and supports allows her to "get the best writing I can get out of each child."

Autobiography

The autobiography is a brief piece of writing that is highly structured and purposeful: It serves as the "author's page" in the finished scrapbook, which must include students' first and last names, their age, city of residence, and favorite hobbies. It can also include a recounting of important events and future plans, and a photograph of themselves.

In preparation for writing the autobiography, and as part of Mrs. Staszak's effort to acquaint children with different genres, students read examples of autobiographies and "about the author" sections. As with most written pieces, students review and revise it until it is clear, correct, well organized, and interesting.

Mathematics Activities

Social sciences commonly make use of graphs, tables, time lines, and other mathematical tools and concepts, therefore, it's natural that Marge Staszak uses several different math activities to help students explore and represent information about their own traditions and heritage and the diversity of the larger society. Learning to represent information in this way is also an important learning standard for the state of Washington and the local school district.

The Venn Diagram

The Venn diagram builds on the interview with a family member. As part of the interview, students seek to learn what life was like for an older relative, typically a parent or grandparent, when that relative was in sixth grade. During the interview students ask their relatives what school was like, what kind of food, music, and clothing were popular, and what children at that age and at that point in time did for fun.

FIGURE 10.4　Students in the Heritage/Traditions Unit use Venn diagrams to represent commonalities and differences across generations.

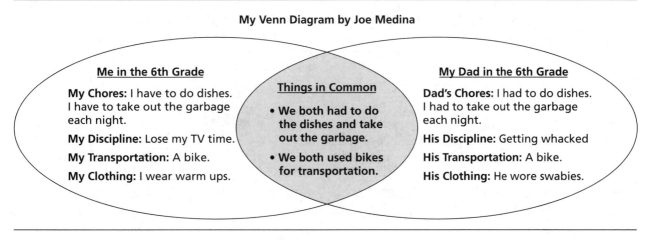

My Venn Diagram by Joe Medina

Me in the 6th Grade

My Chores: I have to do dishes. I have to take out the garbage each night.

My Discipline: Lose my TV time.

My Transportation: A bike.

My Clothing: I wear warm ups.

Things in Common

- **We both had to do the dishes and take out the garbage.**
- **We both used bikes for transportation.**

My Dad in the 6th Grade

Dad's Chores: I had to do dishes. I had to take out the garbage each night.

His Discipline: Getting whacked

His Transportation: A bike.

His Clothing: He wore swabies.

For the Venn diagram activity, students then generate their own responses to the questions they asked from the older relative. Using their own responses and those of their older family member, the students build the set of responses that are shared or similar, and responses that vary or differ. They then represent these sets of information visually in a Venn diagram.

Family Heritage Graphs

Another way students work with mathematical concepts in the Heritage/Traditions Unit is by creating graphical representations of their family background. The graphic can be computer generated or drawn by hand. In either case, it requires students to transform information that they've collected through interviews, a family tree, or other sources by representing it in graphs, charts, and numbers.

What If?

In conjunction with the graphing activity, and also as part of the opening discussion for this unit, Mrs. Staszak asks the children to consider what the United States would look like if no immigration had taken place or if no limitations had been placed on immigration. Students can represent these different hypothetical situations using bar graphs or pie charts and brief narratives.

Arts Activities

Each culture has an array of artistic traditions. So, the Heritage/Traditions Unit naturally provides teachers and students with many wonderful ways to involve the arts. In Glenridge Elementary, learning in the arts during this unit also enables teachers and students to meet some of the local school district's goals. For example, during sixth grade students are expected to understand perspective, unity, balance, and other elements of visual composition. Students are also expected to participate in movement and music. Whether or not your district has such learning requirements, the arts also provide students with ways to learn and represent knowledge about their own and other cultures. For these reasons, the arts play a vital role in the Heritage/Traditions Unit.

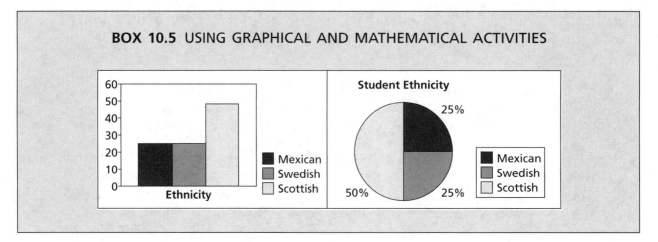

BOX 10.5 USING GRAPHICAL AND MATHEMATICAL ACTIVITIES

Visual and Decorative Arts

For the scrapbook, Mrs. Staszak introduces the idea of memorabilia and heirlooms. She asks students to bring in some of these things for the class to discuss. Sometimes, of course, this isn't feasible: An object may be too big, delicate, or valuable. In those cases, students bring in a photograph of the object. Some students feel that there isn't such an object in their family. In these situations, Mrs. Staszak asks the youngster to choose an object that he or she now values and would want to pass down to younger members of her family. The class then considers what makes these objects special, both in the context of their family and in terms of the object's aesthetic qualities. After this, the students sketch their objects. These drawings, along with an accompanying brief description, are included in the students' scrapbooks.

In addition to the family heirloom, students can opt to produce one or more other visual artworks. For example, they can study family crests and design one that reflects key parts of their own family's heritage and traditions. They can also employ the visual arts in other required elements of the scrapbook, such as its cover and the representation of their family tree.

Performing Arts

Performing arts, including dance, music, storytelling, and drama, exist across traditions and cultures. To help students learn and appreciate the art of different cultures, Marge Staszak collaborates with the music teacher. (In Glenridge, special area teachers regularly consult with classroom teachers so that they can devise ways to support classroom instruction.) As a result of this collaboration, the music teacher taught folk songs and folk dances during the Heritage/Traditions Unit. Students have the option to perform these at the culminating banquet.

The activities described in the previous section offer a starting point for your own thinking. Your own experiences, your colleagues, students, and community will likely bring to mind many other ideas for helping diverse learners to engage in activities that enable them to understand their own, others', and the nation's rich heritage.

CONCLUSION: REVISITING THE FRAMEWORKS

I want students to be able to gather information about themselves and their families in a manner that is comfortable to them. But I also want them to stretch a little bit, to perhaps use those intelligences that may not be their strengths.

—Marge Staszak
Fifth- and Sixth-Grade Teacher
Glenridge Elementary School
Renton, Washington

The following review highlights how MI, the Entry Points Framework, and the Compass Point Practices are incorporated in the Heritage/Traditions Unit.

Linguistic	Spatial	Interpersonal	Intrapersonal	Logical-Mathematical	Musical	Naturalist	Bodily-Kinesthetic	ACTIVITIES
X	X							Scrapbook development: Students create aesthetically pleasing scrapbook pages to present what they have learned in the Heritage/Traditions Unit activities.
X		X	X					Interview: Students interview family members and use the interview material to write stories and poems.
X	X							Writing: Students' writing process includes writing webs to help them brainstorm and connect ideas.
X			X					Autobiography: Students write brief autobiographies.
	X	X		X				Math activities: Students produce Venn diagrams comparing their own and older relatives' childhood, Heritage graphs, and "what if."
	X				X		X	Performing arts: Students learn music and dance of different cultures.
		X	X					Project coordination: Students learn the organizational skills necessary to complete a large scale project over an extended period of time.
X		X	X					Heritage/Traditions Banquet: Students present their scrapbooks to teachers, classmates, and family members at a culminating banquet.

FIGURE 10.5   Multiple Intelligences Engaged During the Heritage/Traditions Unit

MI in This Unit

Activities in the Heritage/Traditions Unit include many intelligences. This means that the concepts of the unit can be engaged by very different learners. It also means that students with different profiles of intelligences are likely to find some activities more appealing than others. The survey, in which they investigate their own heritage, is a particularly good opportunity to engage their interpersonal and intrapersonal intelligences.

Entry Points in This Unit

Helping students understand their own family history, immigration, and the diversity of cultures that have shaped the United States are topics that can be entered and explored through many routes, or entry points. In this unit each of the entry points is used.

Narrative: Students investigate and produce their own autobiography and narratives about their family traditions. Students also read autobiographies and stories about immigrants and immigration.

Aesthetic: Students are asked to attend to the aesthetic considerations of their scrapbook, for example, its design, lettering, and the use of color. They also learn songs and dances from different cultures.

Logical-Quantitative: Students produce graphs and other mathematical representations that reflect the different cultures and ethnicities in their own backgrounds. They are also asked to think about how the United States would be different if no immigrants had been allowed to enter America or if there were no limits on the number of immigrants allowed to enter the country.

Experiential: Students conduct interviews with family members. They are also asked to present one or more pieces of their work at the Traditions Banquet.

Existential: Students consider why their own family lives in the United States, and why other people immigrate/emigrate.

Interpersonal: Students interview family members to gain an understanding of others' experiences and perspectives. Students also work together in pairs to reflect on the strengths of each others' writing and to make suggestions about how to improve it.

Compass Point Practices in This Unit

Compass Point Practices are institution-wide approaches that allow MI to be used in ways that support student learning. These practices are evident throughout Glenridge. Many are clearly in place in the smaller context of Mrs. Staszak's room.

Tool: The content of the Heritage/Traditions Unit focused on family history, immigration, and the wider, multifaceted American culture. MI was a tool for engaging learners in this content: It "provided the structure" for engaging and developing different learners' knowledge and skills.

Arts: The Heritage/Traditions Unit incorporates a number of art forms, including visual arts, poetry, music, and dance.

Choice: Controlled choice is evident in the scrapbook that each student produces. Each scrapbook has required elements as well as optional components. Mrs. Staszak also gives students the opportunity to choose how they demonstrate their learning. For example, children have a choice in selecting which part of their scrapbook they wish to present.

Collaboration: The Heritage/Traditions Unit has been developed and revised over time through discussions with other teachers throughout the school. As Mrs. Staszak described the process, "The more heads you put together, the more ideas you get. . . ." In addition, the music teacher and other special area teachers meet with classroom teachers so that the content of special areas and classroom curricula can be integrated.

Readiness: Students and their parents are provided with planning materials and structures that help students to organize their efforts and carry out the range of learning activities. These preparatory materials are part of the strategy for enabling diverse learners to produce high-quality work.

Culture: In Marge Staszak's room, and throughout Glenridge Elementary School, learning is seen as an adventure or a voyage. At the same time, students are expected to appreciate their own and others' traditions. They are also expected to produce high-quality work.

As this review of the frameworks shows, the curricular and institutional supports are in place to enable teachers and many different students to succeed in this unit. And they do.

11 Searsport Elementary School

The curriculum example we are presenting from the Searsport Elementary School is the Archaeology Dig, or, simply, the Dig. The unit was developed and taught by a team of educators: the school's principal, Doug Lockwood, and two fifth-grade teachers, Charlene Farris and Renée Blodgett. The Dig incorporates hands-on work in science and social studies, as well as an exhibit of the students' findings at the local museum. It also enables many different kinds of learners to engage in science and history and to draw on standards for archaeology and museum practices to produce high-quality work. Before delving into the Dig, it's helpful to see the unit in the context of the surrounding school. In this chapter, we provide an overview of Searsport Elementary and illustrate, through the framework of Compass Point Practices, how the school enables teachers and many different kinds of learners to work at high levels.

OVERVIEW OF SEARSPORT ELEMENTARY SCHOOL

Searsport Elementary School, Searsport, Maine.

Searsport Elementary School is a K-5 school located in Searsport, Maine, a seacoast town about three-and-a-half hours north of Boston. The school is a quarter-mile from the ocean, on a street that includes the Penobscot Marine Museum, a worn clapboard house, the town's middle school, and its high school. In contrast to the neighboring schools, Searsport Elementary occupies a beautiful, new brick building that incorporates many child-friendly features. There are doors with windows at child's-eye level and wide corridors with curved recesses that provide spaces for group activities or small performances. Hanging from the top of the two-story entry hall is a banner that sports the school's mascot, the Searsport Seal, and the school's philosophy, "Success for Every Student."

The school's office is to the left of the entryway and the cafeteria to the right. On the first floor there is a gym, a large music room complete with a performance stage, and a spacious art studio with cathedral ceilings and big windows that look out onto the woods. The media area/library begins behind a glass wall at the back of the entryway. It is two stories high, accessible to classrooms on both levels, and well supplied with new tables, computers, and books. An abundance of artwork is built into the school. The media area houses a collection of colorful circus scenes, painted by a local artist, Waldo Pierce. Large mobiles shaped like sea creatures are suspended from the top of the tall corridors. Walls have been painted with sea murals, and tall, brightly colored, modern sculptures occupy the back lawn.

The school building would be an outstanding asset in the wealthiest district. Here it serves one of the poorer counties in Maine. It is a place where, as Mrs. Wood, a second-grade teacher explained, education has only recently become important, because "people can't make a living by cobbling work together anymore." Many of the students come from rough, rural poverty. Just past the school, the "out back" emerges: trailers and tiny houses, some with uneven hand-made chimneys, tarpaper roofing, and abandoned cars in the yards. About 60 percent of the students, all of whom are white, are on free and reduced lunch. The school's K-5 population shifts with the seasons, moving between 235 and 280 students, as migrant laborers pull up stakes by Thanksgiving and then return to fishing and agricultural work in the spring. Alongside these K-5 students, the school houses a countywide special-needs prekindergarten and a small, region-wide program for students in grades 3–5 who have behavioral difficulties. These students are gradually mainstreamed into regular Searsport classrooms as they learn new social skills.

While the school's students are quite mobile, its twelve classroom teachers are long-term staff, with a minimum of eight years in the school. The school also has a full-time reading specialist. There are two music teachers, an art teacher, a physical education teacher, and a librarian, all on a part-time basis. The school has a federally funded teacher to support migrant family students. It receives Title I funds, which have supported two primary classroom aides who focus on arts enrichment. Title I money was also used to purchase staff-development materials in the areas of literacy, assessment, and MI. The principal, Doug Lockwood, spurs their use by continually encouraging teachers to develop new curricula, take risks, and consider new ideas.

Through efforts to incorporate MI and other useful ideas about assessment and literacy, students in the school show marked improvement over time. Second-graders' average performances on nationally normed achievements tests are usually at about the forty-fifth percentile, but students' average performance in the fifth grade rises to about the sixty-fifth percentile. Over time, disciplinary problems have also markedly improved. In addition, the school has been very successful in involving the students' parents, which in turn helps them to achieve more.

THE COMPASS POINT PRACTICES

The framework of the Compass Point Practices emphasizes the organizational approaches that support Searsport's staff in their efforts to enable diverse learners to succeed in challenging work. The framework also sets a context for the Archaeology Dig, the curriculum described in Chapter 12. We describe the Compass Point Practices in an order that allows Searsport Elementary's experiences to be clearly conveyed.

Readiness

Doug Lockwood's emphasis on staff development and growth was central to the school's adoption of MI. During the early 1990s, the district's superintendent was concerned with giving parents some degree of choice in the type of schooling that their children could receive. To develop choices, the superintendent formed a choice committee, which Doug Lockwood joined, along with educators from all the district's three elementary schools. At each choice committee meeting, a speaker addressed a model of elementary education, such as Montessori, Waldorf, and British infant schools. One meeting focused on MI. Mr. Lockwood said, "When the multiple intelligences model came up, the people on that committee all looked at each other, and though we didn't know what we were looking for [before that point], we knew when we found it."

Mr. Lockwood discussed MI with all the Searsport teachers. They were also attracted to the theory. They understood that children learned in a variety of ways and had different strengths. Many also felt that music and art, as well as elementary grades' focus on reading, were equally important. In part because of the interest at Searsport Elementary, the superintendent approved an MI-influenced choice program for K-1 students at the school. Along with the K-1 program, teachers throughout the school began exploring the theory.

To support this exploration, there was a great deal of professional development. Doug Lockwood, a Searsport teacher, and the district's special education director attended a week-long summer institute held at the Key School, the first school to implement MI theory. The first year of the program at Searsport, 1992–1993, every week's staff meeting focused on understanding the intelligences. Teachers read about the theory and shared ideas about how it could be implemented. In addition, during the spring of that year, two teachers came from the Key School for an intensive two-day staff development meeting. The Key School teachers also held an evening meeting with community members to explain the theory, how it could engage more students, and how real-world roles—ranging from teachers to carpenters to business executives—relied on diverse intelligences.

The following winter, a group of district teachers organized a course on using MI for other teachers in the district who were interested. Almost all the teachers in Searsport Elementary signed up. Doug Lockwood explained that his school's teachers were keen to enroll because he encourages people to grow, rather than forces them to change. "You can't do that. You can [try]. But it doesn't work. So what we said is . . . MI is important. How you use it, and how much you use it in your classroom is absolutely up to you." In line with this philosophy, Mr. Lockwood sees his staff on a continuum, with some teachers implementing ideas that explicitly draw on MI and some incorporating practices that are influenced by the theory, though doing so less explicitly. The district's special education director, Sharon Goguen, expressed the same notion: "In their own way, they are all using the theory."

Culture

As its entry way banner proclaims, Searsport Elementary School is truly dedicated to promoting success for every student. In this school, there is no talk about hopeless cases, despite the extremely difficult circumstances many of these youngsters face. Instead, teachers talk about their students' progress. It is a place marked by a belief in youngsters' potential, caring and respect, joy in learning, and hard work.

Belief in children's strengths. Searsport Elementary School teachers expect that their students can produce high-quality work when they are supported and given the guidance needed to do so. The educators' belief in their students is accompanied by a variety of approaches to tap and nurture their strengths. A fundamental question throughout the school, said one fourth-grade teacher, is "how do we approach every child's needs?"

One way this is done is through the different grade-level groupings the school employs. Providing more than one form of grade-level grouping allows youngsters who need more than a year to master fundamentals to have that time without being held back. (When students are not left back, they are less likely later to drop out of school. See Hauser, 2001; Shepard and Smith, 1989.) As a result, there is a combined class for grades K-1 and grades 2–3. Over the two-year period with their students, teachers also develop a deeper understanding of each child's strengths and needs.

This continuity and flexibility in grouping students has attracted many special-needs students to Searsport Elementary. Special education students are mainstreamed into every classroom. Their needs are met through aides in the classroom and rotations through a resource room staffed by the reading specialist and trained parent volunteers. At the same time, when youngsters come to school with some advanced skills, their needs can also be met. A mother of a child who taught himself to read at age three commented that she was pleased with the way that her son's needs in different areas are being met and strengthened.

Teachers at Searsport draw on MI to have a framework for incorporating activities and media that engage many different students and develop their skills. For example, in the K-1 classroom, poems that are written in large print are often set to music. Chris O'Roak and Karin McKeen, the K-1 teachers, explained that this enables nonreaders to grasp the words and to participate. To develop students' understanding of the relationship between the spoken and written word, teachers and students point to the poem's text during the song and, after it, they work on "code-cracking": learning letter sounds and letter combinations. Teachers in these early grades rely on special training, especially to "beef up language development," said Sharon Goguen, the district's special education director. If a child continues to have difficulty into the middle of first grade, then they participate in Reading Recovery, an intensive one-on-one reading program. By second grade most youngsters are performing at or near grade level in reading.

Care and respect.   Building a respectful and caring climate is an ongoing effort at Searsport Elementary. Because of student mobility, Douglas Lockwood explained, it is especially important to teach and build social skills on a continual basis. "That's a real focus for us," said Mr. Lockwood, "and it will be forever."

Some teachers, for example the K-1 team of Chris O'Roak and Karin McKeen, begin each year by building interpersonal skills with their young students. When students first come to school, "We really need to learn to be a team and . . . to cooperate." Across the grades, educators teach students conflict-resolution skills and also basic manners, such as talking in a kind way and not bumping into others while walking along the corridors. Signs in the hall remind students: "To make our school a nice place to be, be nice." These lessons have paid off. Behavior problems have markedly diminished, and teachers can spend their time on academic matters rather than on refereeing.

Douglas Lockwood reported that he likes to shine a spotlight on students' good behaviors. (This approach was also used by the principals at Governor Bent and Glenridge; see Chapters 4 and 9). He asks children to tell him when behaviors on the playground are improving, and he congratulates children publicly for doing good deeds. "The big announcement happens on Fridays." That's when Mr. Lockwood reads out the names of students who have been "caught in random acts of kindness or manners."

Joy and enthusiasm.   Excitement and enthusiasm for learning are evident among the students in the school. For example, on our first day in the school students noticed us looking at some of their poems and artwork in the hallway. They went into their classroom and brought out even more of it to show us.

Another joyful part of the school experience at Searsport are the regular visits by Mr. Lockwood who comes to sing and teach topic-related songs, which he accompanies with his guitar. For an Under the Sea unit, one which many classrooms participated in, Mr. Lockwood led a sing-along using the tune, "There's a Hole in the Bottom of the Sea." For the archeological dig, he taught students various sea shanties, and for a unit on the Civil War, he performed period songs. Mr. Lockwood thinks that it's important for the students to see him not only as a principal but as someone with enthusiasms and skills. He asserts that a good educator is one who is "passionate about his interests and loves kids, loves them unconditionally."

Hard work.   At Searsport, hard work infiltrates the school from the principal through the teachers to the students. Doug Lockwood provides students with thoughts and goals for the day. These emphasize reading, kind behavior, and doing homework. He has weekly memos just for the students about upcoming events, such as the districtwide effort to read a million pages.

These and other communications, Mr. Lockwood says, are intended to "get kids to invest and internalize" the idea that they need to work hard in order to achieve goals.

Mr. Lockwood and the teachers continually reflect on their own work and strive to improve it. The Dig provides a clear illustration of this. Mr. Lockwood initially got the idea for the Dig while taking a course in archaeology. He approached Mrs. Farris and Mrs. Blodgett about doing the unit, and the three of them agreed to talk on the phone every night to map out a plan. Once the unit concluded, the teachers got together to reflect on what worked and what could be improved, and they set to work revising it. "We're always thinking of ways and working out ways that we can do things better than we're doing," Mr. Lockwood noted.

Teachers also work with students to help them reflect on and improve student work. For instance, before the students' Dig exhibit was installed in the Penobscot Marine Museum, the fifth graders first displayed the exhibit in the lobby of the school. For several weeks, everyone in the school spent time looking at the exhibit and critiquing it. Only when every comment and criticism was addressed by the fifth-grade class—only after "redoing and redoing and redoing until we came to a point where nobody found anything wrong"—was the exhibit moved to the real museum.

One of the things that helps students to perfect their work is the extensive use of rubrics throughout the school (See Goodrich, 1997; Goodrich Andrade, 2000; Wiggins, 1998). The standards for much of the work come from the real world. For example, prior to developing the Dig exhibit, the students visited the museum and then brainstormed what made for a good exhibit. Out of this brainstorm, they ultimately developed a rubric that incorporated key characteristics for a good display, for example, interesting visuals, artifacts, information, and titles. For each characteristic, they discussed qualities that made for strong work. For instance, for titles or labels, they knew the wording had to be concise, contain appropriate information, and be free of grammatical errors.

Collaboration

There are two main ways that collaboration operates within Searsport Elementary School. First, the schoolwide plans and goals are collaboratively determined. The teachers and principal get together early in the year to talk through what they want the year's goals to be and what sort of professional development work should be undertaken to meet those goals. Mr. Lockwood explained, "It's the group who really decides on what staff development we need." For instance, one year the teachers decided that a primary aim would be to integrate the state's learning goals into classroom activities. To do that, teachers got together and looked at how the state's guidelines were being met by activities across the different classrooms and what else might need to be implemented in the classroom to meet the state's goals. Much of this took place at regular staff meetings, where substance comes first and routine business, such as announcements about upcoming events, comes last. "I can always write that in a memo," Doug Lockwood explained.

Other, smaller collaborations among the staff also occur throughout Searsport Elementary. For example, several pairs of teachers collaborated to create greater flexibility in student instruction and grouping. As already noted, two pairs of teachers combined their K-1 and two–three classrooms to address young students' needs across a broad range of development. At the upper elementary grades, fifth-grade Dig teachers, Charlene Farris and Renée Blodgett, collaborate to bring their strengths in science and social studies together into one big interdisciplinary project. In another case, two fourth-grade teachers collaborate on curriculum throughout the entire year. This enables the teachers to jointly plan and reflect on their work.

In line with his belief that real change in practice can't be mandated, Doug Lockwood does not insist on collaboration. He notes that some teachers do very strong work on their own. On the other hand, he does encourage all teachers to visit each other's room to observe and to learn from each other. And, when he sees good collaborative work, he "just tells them [the teachers] how much I appreciate it." Sometimes, collaboration appeared difficult for the part-time specialist teachers. One specialist told Mr. Lockwood he was disappointed people weren't collaborating with him. Mr. Lockwood encouraged him, saying that "the name of that game is, well, you go to them. You come up with the idea, show them the possibilities . . ."

Mr. Lockwood tries to model this process. "You talk about it. Get excited about it, and then . . . even if people are not ready, you might even pull them in anyway, by saying, 'Gee, I'd really like you to do it. I know this is going to be difficult. But boy, your group is ready for this, and I'll help. It's kind of what I did with the Archaeology Dig. I didn't know if the fifth-grade [teachers] would go, 'Oh jeez, here's another thing [to deal with],' or if they'd be enthusiastic about it. What they told me was, you were so darn enthusiastic about it, we couldn't say 'no.'"

Arts

The arts play a vital role within Searsport Elementary School. Art is intrinsic to the building itself, and it is prevalent in the curriculum. The arts are taught as disciplines, regular classroom teachers draw on arts disciplines, and art teachers incorporate other disciplines, in part through collaboration.

Searsport's part-time arts teachers provide instruction within their own disciplines. For example, Mr. Pasvogel, the general music teacher, did a unit

The arts are intrinsic to Searsort Elementary School.

on different musical eras, ranging from Beethoven to contemporary music. During our visit, the students were learning about early rock and roll. In addition to this, the music teacher incorporated into this unit history about popular culture of the 1950s: hairstyles, clothing, dances of the era, and tapes of the long popular TV show, *American Band Stand*. The unit culminated in the creation, rehearsal, and performance by students of 1950s style music videos. The making of the videos incorporated roles for set designers, choreographers, announcers, and "a cameraman," and reflection on how well these roles were carried out ("Did you do a good job? What could you do better?"). This allowed students with different areas of strength to participate and learn about the music.

During our visit, John Balzer's art class was focused on tesselations. These are designs made up of repeating patterns of interlocking shapes. (The artwork of M. C. Escher is a well-known example.) Tesselations provide an opportunity to talk about elements intrinsic to the visual arts: shape, color, line, and composition. At the same time, tesselations intersect with mathematics, and the teacher used them to talk with the students about regular and irregular polygons, symmetry, and how the angles of some shapes readily form tesselations, while the angles of others do not. By drawing on elements of both art and mathematics, Balzer involves and educates students with different proclivities. At the same time, he felt he was actually providing instruction in line with how the world really operates: "Life doesn't exist in little individual elements" of pure subject matters, he explained.

Mr. Balzer has also collaborated with some classroom teachers to bring about a greater integration of different disciplines. For instance, with a modest grant, he and a local artist worked with several classroom teachers to develop a model of the town. Together, they looked at the buildings of the town, and then designed a whole scene of the town in ceramic tiles, which was to be fired, glazed, and then installed. This artwork tied in with the classroom teachers' curriculum and gave the school's students several different ways to increase their understanding of their town and its history.

Regular classroom teachers also seek to incorporate the arts. The K-1 teachers, Chris O'Roak and Karin McKeen, have students create their own interpretations of books using pictures as well as words. For instance, on the wall outside their rooms was a series of students' watercolors entitled "Pablito." These pictures, accompanied by brief text, allowed students to describe and illustrate events from Pablo Picasso's childhood. The Dig, highlighted in the following chapter, also incorporated artistic elements: learning how an exhibit was organized, displayed, and titled. Mr. Lockwood's songs not only entertain, but they engage students and help to round out their understanding. For example, Mr. Lockwood explained that soldiers' songs from the Civil War helped the students to know that "much of the Civil War wasn't spent in battle," but in living, preparing for war, and building morale and patriotism.

Controlled Choice

At Searsport, student choice coexists with efforts to ensure that all students master fundamental literacies. This is true even in the earliest grades. For example, students have many ways to acquire reading skills in the K-1 class: through singing, through drawing representations of works, through decoding efforts, and reading with friends. However, if a child is still not reading by the middle of first grade, then he or she also participates in Reading Recovery. Similarly, students in that class can learn mathematical concepts, such as measuring, graphing, and ordering by rotating through different activity centers. However, youngsters who are having difficulty grasping these ideas are supported to learn them with intensive small-group work in mathematics with the resource room teacher. Either through regular classroom activities, intensive in-class support, or through one-on-one help, Searsport students are all expected to succeed in acquiring essential literacies.

Mr. Lockwood sees two levels of classroom choices. He described some as "basic." For instance, students in the K-1 classroom can choose among a variety of learning centers, but ultimately they participate in each center. In other grades, for example, all students must do time lines, in part to help them learn about history and to grapple with the concept of sequence. However, the format and materials used in the time line are wide open. Similarly, all students must read biographies for a unit on history and language arts, but they are free to pick biographies of people who interest them.

Other choices are more advanced: they demand more individual student input and creativity. For example, there are mandatory student presentations in the biography unit. However, Doug Lockwood explained that "Students have options. It doesn't always have to be a written report." The student can build and present a model, or do a dramatization or make and explain a poster. Another kind of more advanced choice happens in the Dig unit. All students in Mrs. Farris's and Mrs. Blodgett's classroom have to participate in the Dig, but they can choose to take on particular specialties, such as an exhibit designer or an artifact identifier. The range of choices students have allows them to use their different strengths to produce work and demonstrate what they have learned.

To help students produce quality work in these more advanced choices, teachers and students take time to explore the characteristics of particular kinds of good work, review examples of it, and develop rubrics for supporting and evaluating it. By working with students to develop the rubrics, Lockwood argues that teachers get better "buy in" for doing good work. The students have some choice in determining what constitutes a high-quality product. "They are probably going to come up with the same things you would've come up with," he has told teachers, "but the 'buying' is better."

Tool

At Searsport Elementary, the theory of multiple intelligences has been a major influence on how teachers think about their work and about their students. Yet, MI has not displaced the curriculum. Our visit revealed classrooms focused on substantive content: archaeology, reading, writing, the arts, science, math, and history, not on the different intelligences. Teachers don't feel like they "have to be doing MI one hundred percent of every single day and every lesson has to have seven parts," said Mr. Lockwood. Nor do teachers use the language of the theory with students. Doug Lockwood noted, "Kids don't need particularly to have the MI jargon. That's not the purpose."

Instead, the purpose has been to use the theory as a tool to engage and educate a wider range of students. Karin McKeen put it this way, "If you're aware of MI, opportunities for [students'] success are much more accessible." Keeping the theory in mind has substantially altered classroom practice. This has moved from mostly seatwork and paper-and-pencil approaches to more hands-on, interdisciplinary, arts-infused curricula involving greater collaboration among teachers. These approaches were seen as a way to improve the chances that more students would gain knowledge and skills. As a result of these practices, Mr. Lockwood reported, "Teachers are being much more diverse with the products that they're asking for. The products are much richer."

The Compass Point Practices in place at Searsport Elementary School enabled teachers to work with a wide range of learners and to support them to produce high-quality work. The Archaeology Dig, the curriculum unit described in the following chapter, has been supported by these practices across the school. We hope that, as you read the Archaeology Dig, you might find helpful ideas for developing curriculum, alongside colleagues, that serves and educates many different kinds of learners.

12 Archaeology Dig

Searsport students working on a surface dig.

THE ARCHAEOLOGY DIG AT A GLANCE

The Archaeology Dig is a social studies and science unit taught by fifth-grade teachers, Charlene Farris and Renée Blodgett, and their principal, Douglas Lockwood, at the Searsport Elementary School in Searsport, Maine. The three-week unit draws on local resources. As part of this unit, students participate in a surface dig, during which they gather artifacts on a nearby beach. Afterward, the students identify their artifacts and organize them into a display for the local museum. For the Dig and the museum display, the students' work is judged against real-world standards for archaeology and museum exhibitions.

The story of the Dig highlights ways to design curricula that integrate school subjects and real-world activities. It also highlights strategies for interdisciplinary collaboration.

MI in This Unit

- This unit readily draws on spatial, naturalist, linguistic, and interpersonal intelligences. Logical-mathematical, bodily-kinesthetic, and intrapersonal intelligences are also called on.
- Real-world work usually requires contributions by several individuals with different profiles of intelligence.
- In real-world work, there are many roles to fill in the archaeology and museum activities in this unit.
- Several activities in this unit are designed to reach students with different strengths.

Entry Points in This Unit

- This unit can call on all the entry points. It strongly calls on experiential, aesthetic, narrative, interpersonal, and logical entry points.
- The experiential activities of the Dig at first might not seem like school, but they are easily adapted to teach basic skills.
- One entry point may predominate in some parts of the unit, as the narrative entry point does in the initial presentation of the history of Searsport, but all are included at some point.

Compass Point Practices in This Unit

- Many of the compass points are reflected in this unit, including collaboration, choice, arts, the use of MI as a tool, and efforts to support high-quality work.
- The Dig strongly involved collaboration among the educators who designed it and fostered these educators' professional development.
- Compass Point Practices enable the school to use MI in ways that advance students' knowledge, skills, and understanding.

WHAT IS THE ARCHAEOLOGY DIG?

It is local history you can touch. It's hands-on history. It's right in our town. And yet, I'm sure, students know nothing about it . . . I'm not sure the average citizen knows . . .

—Mrs. Charlene Farris
Fifth-Grade teacher
Searsport Elementary School
Searsport, Maine

The Archaeology Dig is a social studies and science unit developed by the principal of Searsport Elementary School, Douglas Lockwood, and two fifth-grade teachers, Charlene Farris and Renée Blodgett. These educators wanted students to understand the rich history of Searsport, Maine, especially the role that shipyards played in the town's development. They also wanted students to understand the nature of a scientific dig. As part of the

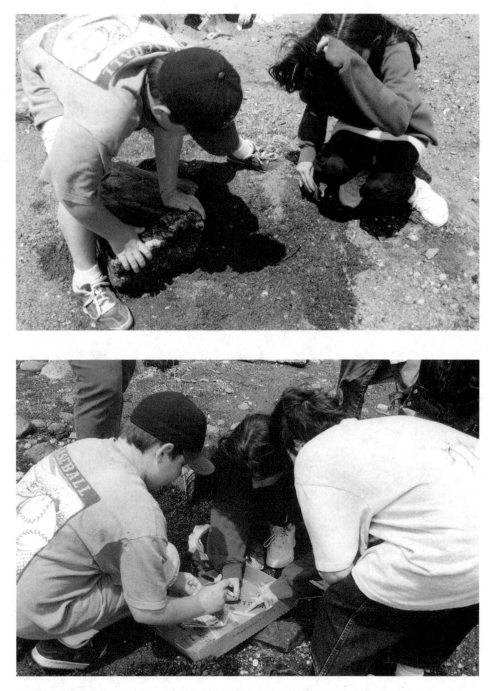

Students digging for artifacts and inspecting them on the site of a former outdoor shipyard.

three-week-long unit, students conduct an actual archeological dig. For the unit's grand finale, students organize their findings from the Dig into a display that is later installed at the local museum.

The Archaeology Dig is more than a neat idea for combining science and social studies. It is also an example of how teachers can collaborate on an interdisciplinary project while still teaching the basics of their own subject areas. If you are interested in doing interdisciplinary work, but fear that it undercuts learning the basics of a subject area, this example will give you courage!

The theory of multiple intelligences is an important part of this unit for two reasons. First, the story of the collaboration describes a group of adults who drew on each other's strengths and interests to design a unit in which each learned from the others. Second, in the Archaeology Dig that they designed, the educators were careful to include opportunities for diverse students to draw on their own strengths. All of this was an effort to support high-quality work, an aim that was continually held in front of both students and adults. The standards for the Dig included not only the state and local education requirements, but also the standards for conducting archaeology and organizing museum displays. In fact, the Searsport dig was an official archeological site, with all found artifacts belonging to the state of Maine.

Even if you don't have a local museum and can't go digging in a nearby shipyard, a close look at this unit will give you ideas for interdisciplinary collaboration. Reading about the Dig will also help you design activities that provide opportunities for a variety of students to engage in work related to real-world roles, while at the same time fulfilling educational standards.

STRATEGIES: CRAFTING AN INTERDISCIPLINARY COLLABORATION

We've got to do more together [as educators] if we're ever to accomplish these learning results. So you open the doors and you model it by doing it. You talk about it, get excited about it. And then you're ready when people are ready. And even if people are not ready, you might even pull them in anyway, by saying, 'Gee, I'd really like you to do it. I know this is going to be difficult, but, boy, your group is ready for this, and I'll help.

—Douglas Lockwood
Principal
Searsport Elementary School
Searsport, Maine

Lots of real-world problems are interdisciplinary in nature. At the same time, teachers can't be experts in everything. Interdisciplinary collaborations are a powerful way to address real-world problems while building strong disciplinary foundations. The story of how the Archaeology Dig started and flourished at Searsport Elementary School illustrates that collaboration can be a great way to combine disciplinary expertise to teach a complex interdisciplinary unit.

This section suggests several considerations and strategies for starting an interdisciplinary collaboration, and explains how reflection and refinements can help a continuing collaboration.

Initially, the different strengths of the three Searsport educators formed a pool of disciplinary and teaching expertise for doing the unit. Not surprisingly, over the course of their four-year collaboration, all learned from each other. So, Searsport's Dig also demonstrates that interdisciplinary collaboration can be a powerful means of on-the-job professional development.

The design of the Dig also shows how, with clear goals, careful planning, and coordination, it's possible to teach to standards of high-quality work in the individual disciplines, as well as the interdisciplinary endeavor, in this case archaeology.

How to Start

Interdisciplinary collaborations start in different ways and change over time. In Searsport, and in many other schools, collaborations start because one person has an idea for a collaborative effort and seeks out—or convinces—others to participate. That's what Douglas Lockwood, the school's principal, did when he thought up the Dig while taking an archaeology course at a local history center. Once the idea for the collaboration came to mind, Mr. Lockwood had to ponder the same questions that all collaborations are likely to raise:

- What do the collaborators offer?
- What topics are worth collaboratively pursuing?
- What activities will motivate students to learn?

What do the collaborators offer?

It's important to see collaboration as an opportunity for teachers to draw on the strengths of colleagues while at the same time developing their own abilities. Deciding who to collaborate with therefore involves some "getting started" questions. Which teachers have expertise in the area? Where do subject interests or personal interests (like wanting to work with someone in particular) intersect? What needs to get taught? What resources are available? These are all good "getting started" questions, and there are certainly others.

The strengths that individual members bring to the group are a critical resource for developing any unit and for sharing expertise. For example, at

FIGURE 12.1

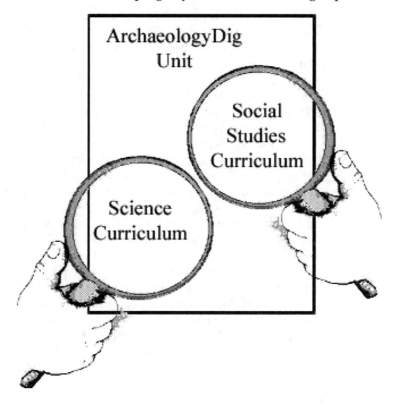

first neither the science nor social studies teachers whom Mr. Lockwood approached knew much about the specifics of a dig. However, each brought particular interests and expertise to the project. The social studies teacher, Mrs. Farris, was already an avid sleuth of Searsport history. (According to Mr. Lockwood, she is an "incredible storyteller who knows all kinds of interesting information about the topics, including which houses in Searsport were believed to be haunted and why.") For Mrs. Blodgett, the science teacher, a study of archaeology that culminated in a real dig offered a way to do more "hands-on science," something to which she is committed.

What ideas are worth pursuing?

Just because a topic is interesting doesn't mean that it will be a worthwhile addition to the curriculum. One way to determine whether it is worthwhile is to look at how the topic intersects with what teachers must teach. How does it build disciplinary skills? What is already taught that can be included?

Both the Searsport teachers thought that the Archaeology Dig sounded like a way to interest students in aspects of the curriculum that they already had to cover. In effect, they looked closely at the proposed unit through the lens of basics skills and knowledge that students needed to learn in the disciplines of science and social studies. State and local standards are another lens with which to decide what's worth pursuing. For example, Mr. Lockwood said, "Think about a great integrated unit. Then really think about all the components, and then go back and think about standards. Think about what the components cover in English, language, arts, and check them off." Regardless of where you start—with an engaging task or what students are required to learn—it's important to consider both early in the planning process.

What activities will motivate students to learn?

Activities that are authentic to a discipline are often inviting to students and help students do quality work. That's because such activities have clear standards for quality: In archaeology, there are standards for carrying out a dig. Similarly, there are museum standards for mounting an exhibit of artifacts.

Alongside these features, real-world activities like the Dig draw on a variety of intelligences and are thus likely to engage a variety of learners. For example, the culminating museum exhibit required many different tasks: Selecting artifacts and writing explanatory labels are tasks likely to appeal to a student's naturalist and linguistic intelligences. Other jobs, like arranging the artifact display, lettering the accompanying labels, and designing the banner lettering are likely to engage students' spatial intelligence. And working with a group, which is part of many of the Dig activities, will draw on students' interpersonal intelligence.

At the same time, real-world tasks readily allow for the study of basic skills. In fact, the Searsport teachers found that the nature and variety of the tasks in the Archaeology Dig frequently provided them with opportunities to teach basics in ways that motivated students and engaged a variety of intelligences. Mrs. Blodgett, for example, saw that learning how to lay out the grids of a dig site (first through practice in the gym and then at the Dig site on the beach) was a perfect chance to teach her class how to calculate ordered pairs of x and y coordinates. She still used paper and pencil to have

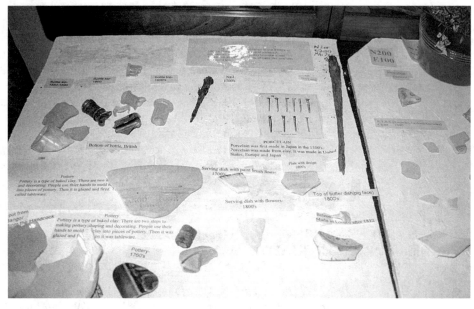

The students' museum display draws on a range of strengths and incorporates real-world standards.

students make calculations and practice the concept of ordered pairs, but this now was in order to calculate how to lay out the grids for the Dig site. At the same time, the nature of the task also required that students walk to trace the measurements and to physically trace and define the space. The logical-mathematical activity that used paper and pencil might appeal to one student, the bodily-kinesthetic activity to others.

Reflect and Refine

Any repeated unit naturally entails design change (see Donna Schneider's comments on this in Chapter 8). Sometimes there is a problem with the early design; other times, teachers gain new insights. Or maybe change is just a way to do something differently the next time. But change without reflection is like sailing a ship without a compass.

Each year Mrs. Farris, Mrs. Blodgett, and Mr. Lockwood reflect on that year's dig as soon as it is over and decide what worked well and what can be improved. For example, for the second year of the Dig, they mounted a whole new museum exhibit. This entailed a huge amount of work! So, for the third year they refined the unit by deciding to add new artifacts to the existing display and to accompany this with a collage of photographs that students took to show the most recent dig. As they reflect and plan for each new year, the collaborators see places for improvement. For the fourth year, they recognized a need to have a smaller group work on artifact identification. On reflection, they also decided to look for more child-friendly reference books that would be more engaging and make it easier for students to identify the objects they've uncovered at the site.

Not surprisingly, the work collaborators do together often changes over time, because each person learns from the others. In the Dig collaboration, for example, Mr. Lockwood's expertise and passion for archaeology provided the spark to get the unit started. The two teachers brought their own subject expertise, and they initially saw themselves as assistants who were learning about archaeology alongside their students. Each year, however, they developed their own capacities to organize a dig and museum display. In fact, Mrs. Farris noted that the thing that has changed most is the amount of time that the unit takes every year. Because they are better at teaching the Dig, many tasks take less time.

To maximize this kind of growth in participants, the collaboration itself should also be the subject of reflective refinements. New collaborators can bring new knowledge and skills from which all the participants can benefit.

WHAT HAPPENS DURING THE ARCHAEOLOGY DIG? SUPPORT FOR HIGH-QUALITY WORK

We are scientists. We are not just beachcombers. That's one of the vocabulary words we introduce that we have never heard of before. We don't lose the stuff. We don't mix it up. We don't say, 'Oh, I don't know where this goes, I'll throw it in this kit.' You can't do that. You must be accountable for it.
—Mrs. Charlene Farris

The activities for the Archaeology Dig that Mr. Lockwood, Mrs. Farris, and Mrs. Blodgett designed and refined encourage their fifth-grade students to do quality work in the real worlds of archaeology and museum curating. If you are interesting in planning a dig, this section will outline activities that will get you started.

Even if you don't have a shipyard or museum nearby, keep reading! Activities like those described here can also be a good starting point for thinking about how to adapt one of your current units to allow students to

BOX 12.1 MATERIALS NEEDED FOR THE DIG

The dig unit requires lots of materials you probably have around already: buckets, toothbrushes, pails for cleaning, plastic bags for collecting artifacts and boxes (pizza boxes are great!) for storing artifacts, newspaper, craft paper, sinks or other source of water, permanent markers, and plastic gloves for students who may want them. Only the reference books for identification might take some time to find. For the Searsport dig, these were borrowed from the Penobscot Marine Museum, but a local library or historical society can probably suggest other sources

learn by doing real work in a discipline. In whatever real-world work that you do, it's important:

- to identify from the outset what the standards for quality work are;
- to apply those standards to the students' work;
- to include a variety of activities that will enable and encourage all students to do quality work.

(Schneider's Ink, Chapter 8, provides another example of real-world work that uses many ways to engage learners and support their doing quality work.)

Keep in mind that the activities for this unit, or for the others in this book, rarely require the majority of each day or need to form a teacher's whole curriculum. A core set of activities for the Dig (or another unit involving the real work of a discipline) can be integrated with other studies and skill building. For example, Mrs. Blodgett coordinates the Dig with science lessons about the seashore, marine animals, and ocean ecology. She also uses the Dig as an opportunity to review the scientific method. At the same time, she continues ongoing skill-building activities. For instance, her students learn vocabulary related to the Dig. Students also continue the journal-writing activities that go on all year. However, during this unit, "dig logbooks" provide the substance for the students' editing, topic development, and sequencing work. As a result of this integration, the teachers incorporate both traditional and less traditional activities into their classrooms. In essence, an activity like the Dig can provide coherence for several otherwise unrelated classroom endeavors.

Steps in the Dig

The Archaeology Dig was designed to include a range of activities that would appeal to students with strengths in many different intelligences. Mrs. Blodgett summarized this when she explained: "In everyday teaching of anything that we do now, we try to come up with more than just a paper-and-pencil task because some kids don't learn that way. Some kids learn best through an activity that is not specifically a paper-and-pencil task."

While the Dig's core set of activities may vary somewhat year to year, the unit as a whole always has opportunities for students to learn in several ways and in ways related to their own individual strengths. As Mrs. Farris observed, there are "some children who are not good readers or writers necessarily, but they are good finders." In fact, one of her more severely

BOX 12.2 TEACHERS' LIST OF DIG STEPS

Dig Steps
(Finish before the last week of school!)

Event	Date
1. Searsport History—Part II (Mrs. Farris—social studies class)	Wed. May 20 & Th. May 21
2. Searsport history slides (Mrs. Farris)	Fri. May 22
3. *Penobscot Marine Museum tour Capt. Merrithew House & Old Town Hall (Mrs. Farris call for museum visit times and to be sure trunk & sword out)	Tues. May 26, 1:00
4. Marilyn Stumpff's visit (artifact talk) (Mr. Lockwood)	Th. May 28, 11:00 AM
5. "Dig" slide show (both classes and Mr. Lockwood)	Th. May 28, 1:00
6. Science vocabulary crossword (Mrs. Blodgett)	
7. Math work: matching pairs/grids	
8. Mock grid in classroom Circle of chairs (Mr. Lockwood)	Mon. June 1, 9:30 AM
9. *Site visit A. Mr. Lockwood, volunteers lay our "grid" B. Walk to site (Mr. Lockwood will call when grid is ready. Then class walks to beach.)	Wed. June 3
10. Demonstration of cleaning and sorting (Mr. Lockwood) Follow through (afternoon) actual cleaning and sorting Next day finish cleaning and sorting	Th. June 4 ,11:00 AM 12:30 Friday June 5
11. *Museum visit See last year's dig exhibit (old Vestry building)	Mon. June 8, 10:30 AM
12. Explanation of Dig scoring rubric (Mr. Lockwood)	Mon. June 8, 12:30
13. Prepare museum display Small groups identify artifacts with resource books (Mrs. Blodgett and Mr. Lockwood plus volunteers) Type display information (Mrs. Blodgett's room) Movie in Mrs. Farris' room for students not involved Mrs. Farris will "edit" typed material	June 9–12, 12:30
14. Set up lobby display in our school Mr. Lockwood will take unused artifacts to museum Mr. Lockwood—student assessment form	
15. Take lobby display to Penobscot Marine Museum	

*volunteer parents/teacher's aid help needed

The teachers' list of steps for the Archaeology Dig provides a time line for the unit's varied activities.

disabled children found the oldest artifact yet collected, a pre-Civil War olive oil bottle. Another very quiet child, but one who loved history, found a great many artifacts and became one of the stars of the Dig.

As you read the following list of core activities, think of how the following activities can be adapted to other units that involve students in real-world work and standards of a discipline, while at the same time teaching them what they need to learn to do quality classroom work.

1. *Introductory lecture and slides*

The Dig unit is introduced with a lecture and slide show in which Mrs. Farris describes Searsport history. During this narrative, students practice their note-taking skills as they learn about the era of shipbuilding, why shipbuilding was prominent in Searsport during that time, and who the founders of the local shipyards were. They also draw diagrams of the shipyards and explore how they were organized.

FIGURE 12.2
Surveyor's map of the official Searsport Archaeology Dig site.

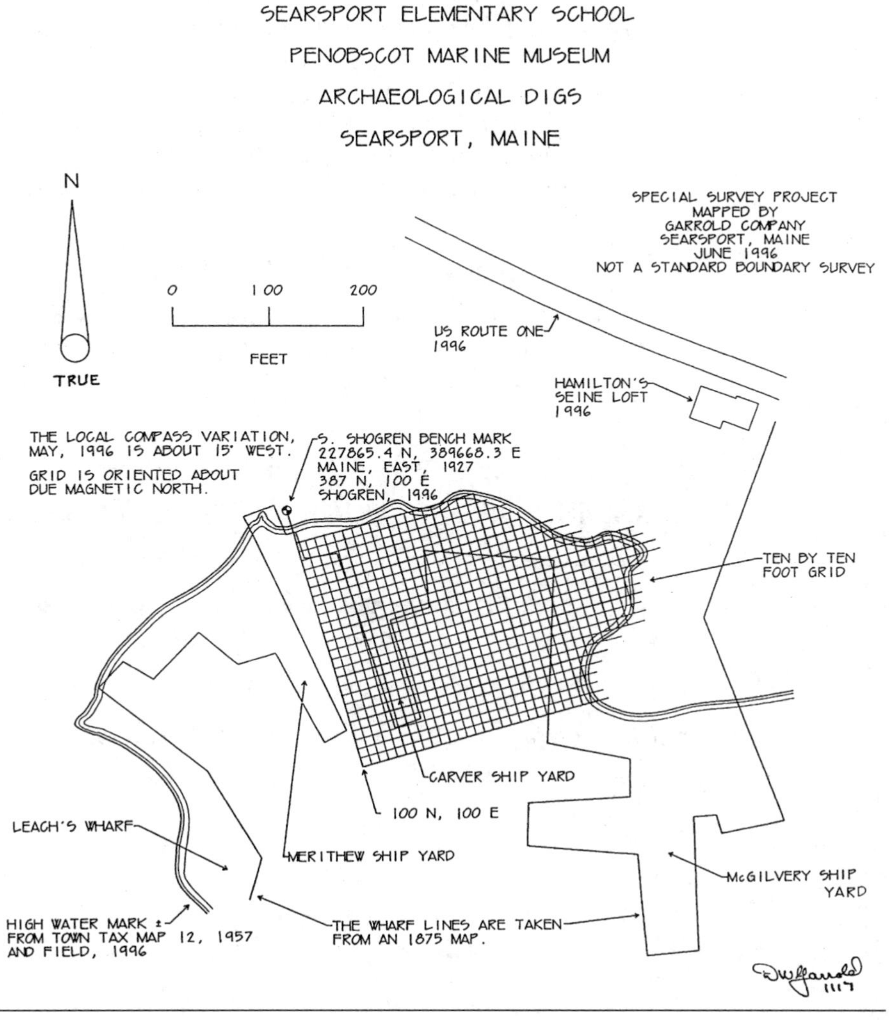

2. *Museum visit*

In the first week of the Dig, both fifth-grade classes visit the Penobscot Marine Museum. Here they learn about Searsport's history from displays of artifacts and see firsthand what makes a quality museum exhibit. For this experiential activity, classes go to two of the buildings in which the museum houses exhibits about Searsport's local shipyards and the town's connection to the sea. They look at the content of the exhibits to learn more about history and at the exhibits themselves to learn about how they are designed. After they return to their classroom, classes brainstorm a list of what makes a quality exhibit, which becomes the basis of a rubric to use in their own work. This rubric will help guide them when they prepare an exhibit of their artifacts for display in the Penobscot Marine Museum.

3. *Guest speaker*

A secretary in the school superintendent's office, a passionate amateur archaeologist, visits the classes to give a talk on archaeology and show her artifact collection. This resident expert goes down to the shipyard site to search for artifacts every lunch hour. Her talk, in which she shows objects and tells where she found them, gives students a sense of what it means to do a surface dig. They begin to think in realistic terms, like having to move rocks and sand to find the artifacts and not being able to find objects in perfect condition. In her collection students get to see artifacts they might later identify as well as artifacts that they might not find. Her talk helps students build their knowledge of the vocabulary and methods of archaeology.

4. *Slide show of the first dig*

During the first year of the Dig, Mrs. Farris organized the production of a slide show so that anyone who visited the students' museum display would have background information on the process. A group of students

---

BOX 12.3 ARCHAEOLOGY DIG MUSEUM DISPLAY RUBRIC

Archaeology Dig Museum Display Rubric
(20 Points Possible for Each)

Visuals (Photos, Drawings, Sketches, Models, Diagrams, Maps) _____

Information (Paragraph Format, Edited, Word-Processed, Laminated) _____

Artifacts (Real and/or Photos) _____

Title _____

Quality _____

wrote the script for the slide show and took many of the photographs. Now the slide show is an invaluable way to give future classes a preview of what they will do because it shows the steps of the Dig: gathering the artifacts, sorting and cleaning, identification and cataloguing. It describes the various jobs students take on during the unit (see Box 12.4). It also explains what a surface dig is and provides guidelines for conducting a dig according to accepted practices for archaeological fieldwork. For example, because the site for the Searsport dig is an official State of Maine site, all artifacts found by the class go to the museum. This means that students must also carefully record their findings.

5. *Job selection*

Prior to visiting the site, students sign up for several dig jobs. Job descriptions (Box 12.4) describes two of the many roles students can fill. The jobs described—a lab technician and a photographer/videographer—are associated with a real archaeological dig, although the descriptions and qualifications are reworked to reflect the abilities found in a fifth-grade classroom. It's easy to imagine very different students signing up for each job. Because there is this kind of choice, activities like the Dig are likely to engage a variety of students. Each description also comes with a list that clearly defines the job's responsibilities. This helps students to choose widely and understand what's expected.

6. *Mock grid and dig pit*

In this practice session, students use what they have learned about ordered pairs to layout a practice grid of x and y coordinates on the gym floor. The grid is made from string laid across the floor according to where coordinates should be. Then objects are put in each quadrant. Students identify these objects and use criteria to determine which they would want to bring back from the site and which they will want to leave. For this activity students are grouped according to grid pits, a grouping that they will retain for the Dig at the site and for the cleaning and sorting of artifacts once they return to the classroom.

7. *Site visit*

Before scheduling the Dig, Mr. Lockwood consults the tide charts to see when a low tide will occur early in the school day. Then, the morning of the Dig, he and a group of students stretch string across the beach site to form quadrants. When students arrive at the Dig site, most fulfill the job of archaeologist, and fan out across the beach to gather, bag, and label artifacts.

8. *Cleaning, sorting, and identification*

For these activities, the classroom is rearranged. Desks are pushed together, screening is added in the sink, and surfaces are covered with craft paper. After the room is set up, there is a demonstration on how to use toothbrushes to clean objects delicately and how to keep artifacts organized. Then students clean, taking care to keep together those artifacts that were

BOX 12.4 JOB DESCRIPTIONS

Job: Lab Technician

Qualifications:
1. Well-organized with an understanding of sorting and classifying
2. Patient, ability to stick with a task until completed
3. Able to work well in a small group and follow directions exactly
4. Able to manage time and materials well
5. Interested in artifacts and artifact identification

Job description:
1. Clean, sort, and classify artifacts according to instructions
2. Count artifacts and figure out percentages of types
3. Accurately label bags, provenience slips, and boxes

This job requires the students to do lab work from 12:00–12:25 and from 2:00–2:50. They need to clean, sort, count, label, and box artifacts for the Penobscot Marine Museum.

Name: _____

Address: _____

Telephone #: _____

Grade 5 Teacher: _____

Reasons why you qualify for this job: _____

_____

Job: Photographer/Videographer

Qualifications:
1. Experience taking pictures/videos
2. Knowledge and skill to take a good picture/video
3. Knows how to take care of camera
4. Able to follow directions
5. Able to work as part of a team

Job description:
1. Take photographs/videos of the dig in progress
2. Take photographs/videos of artifacts found
3. Select/edit photographs/videos for displays
4. Organize photographs for display

Name: _____

Address: _____

Telephone #: _____

Grade 5 Teacher: _____

Reasons why you qualify for this job: _____

_____

Examples of job descriptions spell out what's expected and help students choose tasks that are aligned with their interests.

found in each quadrant of the grid. After cleaning, artifacts are placed on paper to dry, and they are labeled with the quadrant number. When the artifacts are dry, they are put back in bags, and the provenience slip is re-attached. During this process, students work in eight–ten small groups to clean and sort. Only a small group of interested students work with Mr. Lockwood to do the final step of identifying artifacts. For this they use reference books borrowed from the Penobscot Marine Museum.

BOX 12.5 ON THE BEACH

A student runs over to Mr. Lockwood, the principal who set up the grid with students the day before and today has led both fifth-grade classes down to the beach. "What do you think of this?" Mr. Lockwood is crouched over a pile of rocks. As he turns over a piece of pottery, he says to the girl peering with him at the pile, "Oh, that's a real find. It says something 'art shop.' Why don't you try to figure out what it says?" At the same time, another student saunters their way, dangling a mass of seaweed. "I found a crab." Nearby a girl on her knees rubs her hand repeatedly from right to left across the sand looking for artifacts. "Help, what are these things on me?" she screams. And she hurriedly withdraws her hand when a friend nearby says, "They are sea maggots."

Everywhere there are boys and girls in shirts and shorts, some bare-handed, some with gloves. Some wear jackets and are swaddled in layers; some are bare armed. But all are carefully attending to the task at hand as they go back and forth across the beach and periodically stop to carefully scrape away layers of sand mixed with shells and gravel.

Careful record keeping begins with each discovery. A boy who has found a piece of glass balances his bag on a stone as he uses a marker to write on his bag the exact location of his find. Another girl slowly turns over a small gray object for which she has scoured the sand and sighs, "I think that's just a rock."

As they work, some students also try to make identifications in conversations sprinkled liberally with the vocabulary they learned in class. One boy, for example, holds up a piece of glass and wonders if the few letters he sees might be part of a trademark inscription. Three girls circle around Mrs. Farris seeking her advice on what they have found. One says, "This must be older." Before Mrs. Farris answers, she casually looks down and says, "What's that by your foot?" Her expert eyes have spotted a piece of colored glass. Returning her attention to the group, she asks, "How can you tell if it's important?" With this prompt, they begin to recall some of the criteria they learned in class (like looking for a recognizable pattern), the artifacts the superintendent's secretary brought to show them, and what they saw in their visit to the Penobscot Marine Museum. And from their teacher there is also the gentle reminder that they can't take everything back with them!

BOX 12.6 DOING QUALITY WORK IN ARCHAEOLOGY

In archaeology it's important to know exactly where an object was found. To facilitate this at the dig site, a grid of string is used to divide the beach into square areas, each of which is assigned a number. Students must place any artifacts they find in a bag. Each bag is labeled with these coordinates to ensure an accurate record of where each artifact was found. Students record what they find in each square on a provenience slip, one slip for each bag. While cleaning objects, students also have to be careful to keep artifacts with their provenience slips.

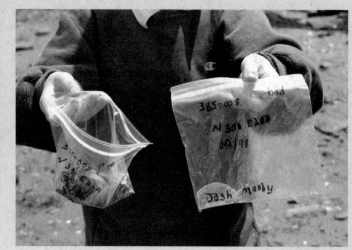

9. *Museum display*

The culminating display of the Dig has changed from year to year. The first two years of the Dig, volunteers from each class constructed an exhibit to display artifacts found during that year's dig. They wrote and edited labels, lettered the display text, and developed the design of the display. The display was exhibited in the lobby of the school for a week, during

---

BOX 12.7 CAN YOU DIG IT? SELF ASSESSMENT

Archaeology Dig Self Assessment

Name: _____

Date: _____

Teacher: _____

Rate yourself by circling the number in each category and explaining in writing your

1. How well did I participate in learning about Searsport history, the shipyards and the sea captains?

1	2	3	4	5
Not at all	very little	expected	actively involved	actively involved beyond class time

Explain:

2. How well did I participate in the collection of artifacts at the dig site?

1	2	3	4	5
Not at all	very little	expected	actively involved	actively involved beyond class time

Explain:

3. How well did I participate in the cleaning and sorting of artifacts?

1	2	3	4	5
Not at all	very little	expected	actively involved	actively involved beyond class time

Explain:

4. How well did I participate in preparing the museum exhibit?

1	2	3	4	5
Not at all	very little	expected	actively involved	actively involved beyond class time

Explain:

My overall grade for the project is _____

Each student assesses and grades his or her own level of effort in the surface dig and the development of the museum exhibit. A final grade is determined in collaboration with the teacher who also assesses each child's work.

which time the rest of the school was asked to comment on the display in general and to point out any specific changes that might need to be made, like misspellings or unclear language. In subsequent years, students have added to the display of the previous year instead of constructing a whole new exhibit. However, each year the additional display is critiqued by the whole school and revised until everything is perfect. At the end of the unit, students use another rubric to evaluate their own performance during the Dig (see Box 12.7). They then give this to their teacher for her input. From this collaboration, teacher and student together decide each student's grade.

As these activities reveal, students are encouraged to do quality work through a number of experiences: visiting the museum, seeing a slide show, hearing about archaeology from a local, dedicated amateur, and instruction in sorting, labeling, and cleaning their artifacts. They are helped to apply high standards in their work, for example, through having a practice session for a surface dig, having specific job descriptions, having their exhibit critiqued by the school, and the use of rubrics. Finally, they also have many ways to engage in the task. So, while there are paper-and-pencil activities (like the logbook and vocabulary and history tests), there is also hands-on work and work with other people. As a result, many different students can learn about their town's history, the science of archaeology, and what goes into making a museum display.

REVISITING THE FRAMEWORKS: AN INTERDISCIPLINARY COLLABORATION FOCUSED ON QUALITY DISCIPLINARY WORK

> *At the beginning both Charlene, the other fifth-grade teacher, and I were just on it.*
> *We were there in a supervisory capacity for the children and trying to help them.*
> *But we were learning right along with them.*
>
> —Renée Blodgett
> Fifth-Grade teacher
> Searsport Elementary School
> Searsport, Maine

This section summarizes how the Archaeology Dig intersects with MI, the Entry Points, and the Compass Point Practices. Thinking about these frameworks is helpful in planning and reflecting on one's own work. Keep in mind that it is not necessary to tap every intelligence, entry point, or compass point in every activity, or even in every unit. It's most important to include only activities that illuminate a topic, and engage learners' strengths in a substantive way.

MI in This Unit

MI is a framework for considering individual students' strengths and for finding ways to engage them. In the Dig, all but musical intelligence is substantively included. Singing songs of the seas, in sessions led by Mr. Lockwood on his guitar, is the only use of musical intelligence during the unit. However, music is an important focus in many other units during the year.

Entry Points in This Unit

Entry Points provide a framework for making the curriculum accessible to different learners. In the Dig, the teachers incorporate all the Entry Points.

Narrative: The Dig includes many stories of historic events, as well as interesting details about various leading sea captains and shipbuilders in Searsport. Students also keep a journal that tells the story of their own class's dig.

Aesthetic: Students study museum displays and exhibits. They also consider the features of artifacts and seek to identify them on the basis of these features. For their own exhibit, students may complete broken pieces of pottery, pipes, or other objects that they have found by drawing the missing portions.

Linguistic	Spatial	Interpersonal	Intrapersonal	Logical-Mathematical	Musical	Naturalist	Bodily-Kinesthetic	ACTIVITIES
X	X							Introductory lecture and slides: This lecture and slide show presents an historical overview of Searsport history.
	X					X		Museum visit: A visit to the local museum helps students to understand how to organize and display objects and how Searsport's natural resources led to its shipbuilding industry.
X	X	X				X		Guest speaker: A special invited guest tells about her passion for looking for artifacts on the beach and shows her collection of artifacts.
X	X					X		Slide show of a dig: This slide show, produced by students and their teacher during the first year of the dig, previews what the class will later do.
	X	X		X			X	Mock grid and dig pit: Students use string to lay out a grid on the gym floor to model what they will later use to mark the beach for their actual dig. They then work in grid pit groups that will be replicated at the dig site.
	X	X				X	X	Site visit: All students search for artifacts at the beach. They carefully put what they find in plastic bags marked with the number of the quadrant in which the artifact was found. Some students also choose specialized jobs.
	X	X		X		X		Cleaning, sorting, and identification: Back in the classroom, students clean, identify, and classify the artifacts.
X	X	X	X			X		Museum display: Carefully labeled artifacts are displayed first at the school and then at the local museum. Students use a rubric to assess their own work.

FIGURE 12.2 Multiple Intelligences Engaged During the Archaeology Dig

Logical-Quantitative: Students learn about ordered pairs. Logical sequences are important in the study of history and science. Several activities ask students to determine cause and effect or draw conclusions from what they read or observe.

Existential: Students consider the fundamental principles of archaeology. In particular, they explore the relationship of an archeological dig to what they see in a museum exhibit. They also consider why some sites, like their own town, are conducive to the development of shipbuilding and what forces led to the decline of that industry's existence.

Experiential: This unit gives students the actual experience of conducting a surface dig, identifying archeological finds, and launching a museum exhibit.

Interpersonal: Students work together and learn from each other in many ways. The Dig itself and subsequent cleaning and identification of artifacts are particularly group-oriented activities, as is the construction of the museum display.

Compass Point Practices in This Unit

Compass Point Practices provide a framework of organizational characteristics for classrooms and schools that enable MI to be used in ways that are associated with improvements for students. The Dig highlights several of these practices.

Collaboration: The story of how the Dig curriculum developed shows how teachers can draw on each other's strengths in collaborative efforts to develop an interdisciplinary unit that serve a wide variety of learners.

Readiness: There were many preparatory efforts to make sure many different kinds of learners could undertake high-quality work in the Dig and the exhibit.

Choice: Students volunteer for specialized jobs during the Dig, choose to do particular parts of the museum display, and can choose to work with Mr. Lockwood to identify artifacts using reference books borrowed from the museum. These choices still require students to do "real work" and to do quality work.

Arts: The museum display highlights the prominent role that the arts play in this unit and throughout the school.

Tool: In the Dig, the theory of multiple intelligences was used to design learning activities that help all students to reach the goals of the unit. However, students are taught history and archaeology, not the theory of multiple intelligences.

Culture: The Dig unit is a good example of how beliefs that all students have strengths can be meshed into a curriculum that allows each student to produce quality work. The unit engages many different strengths and provides many routes for students to learn about archaeology and museum work. At the same time, the learning in this unit is a joyful and exciting adventure!

13 Real Learning, Standards, and State Tests

The work that resulted in this volume began with a single question: What practices are found in schools that associate Gardner's theory of multiple intelligences with benefits for students? That question had two motivating forces. As researchers, we wanted to arrive at a better understanding of how MI theory might be used to support good work in schools and classrooms. In addition, our investigation was driven by hundreds of inquiries from educators who were looking for research-driven answers about how to use the theory wisely.

The answer to our question has been captured in this volume in two forms: It is reflected in the framework called the Compass Point Practices. This framework distills much of what we learned from our forty-one interviews and our site visits about the organizational practices that are used in schools that associate MI with benefits for students. Our answer is also presented in detailed examples of schools, classrooms, and teachers' strategies where these practices are used.

The answers to our question supports the idea that schools can enable many different kinds of learners to produce strong work when they have reasonable organizational practices in place. We've called these Compass Points Practices, and we see them as directions worth heading in: creating an environment marked by caring, respect, a belief in students' potential, hard work, and the idea that learning is exciting (culture); enabling teachers to learn about, discuss, and try out new ideas (readiness); nurturing opportunities for teachers to work and learn together (collaboration); providing students with several meaningful ways to explore a topic (controlled choice); using MI to support, rather than replace, strong curriculum and high-quality work (tool); and fostering an arts-rich education (the arts).

The students in the schools and classrooms we visited demonstrated that they could produce work of exceptionally high quality. For example, in the Governor Bent School, students from diverse ethnic, socioeconomic, and language backgrounds produced extraordinarily strong writing (Language Artists) and gained essential math skills through a curriculum that included hands-on work (Math Labs). In Searsport Elementary, students from hard rural poverty carried out real scientific and historical investigations (the Archaeology Dig). Inner-city students in Pittsburgh's McCleary School grew to understand the complex interactions between natural resources and human societies (the Rivers Study). In each of these examples, and the others in this book, students were held to the highest standards and were supported by the Compass Point Practices to meet those standards. We are hopeful that these examples from practice, alongside research-derived principles, will support many educators' efforts to enable different kinds of learners to produce high-quality work.

At the same time, we are fully aware that there are contemporary forces that run counter to the practices and principles we have highlighted. The most significant of these is the increasing demand by state and federal policymakers for educators to raise students' scores on standardized tests. Such demands, and the high-stakes consequences often accompanying them, often do result in higher test scores. Nevertheless, there is increasing evidence that such demands are not systemically related to improved student understanding or academic achievement. Instead, when students are called on to use the knowledge and skills measured by the state test on different kinds of tests, the pattern of score gains disappears (Amrein & Berliner, 2002; Klein, Hamilton, McCaffrey, & Stecher, 2000; Koretz & Barron, 1998; Neill, 2001). Simply put, students are not generally able to transfer what they've been taught for the state test to any other circumstance, even to a different test in the same subject area.

One explanation for this phenomenon is that policies aimed at producing higher test scores have often yielded very limited, and limiting, forms of instruction, especially for students who are already struggling. One dimension of this problem is that the curricular areas that are not tested tend to be given short shrift. In addition, because the format of the tests is narrow, students are provided with fewer opportunities to apply or develop knowledge beyond the realms of paper and pencil or screens and keyboards (Amrein & Berliner, 2002; McNeil, 2000; McNeil & Valenzuela, 2001).

In contrast, in the schools we have profiled, curriculum and instruction often entail activities that do not mesh neatly with test content or formats: the arts, hands-on learning, group activities, interdisciplinary projects, and real-world products. Educators in these schools have instead incorporated efforts that support the transfer of knowledge from school learning to real-world learning. (We have even seen a few spontaneous instances of young students transferring knowledge from one unit of curriculum to another.) In essence, students are frequently asked to use what they are learning on something besides an exam, and they often can. For example, they are able to take math concepts and skills and use them to develop designs (Math Labs, Schneider's Ink). They are able to take historical facts and principles from archaeology to produce a museum-quality display (the Archaeology Dig). These kinds of activities were far more prevalent in the schools we visited than test preparation, which was, frankly, extremely limited. Nevertheless, in addition to demonstrating high-quality work, the students in the schools profiled in this volume showed either high test scores, or, over time, rising scores.

Policies that call for raising test scores have serious implications for a number of the Compass Point Practices we have identified. Such policies likely have negative implications for the arts, which are rarely tested, but which have played a prominent role in the schools we have profiled. In addition, because testing follows strict disciplinary lines, these policies may undermine the kinds of collaborations that promoted teacher development and yielded engaging curriculum. It is more expedient to pursue score increases (though not necessarily actual learning) through a narrow curriculum, rather than one like Math Labs, the Rivers Study, or any of the others in this book. It is also likely that policies focused on raising scores threaten the kinds of school cultures we have described. When these policies prevail, students who have weak scores may be viewed as a threat to the school (which can sometimes be shut down, or totally restaffed, on the basis of scores), rather than as people who are worthy of respect and capable of contributions. It is hardly surprising that where school cultures are not supportive, dropout rates are higher (DeLuca & Rosenbaum, 2001; Lee & Burkam, 2001), and across a number of states where high-stakes testing is prevalent, dropout rates have increased (Amrein & Berliner, 2002; Clarke, Haney, & Madaus, 2000; Haney, 2000, 2001; Reardon & Galindo, 2002).

We firmly agree with assertions that high standards and high expectations are essential to promote learning. We know there is good evidence for such claims (Chi, Glaser, & Farr, 1988, Ferguson, 1998; Howard & Hammond, 1985). Yet, arguments that high standards and expectations are achieved through demands for higher test scores are made in ignorance of the ways people actually learn. For actual learning to occur, students need to engage content deeply over time and have multiple ways to access and represent content. They also need substantial and diverse opportunities to apply what they learn (Perkins & Salomon, 1989). In addition, through human connections, students and their teachers need to be supported and motivated to deal with increasing intellectual challenges (Chi, Glaser, & Farr, 1988).

These requirements for real learning will not be met by a bottom-line focus on test scores. The evidence is growing that higher test scores do not yield marked increases in students' academic or real-world functioning. Therefore, policymakers need to raise their sights. Above the bottom line, we think that a focus on Compass Point Practices, and on the kinds of teaching and learning illustrated in this volume, might enable policymakers, educators, and students to travel in more productive directions.

Appendix
Description of Schools That Participated in the Project on Schools Using MI Theory (SUMIT)

The data for this book was gathered from educators at the following forty-one schools. The authors deeply appreciate the effort of these educators to help us understand the work that they do and the communities that they serve.

The Briarcliff Elementary School is located in Shoreham, New York, about sixty miles from New York City. It is a K-1 school serving 175 students from middle-income families, 98 percent of whom are white.

Brown Street Academy for Talent Development is located in Milwaukee, Wisconsin. It is a pre-K-5 school serving a student population of 600 that is 1 percent white, 75 percent African American, about 10 percent Hispanic, about 10 percent Asian/Pacific Islander, and about 4 percent other. Ninety percent of the students are on free or reduced lunch.

Centennial Elementary School is located in Littleton, Colorado, near Denver. It is a K-5 school serving a student population of 550 that is 95 percent white, and 5 percent other. Of the school's students, 76 percent are from middle-income families and 24 percent are on free or reduced lunch.

Champlain Valley High School is located in Hinesburg, Vermont, near Burlington. It serves 1,000 students in grades 9–12, almost all of whom are white. About 96 percent of the school's students are from middle-income families and 4 percent are on free or reduced lunch.

Claremont Elementary School (PS 42) is located in the Bronx, New York. It is a pre-K-5 school serving a student population of 600 that is 50 percent African American and 50 percent Hispanic. All of the students are on free or reduced lunch.

Cloud Elementary School is located in Wichita, Kansas. It is a pre-K-5 school serving a student population of 800 that is 18.7 percent white, 14.5 percent African American, 60.5 percent Hispanic, 3.9 percent Asian/Pacific Islander, and 2.4 percent Native American. Ninety percent of the students in the school receive free or reduced lunch.

Dover Elementary School is located in rural Dover, Florida, near Tampa. It is a K-5 school serving a student population of 800 to 1,100 that is approximately 44 percent white, 3 percent African American, and 53 percent Hispanic. Twenty-five percent of the school's students are from lower- to middle-income families and 75 percent are on free or reduced lunch.

Edgemont Elementary School is located in Montclair, New Jersey, a suburb of New York City. It is a pre-K-5 school serving a student population of 350 that is 54 percent white, 36 percent African American, and 10 percent other. The economic background of the students spans the entire continuum: approximately 12 percent come from affluence and 12 percent are on free or reduced lunch.

Elk Elementary School is located in Charleston, West Virginia. It is a K-5 school serving a student population of 600 that is 99.5 percent white and .5 percent African American. Fifty-two percent of the students in the school are from families that are middle- to lower-middle income and 48 percent receive free and reduced lunch.

Fawcett Center for Year-Round Learning is an elementary school located in Tacoma, Washington. It is a K-5 school serving a student population of 600 that is 61.9 percent white, 12.9 percent African American, 5.9 percent Hispanic, 17.5 percent Asian/Pacific Islander, and 1.8 percent Native American. Forty percent of the students in the school are from lower- to middle-income families and 60 percent are on free and reduced lunch.

Freeman School is located in Phillipsburg, New Jersey. It is a grade 1–2 school serving a student population of 207 that is 90 percent white, 5 percent African American, and 5 percent Hispanic. Approximately 62 percent of the students are from lower-to-middle-income families and 38.3 percent are on free and reduced lunch.

Fuller School is located north of Boston in Gloucester, Massachusetts. It is a pre-K-5 school of 752 students that are 95 percent white with 5 percent other. The socioeconomic status of the students' families ranges from lower- to middle-income.

Glenridge Elementary School is located south of Seattle in Kent, Washington. It is a K-6 school serving a student population of 635 that is 85 percent white, 4 percent African American, 2 percent Hispanic, 8 percent Asian/Pacific Islander, and 1 percent Native American. The students in the school are from middle-income families.

Governor Bent Elementary School is located in Albuquerque, New Mexico. It is a K-5 school serving a student population of 730 that is 48 percent white, 5 percent African American, 37 percent Hispanic, 5 percent Asian/Pacific Islander, and 5 percent Native American. Seventy percent of the students are from families ranging from lower-middle to upper income and 30 percent are on free and reduced lunch.

Jessie Wowk Elementary School is located in Richmond, British Columbia, Canada. It is a K-7 school serving a student population of 300 that is 35 percent white, 62 percent Asian/Pacific Islander, and 3 percent other. The students in the school are from middle to upper income families.

John F. Kennedy Elementary School is located in Brewster, New York, about fifty miles north of New York City. It is a K-3 school with 792 stu-

dents who are almost all white. More than 90 percent of the students are from families that range from lower- to upper-middle income and 8.7 percent are on free or reduced lunch.

Josiah Quincy Elementary School is located in Boston, Massachusetts. It is a K-5 school serving a student population of 950 that is 10 percent white, 23 percent African American, 7 percent Hispanic, and 60 percent Asian/Pacific Islander. Thirty percent of the students come from upper-middle-income families and 70 percent are on free and reduced lunch.

Key Renaissance Elementary School is located in Indianapolis, Indiana. It is a K-5 school serving a student population of 150 students that is 55 percent white, 40 percent African American, and 5 percent other. Seventy-five percent of the students in the school are from middle- to upper-middle-income families and 25 percent are on free and reduced lunch.

Key Renaissance Middle School is located in Indianapolis, Indiana. It is a grade 6–8 school serving a student population of 150 students that is 50 percent white, 45 percent African American, and 5 percent other. Fifty-five percent of the students in the school are from middle to upper middle income families and 40 percent are on free and reduced lunch.

King's Park Elementary School is located in Springfield, Virginia. It is a pre-K-3 school serving a student population of 750 students that is 70 percent white, 7 percent African American, 10 percent Hispanic, 10 percent Asian/Pacific Islander, and 3 percent other. About 95 percent of the school's students are from middle-income families and 5 percent are from lower- to middle-income families.

Liberty Elementary School is located north of Seattle in Marysville, Washington. It is a K-5 school serving a student population of 550 students that is 86 percent white, 7 percent Hispanic, and 7 percent Asian/Pacific Islander. Approximately 35 percent of the school's students are from lower- to middle-income families and 65 percent are on free and reduced lunch.

Limona Elementary School is located in Brandon, Florida, near Tampa. It is a K-5 school serving a student population of 1000 students that is 88 percent white, 10 percent African American, and 2 percent Hispanic. Sixty-eight percent of the school's students are from lower- to middle-income families, and 32 percent are on free and reduced lunch.

Madrona Non-Graded School is located in Edmonds, Washington, near Seattle. It is a pre-K-8 school serving about 700 students that are 93 percent white and 7 percent other. Approximately 80 percent of the school's students are from lower-middle- to upper-middle-income families, 13 percent are from lower income families, and 7 percent are on free and reduced lunch.

McCleary Elementary School is located in Pittsburgh, Pennsylvania. It is a K-5 school serving a student population of 180 that is 67 percent white, 30.5 percent African American, 0.3 percent Hispanic, 1.7 percent Asian/Pacific Islander, and .3 percent Native American. Twenty-three percent of the school's students are from lower-income families and 77 percent are on free and reduced lunch.

McWayne Elementary School is located in Batavia, Illinois, about sixty miles northwest of Chicago. It is a K-5 school serving a student population of 200 that is 98 percent white, 1 percent African American, and 1 percent Hispanic. Ninety-eight percent of the school's students are from upper-middle-income families and 2 percent are on free and reduced lunch.

Moore Alternative School is located in Winston-Salem, North Carolina. It is a K-5 school serving a student population of approximately 650 that is 58 percent white, 41 percent African American, and 1 percent Asian/Pacific Islander. The economic background of the students spans the income continuum. Ten percent are on free and reduced lunch.

Mountlake Terrace High School is located north of Seattle in Mountlake Terrace, Washington. It is a grade 9–12 school serving a student population of 1700 that is 85 percent white and 15 percent Asian/Pacific Islander. About 16.5 percent of the students are on free and reduced lunch.

New City School is a private school in St. Louis, Missouri. It is a pre-K-5 school serving a student population of 350 that is 70 percent white and 30 percent African American. The economic backgrounds of the students range from 30 percent upper-income families to 10 percent from lower-middle-income families.

Russell Elementary School is located in Lexington, Kentucky. It is a pre-K-5 school serving a

student population of 274 that is 36 percent white and 64 percent African American. Ninety-four percent of the students are on free and reduced lunch.

Searsport Elementary School is located in Searsport, Maine. It is a K-5 school serving a student population of 235–280, which fluctuates because of its migrant labor families. The student body is 100 percent white. Forty percent of the students are from middle- to lower-income families and 60 percent are on free and reduced lunch.

Sharon Elementary School is located in Charlotte, North Carolina. It is a K-5 school serving a student population of 585 that is 60 percent white and 40 percent African American. Approximately 65 percent of the students are from middle-income families and 35 percent are on free and reduced lunch.

Skyview Junior High is located Bothell, Washington, near Seattle. It is a grade 7–9 school serving a student population of 875 that is 92 percent white and 8 percent Asian/Pacific Islander. Approximately 12 percent of the students are from middle-income families, 80 percent are from lower-income families, and 8 percent are on free and reduced lunch.

Southhampton Elementary School is located about eighty miles east of New York City in Southhampton, New York. It is a K-4 school serving a student population of 600 that is 65 percent white and 35 percent African American, Hispanic, and Native American. The students' families span the economic continuum; 25 percent of the students are on free and reduced lunch.

Spectrum School is a private school located in Rockford, Illinois, about fifty miles from Chicago. It is a pre-K-8 school serving 176 students who are mostly white and 5 percent other. Five percent of the students are from upper-income families, close to 95 percent from middle-income families.

Stanton Elementary School is located in the Appalachian Mountains of Kentucky. It is a K-5 school serving a student population of 400 that is 100 percent white. Thirty percent of the students are from lower- to middle-income families, and 70 percent are on free and reduced lunch.

Tuscan Elementary School is located in Maplewood, New Jersey. It is a K-4 school serving a student population of 425 that is 60 percent white and 40 percent minority. The economic backgrounds of the students range from 10 percent from upper-income families to 10 percent on free and reduced lunch.

Union Elementary School is located in Maumee, Ohio, near Toledo. It is a K-5 school serving a student population of 325 that is 80 percent white and 20 percent African American. Eighty percent of the students are from lower-middle- to upper-income families, and 20 percent are on free and reduced lunch.

Valerie Elementary School is located in Dayton, Ohio. It is a K-6 school serving a student population of 325 that is 30 percent white and 70 percent African American. Approximately 40 percent of the students are from lower- to middle-income families and 60 percent are on free and reduced lunch.

West Boylston Elementary School is located in West Boylston, Massachusetts, near Worcester. It is a K-5 school serving 274 white students. Almost all of the students are from middle- to upper-income families, three percent from lower-income families, and two percent are on free and reduced lunch.

Wheeler Elementary School is located in Louisville, Kentucky. It is a K-5 school serving a student population of 637 that is 75 percent white and 25 percent African American. Seventy-four percent of the students are from lower-income families, and 24 percent are on free and reduced lunch.

Whitfield Elementary School is located West Lawn, Pennsylvania, near Pittsburgh. It is a K-6 school serving a student population of 630 that is 86 percent white and 14 percent African American, Hispanic, and Asian/Pacific Islander. Approximately 90 percent of the students are from working-class to middle-income families, and 10 percent are on free and reduced lunch.

References

Amrein, A. L., & Berliner, D. C. (2002). High-stakes testing, uncertainty, and student learning. *Education Policy Analysis Archives, 10*(18) [On-line]. Available: *http://epaa.asu.edu/epaa/v10n18/*

Chi, M. T. H., Glaser, R., & Farr, M. J. (Eds.). (1988). *The nature of expertise.* Hillsdale, NJ: Erlbaum.

Clarke, M., Haney, W., & Madaus, G. M. (2000). *High-stakes testing and high school completion.* Chestnut Hill, MA: National Board on Educational Testing and Public Policy.

Costa, A. L. (1991). The school as a home for the mind. Palatine, IL: IRI/Skylight.

DeLuca, S., & Rosenbaum, J. (2001, January). *Are dropout decisions related to safety concerns, social isolation, and teacher disparagement?* Paper presented at the Conference on Dropouts in America. Harvard Graduate School of Education, Cambridge, Massachusetts.

Eisner, E. (1992). *The DBAE handbook: An overview of discipline-based art education.* Santa Monica: The J. Paul Getty Trust. Note: Examples of DBAE-influenced curriculum can be found at ArtsEdNet website: www.getty.edu/artsednet/home.html.

Eisner, E. (2002). *Arts and the creation of mind.* New Haven: Yale University Press.

Ferguson, R. (1998). Teachers' perceptions and expectations and the black-white test score gap. In C. Jencks & M. Phillips (Eds.), *The Black-White Test Score Gap* (pp. 318–374). Washington, DC: The Brookings Institution.

Gardner, H. (1983/1993). *Frames of mind: The theory of multiple intelligences.* New York: BasicBooks.

Gardner, H. (1990). *Art education and human development.* Los Angeles: The Getty Center for Education in the Arts.

Gardner, H. (1991a). *The unschooled mind: How children think and how schools should teach.* New York: BasicBooks.

Gardner, H. (1991b). Assessment in context. In B. R. Gifford and M. C. O'Connor (Eds.), *Changing assessments: Alternative views of aptitude, achievement, and instruction.* Boston: Kluwer.

Gardner, H. (1993). *Multiple intelligences: The theory in practice.* New York: BasicBooks.

Gardner, H. (1999). *Intelligence reframed: Multiple intelligences for the 21st century.* New York: BasicBooks.

Goodrich, H. (1997). Understanding rubrics. *Educational Leadership, 54*(4), 14–17.

Goodrich Andrade, H. (2000). Using rubrics to promote thinking and learning. *Educational Leadership, 57*(5), 13–18.

Haney, W. (2000). The myth of the Texas miracle in education. *Education Analysis and Policy Archives, 8*(41) [On-line]. Available: *http://epaa.asu.edu/epaa/v8n41/*

Haney, W. (2001, January). *Revisiting the myth of the Texas miracle in education: Lessons about dropout research and dropout prevention. Initial estimates using the common core of data.* Paper presented at the Conference on Dropouts in America. Harvard Graduate School of Education, Cambridge, Massachusetts.

Hauser, R. M. (2001). Should we end social promotion? Truth and consequences. In G. Orfield & M. L. Kornhaber (Eds.), *Raising standards or raising barriers? Inequality and high-stakes testing in public education* (pp. 151–178). New York: Century Foundation.

Howard, J., & Hammond, R. (1985). Rumors of inferiority: The hidden obstacles to black success. *The New Republic, 3686,* 17–21.

Klein, S. P., Hamilton, L. S., McCaffrey, D. F., & Stecher, B. M. (2000). *What do test scores in Texas tell us?* Santa Monica, CA: Rand Corporation.

Koretz, D., & Barron, S. (1998). The validity of gains in scores on the Kentucky instructional results information system (KIRIS). Santa Monica, CA: Rand Corporation.

Kornhaber, M. L. (1999). Multiple intelligences theory in practice. In J. Block, S. T. Everson, and T. R. Guskey. (Eds.) *Comprehensive school reform: A program perspective* (pp. 179–191). Dubuque, IA: Kendall/Hunt.

Kornhaber, M. L., & Krechevsky, M. (1995). Expanding definitions of teaching and learning: Notes from the MI underground. In P. Cookson & B. Schneider (Eds.), *Transforming schools* (pp. 181–208). New York: Garland.

Lee, V. E., & Burkam, D. T. (2001, January). *Dropping out of high school: The role of school organization and structure.* Paper presented at the Conference on Dropouts in America. Harvard Graduate School of Education, Cambridge, Massachusetts.

McNeil, L. (2000). *Contradictions of school reform: Educational costs of standardized testing.* New York: Routledge.

McNeil, L., & Valenzuela, A. (2001). The harmful impact of the TAAS system of testing in Texas: Beneath the accountability rhetoric. In G. Orfield & M. L. Kornhaber (Eds.), *Raising standards or raising barriers? Inequality and high-stakes testing in public education* (pp. 127–150). New York: Century Foundation.

Neill, M. (2001). Do high-stakes graduation tests improve learning outcomes? Using state-level NAEP data to evaluate the effects of mandatory graduation tests. In G. Orfield & M. L. Kornhaber (Eds.), *Raising standards or raising barriers? Inequality and high-stakes testing in public education* (pp. 107–125). New York: Century Foundation.

Perkins, D. N., & Salomon, G. (1989). Are cognitive skills context-bound? *Educational Researcher, 18*(1), 16–25.

Reardon, S. F., & Galindo, C. (2002). *Do high-stakes tests affect students' decisions to drop out of school? Evidence from NELS.* Paper presented at the Annual Meeting of the American Educational Research Association, New Orleans, Louisiana, April, 2002. Online: http://www.personal.psu.edu/faculty/s/f/sfr3/papers/aera2002.pdf

Renzulli, J., & Reis, S. (1997). *The schoolwide enrichment model.* Mansfield Center, CT: Creative Learning Press.

Resnick, L. (1987). Learning in school and out. *Educational Researcher, 16,* (9) 13–20.

Schön, D. A. (1983). *The reflective practitioner: How professionals think in action.* New York: Basic Books.

Shepard, L. A., & Smith, M. L. (1989). *Flunking grades: Research and policies on retention.* London: Falmer Press.

Sternberg, R. J. (1996). *Successful intelligence: How practical and creative intelligence determine success in life.* New York: Simon & Schuster.

Wiggins, G. (1998). *Educative assessment: Designing assessments to inform and improve student performance.* San Francisco: Jossey-Bass.

Winner, E. (1996). *Gifted children: Myths and realities.* New York: Basic Books.

Name Index

Subject Index

Photo Credits